The Nourished So

Nurturing Your Mind to Grow Unending Health and Happiness

PAUL GAUTSCHI AND **JAMES BARS**

****

"So I commend the enjoyment of life, because there is nothing
better for a person under the sun than
to eat and drink and be glad.
Then joy will accompany them in their toil
all the days of the life God has given
them under the sun." Ecclesiastes 8:15 NIV

****

Portions of this book were also
released under the titles:
Exploring God's Love & Health and Happiness In A Broken world

****

Cover design: James Bars
Cover Photo:
Technical Supervision: Nathaniel Tainter - Golden Apples Design
Drawing of Jesus: Kip Ayers - www.kipayersillustration.com

ISBN: 979-8-9851732-3-9

"Come to me, all you who are weary and burdened, and I will give you rest. Take my yoke upon you and learn from me, for I am gentle and humble in heart, and you will find rest for your souls. For my yoke is easy and my burden is light." Matthew 11:28-30 NIV

INTRO

"Whether you think you can, or you think you can't—you're right." – Henry Ford

"Now faith is the substance of things hoped for, the evidence of things not seen." – Hebrews 11:1 NKJV

If these two quotes are accurate and most would agree that they are, then what is blocking many broken souls from enjoying the richness of vibrant health and happiness? Is it their belief systems or patterns of thinking? Often, the answer is yes.

During all your years of schooling, were you ever offered a course on developing thinking patterns that would enable you to live in a state of health and happiness? It is here now. Built upon the dual foundations of Scripture and Neural Science, the collected expertise unveiled upon the following pages took nearly thirty years to decipher, test, and assemble. A steady stream of breakthrough discoveries concerning brain function exploded during the years spent organizing the knowledge gathered in this book. We have included much of this new information in easily understood and readily absorbable concepts. Additionally, the Scripture components are embedded as vital bridges across the chasms of human wisdom, knowledge, and understanding.

Although this book came through two different men, the content is inspired by one Source; our great God of love. This book is not about eliminating every struggle and trial in your life but enlisting both the good and the challenging events to empower upward growth. Scripture instructs: *"Dear brothers and sisters, when troubles of any kind come your way, consider it an opportunity for great joy. For you know that when your faith is tested, your endurance has a chance to grow. So let it grow, for when your endurance is fully developed, you will be perfect and complete, needing nothing."* James 1:2-4 NLT

Your soul is a garden. You harvest what you plant, germinate, nourish, and grow. *"The fruit of God's Spirit is, love, joy, peace, patience, kindness, goodness, faithfulness, gentleness, and self-control."* Galatians 5:22-23

These are the crops that will enrich your life and enable you to prosper during the good, the bad, and the ugly experiences of your earth-bound journey.

Your faith will grow firmly in the Spirit's soil of power, love, and self-discipline. Especially amidst the pains and struggles that come your way in this life's once-in-forever opportunity.

The great news is that life on earth provides many necessary difficulties. These you will come to know as health enabling vehicles. As Carl Jung, the founder of analytical psychology, declared, *"Man needs difficulties; they are necessary for health."*

Although much of the science utilized on this adventure is new, the well-used guidance offered in Scripture is not. Along the way, a new competence will activate previously unrealized access to the mental and spiritual pathways that work best for you. Through practice, you will overflow the walls of ineffectiveness that may be suppressing your attempts at happiness and health.

Remember, this is *your* journey. Only *you* can make *your* journey a glorious revelation of the love that heals. This book is a heaven-bound landmark map—you will benefit best by taking your unique pathway through it with God as your benefactor and guide.

Note: The word health, when used in this book, is intended to express the most achievable overall health, encompassing the elements of spiritual, mental, and physical wellness.

The Nourished Soul

Nurturing Your Mind to Grow Unending Health and Happiness

Contents

Chapter One

The Garden of Your Mind

"Then the Lord God formed a man from the dust of the ground and breathed into his nostrils the breath of life, and the man became a living being. Now the Lord God had planted a garden in the east, in Eden; and there he put the man he had formed." Genesis 2:7-8 NIV

"More than anything you guard, protect your mind, for life flows from it." Proverbs 4:23 CEB

The incomprehensible powers and abilities of your brain are without equal among earth's other organisms. Your mind is your brain in action. Physically, you are a combination of earth, water, and that elusive yet ever-present power of our Creator—God, known as the breath of life. Spiritually, you are a force for good or evil. Who you become here and hereafter will be determined by the crops you plant in the garden of your mind.

Your extraordinary brain is a mere three-pound (1.4 kilograms) mass of jelly-like fats and tissues, yet it's the most complex of all known living structures. It comprises less than three percent of your body's weight but uses 20 percent of your body's energy. [E] Your extraordinary brain decidedly sets you apart from all other earthly creatures. [F]

Your brain holds approximately 1.25 terabytes of data and performs at around 100 teraflops (one hundred trillion point operations per second).

No computer built by man can do what your brain can do. Designed and built by God, your brain can choose to move its body from place to place. A computer cannot. Your brain can experience emotions, rewire itself based on new experiences or changes in understanding, and even grow new components (neurons). A computer cannot. Ultimately, your brain is the most marvelous, sophisticated, biological piece of engineering known, far beyond human ingenuity and immeasurably more complex than anything built by man.

Your ability to love and care is primarily located in the front portion of your brain and is referred to as your prefrontal cortex. This area processes most of your conscious decisions and produces nearly all of your love-based emotions. [A] This is the part of your brain where wisdom and understanding create sound judgment, and your soul is either blessed, or you experience the unhealthy consequences of veering from God's laws of love and liberty. It is in the prefrontal cortex that the proverbial heart and soul of a person appear to be located and where your free-choice decisions are planted and nourished.

If you seek them, God's soul-enriching assets of wisdom, knowledge, discretion, and understanding will be planted in your mind to preserve you and deliver you from the ravages of evil. *"When wisdom enters your heart, and knowledge is pleasant to your soul, discretion will preserve you; understanding will keep you, to deliver you from the way of evil."* Proverbs 2:10-12 NKJV

It is interesting to note that the mark of the beast as well as the seal of God, mentioned in the book of Revelation, both occur in the forehead where your prefrontal cortex is located. Your free-choice decisions are planted and nourished in this area of your brain. Plant good seeds, my friend, and nourish them with wisdom, knowledge, discretion, and understanding.

God created your brain to coordinate all of your physical actions and mental processes and to function as a communication device. Through your brain, you are enabled to communicate with other beings and commune with the Creator of the Universe—directly. Fascinating, isn't it?

Your **M**otives, **A**ffections, **D**esires, **F**eelings, **A**ctions, and **T**houghts (Your *MADFATs*—to be discussed at length throughout this book) are rooted in your brain through neural pathways.

Many of your neural pathways were inherited; many more were planted the first time you thought something, felt something, sensed something, tasted something, heard something, touched something, saw something, or smelled something. Actually, anytime you experienced anything.

As an experience occurs, a thin neural fiber is physically created in your brain. If you looked at your brain under a high-powered microscope, you could see these fibers. There are hundreds of millions of them. [H] These neural pathways are in a state of continual flux. Some will survive, and some will dissolve. Every time you re-experience the same event, that particular neural pathway is fertilized and more likely to be retained as a character trait, belief, or choice pattern. [A]

Planting and nourishing neural pathways that promote thriving health and happiness can be compared with how raindrops produce rivers. The more raindrops that seep into a pathway, the easier it is for subsequent raindrops to travel down that same pathway. This is how rivers are formed, and it is the way many of your *MADFATs*, habitual behaviors, and beliefs are developed—through repeated use of the same pathways.

You assign pleasure or pain to each experience and either seek it again if you believe it is pleasurable or avoid it if you believe it is painful. Nearly everything your mind-garden produces is based on and controlled by these two simple yet powerful desires:

1) The desire to avoid discomfort and pain.
2) The desire to obtain happiness and pleasure.

With each new experience and each new neural pathway planted in your brain, you may create a river of habit if you decide it is pleasurable. However, if you decide the experience is too painful, either immediately or if you can see that it will create too much pain in the long run, that trickle or river (neural pathway) will dry up and be eliminated from your nourished life patterns. As you follow God into the light, your *MADFATs* change, which causes physical changes in your brain. God created you to experience security, health, happiness, love, joy, peace, and pleasure when you live in harmony with His original Garden-of-Eden design. [A]

The brain God gave you releases chemicals through neural pleasure circuits that enable you to feel good when participating in thought patterns and behaviors necessary to live, enjoy life, and procreate. A few familiar joy-givers include; romance, love, marriage, marital sex, family, nutrition, exercise, prayer, meditation, charitable endeavors, sunny days, cheerful people, and relaxation. Daring adventures into superior lifestyle choices will elevate joyous delights within you and flow peacefully to the world around you. Invest time and energy often in these types of activities, and both your brain and your body will reward you with happy, healthy days.

The inspiring chemicals these activities release in your brain are known as neurotransmitters and are beneficial for your physical heart as well as your spiritual heart.

Your (spiritual heart) encompasses your beliefs and worldviews, including your motives, affections, desires, feelings, actions, and thoughts. It has much to do with determining your well-being. Your spiritual heart is often the guide who chooses your mental and physical activities. When your spiritual heart is healthy and happy, your physical heart is more likely to experience the same conditions.

Your spiritual heart weighs and selects competing thought patterns and behaviors. The subsequent payoffs they produce will determine your states of being through the release of neurotransmitters and hormones. Two of the most potent and necessary neurotransmitters are serotonin and dopamine. These two neurotransmitters are responsible for most of your feelings of wellness, inner peace, and happiness.

Good *MADFATs* often release pleasurable neurotransmitters. Bad *MADFATs* often release stress hormones that involve the brain's fight or flight systems, such as adrenaline, cortisol, and norepinephrine. These stress hormones, if overused, can be destructive and deadly.

Inner peace enhances your life. Excessive stress damages your brain and body.

Research indicates that the average person experiences somewhere between 12,000 and 60,000 thoughts per day, most of which are a repeat of standard habitual thoughts. [K]

The sad news is that the majority of your habitual thoughts are negative! This condition affects nearly every human on the planet and is known as the negativity bias. The negativity bias is a human propensity to prefer to assimilate and dwell upon negative experiences over positive or neutral ones, even if the negative experiences have little relevance. This tendency leaves us feeling the burn of being scolded more intensely than the delight of being celebrated.

Planet earth can be a dangerous place. You likely discovered this long before you were out of diapers. Your brain began building danger warning neural pathways at a very early age. These danger warning neural pathways and the fight or flight components in your brain's onboard warning systems are activated early and often. So it seems natural for you to develop dominant neural pathways that focus on avoiding danger, thus generating a negativity bias.

You may also delegate space and time to worry about negative experiences others may have, particularly those you love and care for, especially your children and theirs.

People worry. It may be a symptom of the negativity bias humans contend with in this challenging world.

Life is full of positive as well as negative experiences. You record both and often award the negative one's greater worth as you navigate the rough edges of your earthly existence. Negative thoughts can get more nourishment than positive thoughts because they are often repeated repeatedly until they have firmly infested large areas in the garden of your mind.

This habit of repeating the same negative thoughts day after day may be one of the primary reasons why legal and illegal mind/mood-altering drugs are so popular. People often suffer from continually watching for danger and from the relentless stress generated by the negativity bias. As a result, their brains may get battle-weary and so low on beneficial neurotransmitters that they can't seem to feel happy, healthy, or even well.

According to the Center for Disease Control and Prevention (CDC), nearly 13% of the world's population took anti-depressants between 2015 and 2018. [L]

While there are people who do suffer from clinical depression, others may simply be down in the dumps due to negative thinking and the actions that follow. If you struggle with depression, medication may help or may make things worse. You should seek professional assistance. Be prayerful and careful. God instructs us to guard and protect our minds. Remember: *"More than anything you guard, protect your mind, for life flows from it."* Proverbs 4:23 CEB

Whether you take medications or not, positive thinking and lifestyle choices are highly likely to help. Solomon was right when he wrote, *"A cheerful look brings joy to the heart, and good news health to the bones."* Proverbs 15:30 NIV

With this thought in mind, you may wish to consider avoiding the seeds of negativity blown into the garden of your mind from sources such as the news, gossip, and the media. A large percentage of all mental and physical illnesses are often generated or worsened by a person's own bleak thoughts and perspectives. [B]

The good news—it is possible to rewire the habit patterns of your brain. Planting and nourishing positive, uplifting, faithful, and faith-filled neural pathways of love, joy, peace, patience, kindness, goodness, faithfulness, gentleness, and self-control will choke the weeds of negativity, fear, and rebellion against God's perfect laws of love, liberty, and life.

The Apostle Paul's directive concerning your restoration process can become increasingly realized in your life. He wrote: *"Do not conform to the pattern of this world, but be transformed by the renewing of your mind. Then you will be able to test and approve what God's will is—his good, pleasing and perfect will."* Romans 12:2 NIV

Place your soul in God's care and allow His Spirit to guide you in the replanting of your *MADFATs*. Participating in this cream-of-the-crop process will facilitate the transcendent renewing of your mind and progressively transform your life into a well-watered garden of health and happiness. *"The Lord will guide you always; he will satisfy your needs in a sun-scorched land and will strengthen your frame. You will be like a well-watered garden, like a spring whose waters never fail."* Isaiah 58:11 NIV

Being transformed by the renewing of your mind is a concept you will consistently encounter throughout this book. You will also occasionally uncover replays of a variety of pertinent thoughts, Scripture verses, and phrases. This is intentional and has been done as a means of assisting in the process of planting, nourishing, and watering vital neural pathways in the garden of your mind.

You will perform your newly enlightened spiritual skills at a higher level as you practice them.

You are good at many things. A few of your talents were granted at birth. However, many of the skills you perform well require continual practice. Even the skills you have naturally will fade if unused. This is also intentional. God designed your brain. It has features you may not be aware of. Your brain is designed to dissolve patterns you don't use and fertilize those you do. God engineered your brain to be re-programmable. It will displace old patterns as new ones are given priority. Your brain is the most fascinating, complex, and powerful man-operated device on the planet.

A study by the National Institute of Health reveals that negative thoughts stimulate the area of the brain where depression, fear, and anxiety arise—the right prefrontal cortex. Conversely, positive, uplifting, and joyful thoughts take place in the left prefrontal cortex. [M]

You can consciously regulate whether your right or left prefrontal cortex is stimulated by how you focus your thoughts. As your thought patterns change, the physical structure of your brain changes. This is because of brain neuroplasticity, which is its ability to be rewired. Your brain continues to adapt and change throughout your lifetime. So the old saying, *"You can't teach an old dog new tricks,"* is not true regarding your brain.

You can learn to be healthy and happy in the same way you learn to enjoy new tastes—through practice. Your brain and daily life can and will change as you practice and focus your thoughts on positive, God-inspired inclinations.

Your brain is the distributor of the happy drugs—dopamine and serotonin. [N] These drugs are natural anti-depressants. You can help enable your brain to release these happy drugs through exercising positive, uplifting thoughts, physical exercise, eating healthy, nourishing foods, drinking plenty of pure water, spending time out in the clean, fresh air and sunshine, getting enough sleep, as well as other positive lifestyle choices.

Serotonin and dopamine levels are reduced as a result of stress, sleep loss, lack of exposure to sunlight, poor nutrition, and lack of exercise. Low levels of serotonin and dopamine can be the source of issues such as restlessness, tiredness, irritability, obsessive compulsions, weight gain, anxiety, chronic body pains, depression, and aggressiveness.

Lifestyle choices do affect your life. God designed you for optimal functioning when you properly maintain your systems as a whole and observe His laws of life, love, and health.

You may have made some negative life choices—you are human. Don't be discouraged by your past or current failures. You will come to view them as some of your greatest assets. Few souls are transformed instantly. The restoration of your heart, mind, and body will take time, effort, and practice. Enjoy the journey—delight in your successes and view failures not as losses but as opportunities to learn.

In pursuing any worthy endeavor—vision, sincere effort, and diligent practice are essential. Just like learning any new skill—heart, mind, and body renewal will take commitment and practice.

Anything you visualize as real, and repeatedly practice, is more likely to become a natural and automatic part of your daily life as those specific neural pathways are reinforced. [Q] Studies reveal this to be especially true when you meditate, pray, visualize and engage in contemplative activities.

An investigation by the Institute of Noetic Research revealed that meditation and other forms of mindful concentration strengthen and improve function in two critical brain areas—the prefrontal cortex and the insula. These improvements produced increased abilities in attention to one's own interior condition as well as enhanced empathy toward others. [R]

As you meditate on God and His word, practice His loving, peace-filled presence, visualize the uplifting realities of Him, and engage in contemplative, other-focused, as well as healthy activities, your brain becomes physically altered. Purposely focusing your mind on the incredible truths and blessings granted by God elevates your thoughts and ennobles both your interior and public lives. Positive, uplifting, Spirit-inspired neural pathways are created and nourished. You become better able to track the internal state of your being and the feelings of other people. Your level of empathy increases and your life's core motivations shift. Your preferences are brought into alignment with God's will for you. You become spiritually, mentally, and physically transformed. This happens by God's design. He created your brain with the capacity to improve your life—limitlessly.

Neuroplasticity, your brain's fascinating mechanism for constant restructuring, can refer to changes in neural pathways and synapses due to changes in beliefs, behavior, environment, and ways of thinking.

Seeking and following the advice and guidance of God will help renew the physical connections in your brain. Allow Him to demonstrate and teach you His *MADFATs,* and they may become your *MADFATs.* Through this process, your mind, purposes, appetites, and passions will flow naturally into the path of healthy, happy restoration. You will be reborn. The old will go—the new will come. You will be transformed by the renewing of your mind. Negativity, self-centeredness, rebellion, and fear are diminished as they are replaced with God-centeredness, other-centeredness, humility, caring, and love.

This book regularly addresses the devastating repercussions of negativity, self-centeredness, rebellion, and fear that often attend unhealthy lifestyle choices. As God restores you, these dark aspects will slip away.

Unhealthy stress hormones often flood the brain when it is negatively or fearfully focused on the past or the future. In these places, you can get into trouble. Don't do that. *Be Here Now!*

Each moment contains elements of good and evil. You decide which will feed your thoughts.

Most moments of life are perfect opportunities to rejoice. Why not enjoy each educational moment rather than torment yourself with disturbing thoughts about the past and the future?

God exists in the present. Breathe deep these words: *Be here now!* It is a peaceful place.

Have you ever taken a drive on a beautiful day through some gorgeous scenery and not even noticed it because you were lost in your head worrying about something? Do you know why?

It is likely due to the system of neural pathways and circuits that populate your brain. Often these include a storehouse of resentments over harms done (real or imagined), regrets over issues from the past, or fears over issues that may or may not occur in the future. These are frequent repeats of the resentments, regrets, and fears that you resented, regretted, and feared the day before, and the day before that, and the day before that—you get the picture. If you continually plant the same crops in the garden of your mind, you'll habitually harvest the same produce.

Your brain may be trained to focus on negative, fearful, worrisome thoughts. The more you use these neural circuits, the stronger they become, and the more often you experience the resentments, regrets, fears, and worries associated with them. You go where you focus. Where is your focus? What is the fruit of a negatively focused brain? Fear!

Fear and its devastating fallout upon your heart, mind, soul, and body will diminish your ability to love, grow, develop, and experience healthy thinking. Fear, and its ruinous, self-centered manifestations of pride, greed, anger, lust, envy, gluttony, and sloth, will reduce your potential as a child of God. Fear ignites your alarm center and increases insecurity, selfishness, rage, jealousy, envy, and aggression. [A]

Love and its flourishing, God-centered, and other-centered manifestations of joy, peace, patience, kindness, goodness, faithfulness, gentleness, and self-control will envelop your heart when nourished and leave you pleasantly fulfilled and content. Healthy love relaxes your limbic system, counters the effects of fear, and assists you in reaping a healthful, well-watered harvest of joy.

As you free love—love will free you. Developing tangible, well-practiced, alternative neural pathways of love and care will override your inherited and cultivated neural pathways of fear and selfishness, and you will begin to enjoy life like never before. When you leave unhealthy, self-centered neural circuits idle, your brain trims them back. [A]

God has given you His Spirit of ingenious power and a talented mind that *can* be made increasingly wise and robustly new. His laws of love *can* be written on your heart. You *can* increase your levels of health and happiness. God and you together *can* rewire your *MADFATs!* Your brain *can* be renewed because of the God-designed process known as neurogenesis.

Early discoveries in the process of neurogenesis (birth of neurons in the brain) began during research in songbirds. The Society for Neuroscience developed theories concerning the ability of the human brain to participate in the process of neurogenesis by studying the ability of songbirds to learn new songs. They upheld the theory that humans do generate new neurons, but these new neurons don't survive for very long if they aren't put into use by connecting with other neurons. [V]

Neuroscience has shown that the most active area of neurogenesis is the hippocampus, a region deep within the brain involved in learning and memory. The multitude of new cells released by the hippocampus each day must be put to work in order to survive and thrive. If they don't connect, they wither and die. [W] An inspiring way to put new neurons to work is to actively seek out and focus on positive, uplifting thoughts and activities. This will help enable you to rise above the negativity bias that most humans must contend with.

Neurogenesis involves neuroplasticity, which, in part, is the idea that as your thoughts change, the physical connections in your brain change. [X]

The practice of any thought or action connects neurons and ensures their survival. Refraining from any thought or action deprives neurons of connection and ensures their death. You become what you think about, and what you think about is what you feed your heart, mind, and soul.

One purpose of this book is to provide a means to help nourish your heart, mind, and soul with a consistent gourmet feast at the banquet table of God. Delightful delicacies of Eden treats—yum! *"Taste and see that the Lord is good; blessed is the one who takes refuge in him."* Psalm 34:8 NIV

As you partake of the sweet fruit of His Spirit, God satisfies the deepest hunger of your soul.

You will more readily plant new neural pathways in your brain through visualizing, meditating on, writing, and practicing the use of them. As you consistently meditate on the truths God reveals to you, visualize them as your reality, record them on paper and embody them repeatedly in thought and action, new neural circuits will connect in your brain and survive. This is the process by which your *MADFATs* are rewired. God and you together will displace the darkness by filling your heart, mind, and soul with an abundance of light-bearing truth. This is an automatic process because of the way God designed your brain to be re-programmable. He knew you would need this ability when He created Adam and Eve and put them in the Garden-of-Eden.

God knows the end from the beginning. Since the foundation of the world, He prepared a plan for your redemption and renewal. God has given you everything you need for life and godliness. This includes a heart that can be restored, your beautiful, re-programmable brain, and the unending power He gives you through His Holy Spirit.

Ralph Waldo Emerson encapsulates the importance of allowing God to renew your thinking patterns in his famous quote: *"Sow a thought, and you reap an action; sow an action, and you reap a habit; sow a habit, and you reap a character; sow a character, and you reap a destiny."* [AAA]

As God's Spirit inspires, enables, and empowers you to assist Him in rewiring your motives, affections, desires, feelings, actions, and thoughts, the physical connections in your brain are renewed. The result will be ever-expanding—purity in your character, happiness in your days and, overall health in your life.

These are the natural results of following Him and His directions. The path of purity, happiness, and health is often a bumpy one—but it is the most rewarding journey of your earthly life and the challenge of this spiritual quest.

"How can a young person stay on the path of purity? By living according to your word. I seek you with all my heart; do not let me stray from your commands. I have hidden your word in my heart that I might not sin against you. Praise be to you, LORD; teach me your decrees." Psalm 119:9-12 NIV

Through planting, meditating on, visualizing, and storing God's guidance in your heart, self-centeredness is diminished, rebellion is dissolved, fear is replaced with love, and the path of purity, health, and happiness is cleared.

The *Nourished Soul Eden Treats Sheets* (located in the back half of this book) were designed to provide a place to garden your mind and focus it on allowing God's Spirit to plant, nourish, and water valuable, new neural pathways that can enable you to walk according to the vital wisdom He has revealed. It is by consistently exposing yourself to and walking in God's love and light that you become enlightened, and your heart, mind, and soul are nourished and refreshed.

The act of visualizing and recording events in writing holds particular interest. It seems that visualizing and writing affect the brain's ability to retain information in unique ways.

Writing something down while considering the concepts behind the content creates a phenomenon in the brain that makes it believe the event is real. This is similar to the experience that occurs when you visualize performing a skill at a higher level—you often improve. [T]

Writing things down enhances the brain's ability to store them, especially if the message is emotionally generated. Experiences are retained in your brain more readily and solidly if they occur in an emotional context. It seems that most decisions are charged with emotion. So do that. Get emotional about the beautiful garden you and God are replanting in your mind. Don't worry, be happy! When you're happy and healthy, you are in a better emotional state and are more likely to make sound decisions.

It is common knowledge that those who have specific written goals are more likely to achieve them. This is one reason why daily completing the *Nourished Soul Eden Treats Sheets* is so vital to your soul's regeneration process. While consuming the nutrients unearthed in your *Nourished Soul Eden Treats Sheets* and snacking on them throughout each day, you will embody God's transformation of your being. During this process, it is critical that you see God clearly. Your insight into His love-based character and movements is fundamental to who you will become.

As you proceed in gardening and nourishing your mind, you hopefully have a clear portrait of who God is. God has three towering characteristics that define His essence:

(1) God is love. (2) God is light, and (3) there is no darkness in him at all. 1 John 4:8 NLT & 1 John 1:5 NLT

There is a lot of misinformation about God's character. It is clear that He longs to lift you above any misconceptions you may have about Him and how He is dealing with the rebellion we are all born into. Scripture reveals that a personal, knowing relationship with God is the Way to eternal life. Jesus explains: *"Now this is eternal life: that they know you, the only true God, and Jesus Christ, whom you have sent."* John 17:3 NIV

Revelations concerning God's character and the depth of His love for you will unfold as you weed, water, and nourish your soul. May you know Him well.

Rebellion, self-centeredness, and fear are the core patterns of life in our world. Scripture declares:

"Do not conform to the pattern of this world, but be transformed by the renewing of your mind. Then you will be able to test and approve what God's will is—his good, pleasing and perfect will." Romans 12:2 NIV

The preceding verse's instructions are achieved more easily when you see God as He truly is—love and light. If your perception of God is fear-based, this style of thinking may cause damage to your brain. You will find a clear case for love-based living by observing the example set by Jesus Christ, Who demonstrated God's true character. He did this by walking in, living in, and directing you to follow Him in—love and light. In following Him, your focus can shift from fear to love, from sickness to health, and from depression to happiness!

God will plant your garden in the soil of love; if you approve. He will not force Himself upon you at any time. He cherishes your freedom of choice. You will be the deciding factor. Your cooperation is paramount to His success in nourishing you. You decide whether to follow Him or not.

You decide which neural circuits get fed and survive. You decide whether your brain is full of positive or negative thought and belief patterns. Strive to keep your motives, affections, desires, feelings, actions, and thoughts focused on instilling God's positive, uplifting, and boundless qualities of love and care into your *Nourished Soul.* As a result, health and happiness will ripen like a bowl of sweet, refreshing, succulent goodness—Yummy!

God's love for you is as real as the ground you stand on. His desires for you to know Him well and enjoy the satisfying fruits of an intimate and caring relationship with Him rain profusely from the hearts of Him and His. In Him reside complete joy and able health.

Through the acts of visualizing, practicing, meditating on, and recording your *Nourished Soul Eden Treats* in writing regularly, the delights revealed in this book will assist you in focusing your mental energies on crucial areas of God's will for your spiritual, mental, and physical health and happiness.

When you utilize and reinforce positive, God-focused, and other-focused neural pathways, these are strengthened, and your interior and public lives are healed. Your very presence becomes a joyful experience where God, you, and others are honored.

Alternatively, when you utilize and reinforce negative, fear-based, self-centered neural pathways, these are strengthened, and your interior and public lives are robbed of the best God hopes for you. Your world becomes a dark place where God, you, and those whose lives you touch struggle and often clash. This is the turbulence that rumbles between the dark one as he attempts to rule over this world and God's kingdom of love and light as it draws you away from the dark side.

You are the determining variable in the skirmish over your soul.

An ancient Native American legend illustrates the conflict that may arise in you as you seek the path of health, happiness, purity, and honor. The tale goes something like this:

A young warrior found himself struggling with uncontrollable urges and unhealthy desires. He went to the spiritual leader of his Tribe and explained his troubles. He wanted to live a happy, healthy, pure, and honorable life, but he continued to lose the battle against his character defects.

The elder drew him into a lush meadow where they could be with the Creator. He asked him to sit, close his eyes and breathe in the sweet, loving presence of the One Who knows all.

The young warrior relaxed and drifted readily into a state of transcendence as he connected his soul with the Spirit of God. Love and light filled the corners of his being with peace. Acceptance enveloped his troubled heart and washed away his isolation.

As he drank in the consuming flood of love and care emanating from the Creator's heart, the elder spoke softly. "You have two wolves inside of you. A white wolf and a dark wolf—they are striving for your allegiance. One will be victorious over the other."

The elder then rose quietly and drifted into the woods toward a stream. As he knelt, he cupped his hands, filled them with refreshing, pure water, and began to drink. The warrior appeared silently beside him. The elder knew his thoughts but said nothing.

After a moment, the warrior asked. "Which one wins?"

The elder took another drink, sat beside the stream in the soft grass, raised his face toward the warm, summer sun, and said. "That's easy, my son—the one you feed."

Which one will you feed? Whose warrior are you? Solomon wrote: *"Whoever seeks good finds favor, but evil comes to one who searches for it."* Proverbs 11:27 NIV

It is within the heart, mind, soul, and strength of a person that destiny is determined. This is why Jesus instructs you to: *"Love the Lord your God with all your heart and with all your soul and with all your mind and with all your strength."* Mark 12:30 NIV

Love-based living is a parent of health and happiness and a pathway to a peaceful, free spirit.

Even though you were born broken, you can be renewed, rewired, and eternally restored. However, you have a serious dilemma—you lack the appropriate power.

To garden your soul correctly, you will want to continually access and receive the indwelling presence of God's Holy Spirit. It is His Spirit Who bestows upon you vital, life-changing power! Feed your heart at the table of His unending feast of love and light, and your spirit will be contentedly refreshed.

Your heart, mind, and soul hunger for vital nutrients to be fed regularly into your love-based neural circuits. As you continue to apply your focus to whatever is healthy, happy, true, noble, and right, your brain will automatically begin to vanquish the dark wolf's negative patterns.

If fed a clean diet of only healthy programming, your brain will dissolve unused, negative neural circuits and nourish, enrich and secure the neural circuits that ensure victory for the white wolf within you. Your health is affected by what you eat—spiritually, mentally, and physically. Eat well, my friend. When you do, your soul will soar high above the grey, acrid stench of sickness, sadness, and the darkness that seeks to annihilate your secured, heavenly future. Instead, your healthy, happy heart will overflow with love, joy, peace, and patience. You will be transformed by the renewing of your mind. Your time here on earth and your eternal destiny will brighten.

You are not here by mistake. You are here by design. The architect of life created all and upholds all—including you. The Creator is the Source of all life, power, wisdom, knowledge, and understanding. Perhaps the single most valuable truth a human soul may come to know is contained in the following verses. It is written:

> *The Son is the image of the invisible God, the firstborn over all creation. For in him all things were created: things in heaven and on earth, visible and invisible, whether thrones or powers or rulers or authorities; all things have been created through him and for him. He is before all things, and in him all things hold together. And he is the head of the body, the church; he is the beginning and the firstborn from among the dead, so that in everything he might have the supremacy. For God was pleased to have all his fullness dwell in him, and through him to reconcile to himself all things, whether things on earth or things in heaven, by making peace through his blood, shed on the cross.*
>
> *Once you were alienated from God and were enemies in your minds because of your evil behavior. But now he has reconciled you by Christ's physical body through death to present you holy in his sight, without blemish and free from accusation—if you continue in your faith, established and firm, and do not move from the hope held out in the gospel.*
>
> *This is the gospel that you heard and that has been proclaimed to every creature under heaven, and of which I, Paul, have become a servant.* Colossians 1:15-23 NIV

May God grant you an abundance of wisdom, willingness, and spiritual power as together, you garden your soul and transform your life through the heavenly art of mind renewal. May, His most relevant promise, delivered through Isaiah, become your reality: *"You will keep in perfect peace all who trust in you, all whose thoughts are fixed on you!"* Isaiah 26:3 NLT

Mr. Paul's Insights, Inspirations, and Experiences
Chapter One

(As each Chapter neared completion, Mr. Paul would review it. Then, we would discuss it. I recorded our post review discussions. What follows are poignant and interesting excerpts from his recorded comments.)

* I was amazed at the statistics about how many people are depressed. I had no idea it was so common.

I went through a severe time of depression. You know what got me over it? It was that scripture verse: *"Bring every thought into captivity to the obedience of Christ."* It took years. It was a long, drawn-out process. It was a major exercise. We're talking a significant exercise. But it worked!

My wife and I are not into any type of drugs; however, she got serious about having me take medication, but I said, "Carol, no way! God's word is either true, or it's not. And I'm gonna push through and stay with it."

You see, the word is very clear: *"As a man thinks in his heart, so is he."* Your thoughts create your reality.

And I'm telling you, it was a struggle, but it worked. I had to really, really work at it. *"Bring every thought into captivity to the obedience of Christ."* Allow no thought that is not in line with Him. Give no place to it.

The thing that really spoke to me about Chapter One was the realization of how free I am. I no longer deal with those issues. I don't have depression. And I live a really amazing life because I have a relationship with the Father. We communicate all the time. It's amazing how He lifts me above all that stuff. It's really awesome!

The Bible instructs us to be in the world, but not of the world. It's so true. I keep telling people; the Bible says we are pilgrims and strangers here, and we should act like it. We really should act like we don't belong here. It is so true.

* I see the principles of God in everything. Like, *"You reap what you sow." "God is not mocked: whatever a man sows, he reaps."* And I've seen these principles in everything: in agriculture, in life. God is so ordered. It's really amazing. The thing that so speaks to me is God's incredible order in nature. He's an orderly God.

* Man is transformed by the renewing of his mind. Change your thought patterns. What I'm seeing, as you do that, everything changes. It's that reaping and sowing thing. When you start bringing thoughts into alignment with God's word, you are changed.

King David asked, *"How can a young man cleanse his ways?"* The answer is by taking heed, by paying attention to the word. David proclaimed: *"Thy word have I hid in my heart that I might not sin against thee."*

* I'm finding that the Holy Spirit is so faithful. When you have issues, the Holy Spirit will bring the word to mind. It's awesome. I'm just amazed. You don't even have to look for it; it just shows up. And there's the answer. It's like, yes! That's it!

* My experience is, your thoughts fit your reality. It's essential to bring every thought into captivity to the obedience of Christ. It's such an asset when you memorize the word because the Holy Spirit is so faithful to bring it to mind at the time you need it to give you direction, to give you answers. It's a wonderful reality to live in.

* For so long, I didn't think I could hear God because everybody talks about a still, small voice. I was trying to find that still, small voice. But there wasn't any. I was so frustrated. Then my wife came across these teachings from a man named Mark Virkler about how to hear the voice of God.

His testimony was so similar to mine. I read the word; I pray; I never hear God. But when he made the statement: "God's voice comes as a spontaneous thought." All of a sudden, the door was open! It was like the light came on, and there He was! I've always heard. I just didn't know what it was. For me, that really changed everything. It completely changed my whole life. And I tell people the word is so clear. You see it three times in the Bible, first in Psalms and twice in Hebrews: *"Today, if you hear His voice, harden not your hearts."*

Today is a very present tense. God is speaking to us every day and why we don't hear is: we have agendas, we have preconceived ideas, and we're not paying attention. I'm finding that He's always there. He's always speaking. I just need to listen and pay attention.

I ask Him questions. "What do you think about this? What do you think about that?" The word says: *"If you ask, you receive. If you seek, you find. If you knock, the door is opened. You have not because you don't ask."*

* In Proverbs, it says: "In all your ways acknowledge Him, and He will direct your path." What does all leave out? It's so obvious—nothing.

* What I'm finding in my experience is that He is so there. He's so there for us if we come to Him and ask. But He waits on us to ask. That's the thing that really spoke to me, is how He so honors free-will agency. He never overrides our will. He waits on us to ask.

In the Scripture, God says: *"Draw near to God, and He will draw near to you."* In 1st Peter, it says: *"Work out your salvation for God works in you to will and to do His good pleasure."* How I see it: the ball is in our court. Jesus made the move to reconcile us to God, and now the ball is in our court. We have to draw near to Him. Come to Him.

Chapter Notes and Discussion Topics

Notes

How did this chapter affect you? And why?

Did you gain any new perspectives or perceptions?

What changed in you after reading this chapter?

How can you use this knowledge to help improve your relationships with God, yourself, and others?

Chapter Two

Prelude to the

Nourished Soul Gardening Guides

"Happiness is when what you think, what you say, and what you do are in harmony." Mahatma Gandhi

"The Lord will guide you always; he will satisfy your needs in a sun-scorched land and will strengthen your frame. You will be like a well-watered garden, like a spring whose waters never fail" Isiaih 58:11 NIV

The *Nourished Soul Gardening Guides* that follow this preparation embody the soil of your neural plantings as your *Nourished Soul* absorbs nutrients to feed the seeds of eternity. They are intended to expose your mind to God's restoring directions and infinite healing power. They will insulate you in a cocoon of light as you consistently wrap your mind around their landscapes of love. These *Gardening Guides* will help send roots deep into the nurturing soils of God's love, joy, peace, patience, kindness, goodness, faithfulness, gentleness, and self-control. Much, if not most, of the troubling blight of a human's spiritual birth and maturation process is addressed through the *Remedy* revealed in them.

The flower of your soul will bloom in radiant petals of love-based health and happiness. The fruit of your life will drip lusciously with satisfying heaven-sourced waters. Empowering buds of faith and grace will rise upward in your soul's garden and stretch toward the Son-light.

These guides will focus on life transformation through mind renewal under the power and protection of heaven's Master Gardener—Jesus and His sweetening Spirit of love.

You will learn to live the happy, healthy, well-watered, richly-nourished, and fulfilling life God intends for you to live the same way you learn to play a musical instrument—through practice.

By using the *Nourished Soul Eden Treats Sheets* in the back half of this book, you will help create an environment within yourself where you, under the power and influence of the Spirit of God, will assist Him as He performs His soothing, life-enhancing, transformative work.

The *Nourished Soul Gardening Guides* and the *Nourished Soul Eden Treats Sheets* will give you the opportunity to focus your mind on, walk in, and relish the steady presence and direction of the Master Gardener. In doing this, the garden of your mind will progressively bloom His love-based fruits of health and happiness.

As you persistently and consistently incorporate the spiritual and scientific information presented here into your heart, mind, and soul, understand that you, like the rest of us, will always learn new skills best through practice.

Recall the words of Aristotle, *"We are what we repeatedly do. Excellence, therefore, is not an act, but a habit."* [BBB] This is why the echoes of poignant Scripture verses and Biblical concepts resonate throughout this quest. As you experience the abundant rain from these Scriptures and concepts, they will assist you in freely planting, sprouting, and nourishing perennial vines of life-enhancing neural pathways in the garden of your mind.

The new, uplifting, heaven-inspired neural pathways God and you together will plant, sprout, and nourish in your brain will become stronger as you regularly practice them. They will become the heart of your reality.

You are seeking to happily and healthfully renew your mind with positive energy, creative focus, and refreshing, heaven-enlightened motives, affections, desires, feelings, actions, and thoughts. *(MADFATs).*

Remember, nearly all human behavior is controlled by two fundamental desires:

1) The desire to avoid discomfort and pain.

2) The desire to obtain happiness and pleasure.

During your transformation process, you will notice increasingly painful associations to dark, fear-based, self-centered *MADFATs.* Conversely, you will be simultaneously generating and reinforcing pleasurable associations to positive, heaven-inspired ones.

Within the *Nourished Soul Gardening Guides,* you will discover the value of this process. The love-based fruits of health and happiness will enliven and enhance your *Nourished Soul* daily. As the roots of your spirit reach for living water, God's Holy Spirit opens your mind to the renewal procedure, and you become amazingly and increasingly set free while God grows your *Garden Fresh MADFATs.*

As you progress, you will come to understand that the easiest way to dissolve negative life patterns is by focusing your mind on new, positive ones. Therefore, daily practice is critical to your success. Darkness is dispelled by entering into and assimilating the light.

As your mind focuses on God's light, you will stop focusing on old, negative life patterns. When you stop using these negative life patterns, your brain will automatically begin dissolving them.

By surrendering fear-based, self-focused *MADFATs,* filling your mind with God's light, and bringing captive every thought to the obedience of Christ—your mind will be renewed.

Always remember, it is God's Spirit Who enables you to walk in the light of the kingdom of light. Your *Nourished Soul* will be refreshingly filled with Him and His power, love, and self-control as you increasingly grant Him the supervision of your will and all of your life.

A primary objective of this quest is to provide a way for you to expose yourself to the light of God's Spirit and grant Him authority over more and more and more of you. This exposure and progressive surrender of your rebellious, broken self dissolves negative *MADFATs.*

Fear vanishes in the vaporizing love-light emanating from God's purifying presence.

As a part of your *Nourished Soul's* ever-deepening surrender to God's ways, you will experience the thrilling freedoms and joys found in living protected within His beneficial laws of love and liberty.

You will comprehend what the psalmist did concerning the amazing treasures available to you as you walk in willing compliance with your Creator's love-based laws. It is written:

The law of the LORD is perfect, refreshing the soul.
The statutes of the LORD are trustworthy, making wise the simple.
The precepts of the LORD are right, giving joy to the heart.
The commands of the LORD are radiant, giving light to the eyes.
The fear of the LORD is pure, enduring forever.
The decrees of the LORD are firm, and all of them are righteous.
They are more precious than gold, than much pure gold; they are sweeter than honey, than honey from the honeycomb.
By them your servant is warned; in keeping them there is great reward. Psalm 19:7-11 NIV

Living by God's design, you will naturally experience a state of nearly constant peace with others, peace within, and peace with Him that expands harmoniously with each new sunrise.

The power of God will enable you to open doors in your soul and allow His Holy Spirit to begin the process of restoring you to the Garden-of-Eden-being you were meant to be.

The joy exposed in living life God's way often attracts others to Him through the magnetic love His sweet presence brings. As others are drawn toward the light, you are presented with opportunities to share His joy. Thus, you will become a progressively effective ambassador of His kingdom. Jesus tells you to improve yourself before you reach out to help others. *"First take the plank out of your own eye, and then you will see clearly to remove the speck from your brother's eye."* Matthew 7:5 NIV

The Spirit-based adventures contained in this soul-gardening quest will solidly construct in you the God-blessed, humility-led ability to take the plank out of your own eye. Then, as God directs and enables, you will see clearly how to help remove the speck from your brother's eye. As you do this, you will begin to understand why God inspires you to become more like Jesus. Your joy will know no bounds when the motives of your heart are to love, live for, and care for others.

Always keep in the forefront of your consciousness the reality that you can do nothing without God's power and sustaining grace, but you can do all through Him who strengthens you.

Jesus said: *"Yes, I am the vine; you are the branches. Those who remain in me, and I in them, will produce much fruit. For apart from me you can do nothing."* John 15:5 NIV

Paul declares: *"I can do all things through Christ who strengthens me."* Philippians 4:13 NKJV

You are dependent upon Him for everything—whether you believe it or not.

Perceive sacred insight! See all through the lens of love. Let the eyes of your heart discern the lessons revealed through the symbolic, ancient tribe of Israel. Don't be stiff-necked like they were. Follow God humbly, in faith and trust. It is the Lord Who—defeats your captors—leads you out of the house of bondage—protects you through the deserts of life—and guides you into the promised land—the land flowing with milk and honey. God proclaims: *"I am the LORD your God, who brought you out of the land of Egypt, out of the house of bondage."* Exodus 20:2 NIV

"And I have promised to bring you up out of your misery in Egypt into the land of the Canaanites, Hittites, Amorites, Perizzites, Hivites and Jebusites—a land flowing with milk and honey." Exodus 3:17 NIV

It seems to be a human tendency to take credit for our goodness and accomplishments. This is dangerous ground. Never forget the wisdom revealed by Solomon on the matter of self-sufficient pride: *"Pride goes before destruction, and a haughty spirit before a fall."* Proverbs 16:18 TNIV

It would benefit you to keep humility as your guide while you progress in your renewal process. Remember, it is God who has given you everything you need for life and godliness.

Paul tells us, *"It is by grace you have been saved, through faith—and this not from yourselves, it is the gift of God—not by works, so that no one can boast."* Ephesians 2:8-9 NIV

By living humbly and freely, you demonstrate to all that what has been done in you has been done through God. Comprehend the words of the Lord as recorded by Jeremiah:

> *Cursed is the one who trusts in man, who depends on flesh for his strength and whose heart turns away from the Lord. He will be like a bush in the wastelands; he will not see prosperity when it comes. He will dwell in the parched places of the desert, in a salt land where no one lives. But blessed is the man who trusts in the Lord, whose confidence is in him. He will be like a tree planted by the water that sends out its roots by the stream. It does not fear when heat comes; its leaves are always green. It has no worries in a year of drought and never fails to bear fruit.* Jeremiah 17:5-8 NIV

It makes sense that God wants to rid the fertile soil of your heart, mind, and soul of the deadly denizens that dwell there as He did for symbolic, ancient Israel. He crossed the Jordon River ahead of them to dispossess the darkness that resided within the fruitful land.

He will go ahead of you into the promised land, grant you possession of it, and enrich you with prosperous abundance. *"But recognize today that the LORD your God is the one who will cross over ahead of you like a devouring fire to destroy them. He will subdue them so that you will quickly conquer them and drive them out, just as the LORD has promised."* Deuteronomy 9:3 NLT

Notice that the Lord led the way, and the children followed. But both were involved. You must arm your soul with the only effective weapons in this warfare—effort, faith, love, and light. The greatest of these is love.

Regularly recording your progress as God leads you into the promised land of eternal abundance is essential. The science and purpose behind your *Nourished Soul Eden Treats Sheets* is to assist you in establishing and reinforcing the battle-tested, Holy Spirit-empowered neural habits of effort, faith, love, and light. As you witness unbelievable victories unfolding in your life, you will be continually reminded of His grace. At the same time, together, you and God will subdue and conquer the spiritual forces of negativity blocking your path. It is God's Spirit that will dispel and dispossess the deadly denizens of darkness that bring spiritual, physical, mental, and financial poverty to your life.

Your daily victories will flourish. Your life will be progressively enriched. Your *Nourished Soul* will grow in perfect symmetry as your spiritual roots reach deep into the fertilizing soils of effort, faith, love, and light, and you will come to fully realize and echo these heart-calming, vital truths:

> *"Today you are going into battle against your enemies. Do not be fainthearted or afraid; do not panic or be terrified by them. For the Lord your God is the one who goes with you to fight for you against your enemies to give you victory."* Deuteronomy 20:3-4 NIV

> *To him who is able to keep you from stumbling and to present you before his glorious presence without fault and with great joy—to the only God our Savior be glory, majesty, power and authority, through Jesus Christ our Lord, before all ages, now and forevermore! Amen.* Jude 1:24-25 NIV

While on this soul-gardening quest, you will encounter a journey unlike any other. It is a migration toward home. This may very well prove to be the most exhilarating, satisfying adventure of your life here on earth. It is the only journey you may continue beyond this world. On your pilgrimage, you will face some rugged terrain. But do not fear. You have a leader who has completed the voyage before you. He will not only show you the way. He is the Way, the Truth, and the Life.

The *Nourished Soul Gardening Guides* will coach you as you seek to plant, germinate, nourish, and grow the eternal kernels of the Garden-of-Eden soul you are meant to be.

The *Nourished Soul Eden Treats Sheets* that follow these guides will fertilize your soul's garden of love as the Spirit of the Master Gardener covers and protects the soil of your soul and allows heaven's rain to sprout succulent joys from the seeds of life.

This journey focuses on seven primary areas that many, if not most, earth-bound citizens of God's kingdom may wish to grow in as they prepare for heaven. Many searching souls find these areas of growth challenging, especially as they seek health and happiness in this broken world.

The seven *Nourished Soul Gardening Guides* (one for each day of the week) will shed light upon your days as you travel the path of the Way, the Truth, and the Life. They include:

1) Growing Garden Fresh MADFATs
2) The Good Soil Promise
3) Amazing Grace and the Touchstones
4) The Covering and the Way Up
5) Untangling the Night
6) IOU Love
7) Happy You, in God's Temple of Light

These seven areas of focused growth are the titles of the following seven chapters. They are each one of the *Nourished Soul Gardening Guides.* These orchards of opportunity will refresh your *Nourished Soul.* They are the groundwork upon which God and you together will build a bridge back to your spirit's sacred homeland. As you diligently study and practice planting them firmly in the garden of your mind, the seeds of your renewal will sprout in the healthy, nourishing soil of God's joyful love and light.

Within your *Nourished Soul Eden Treats Sheets*, you will seek the Holy Spirit's influence as you focus your efforts on one of the *Nourished Soul Gardening Guides* each day. With God's Spirit as your mentor and guide, you will write down, meditate on, visualize, practice, and embody what the fruit of your life's harvest will be. Together you will plant, germinate, nourish, grow, and harvest the eternally blooming crops of love-based happiness and health.

Darkness will flee as God fills you with the enlivening love-light that draws your soul homeward.

The directions for fertilizing and watering your soul are detailed on your *Nourished Soul Eden Treats Sheets* and revealed in the following seven chapters—the *Nourished Soul Gardening Guides.*

May the garden of your *Nourished Soul* produce heavenly rewards. And may you bring God glory as you relish His enduring fruits of love, joy, peace, patience, kindness, goodness, faithfulness, gentleness, and self-control.

Mr. Paul's Insights, Inspirations, and Experiences
Chapter Two

(As each Chapter neared completion, Mr. Paul would review it. Then, we would discuss it. I recorded our post review discussions. What follows are poignant and interesting excerpts from his recorded comments.)

* In considering this Chapter, I keep coming back to this truth: (health is such a critical principle). When things are healthy, they are resilient. They are not taken out by offenses. It all comes back to God's design in nature.

* I would like to comment on the paragraph that states: "The joy exposed in living life God's way often attracts others to Him through the magnetic love His sweet presence brings. As others are drawn toward the light, you are presented with opportunities to share His joy. Thus, you will become a progressively effective ambassador of His kingdom." We used to have this Pastor that people would watch. Wherever he went in life, he was giving the gospel. And they always asked him, "Arthur, how come it's so easy for you to witness?" And I love his statement. He said, "If you always tell the truth, you will end up with Jesus. Cause Jesus is the way, the truth, and the life." I love that! It's such a powerful statement.

* If someone compliments you, you have to acknowledge that: *"Every good gift comes down from the Father of light."* It always goes back to God. The statement: "If you always tell the truth, you will always end up with Jesus," is a very powerful statement. It has really blessed me. If

you always tell the truth, you will always have opportunities to end up with Jesus.

* There is something about testimony that's such a powerful witness. I love the phrase from the book of Revelation, *"Believers overcame the devil by the blood of the Lamb and by the word of their testimony."* The Bible says, *"Faith comes by hearing the word."* When you give testimony, it causes faith to rise up in you.

* I want to bring something to your attention about translations. Around the middle of the Chapter, it says: Paul declares: *"I can do all things through Christ who strengthens me."* But the King James version reads: *"I can do all things through Christ which strengthens me."* Do you see how that changes the whole meaning of the verse? You see, the one passage makes it passive—God does it all. But King James says: It's active! It empowers you. Relying on Him empowers you. That one word changes the whole meaning.

* The same thing happens in 1 Corinthians 15:57. The NIV says: *"Thanks be to God; He gives us the victory."* But the King James says: *"Thanks be to God; which gives us the victory."* Do you see how that changes the issue?

I give thanks. That's how I get strength and get the victory. God doesn't do it for me; I get it by giving thanks. That's why you read in 1 Thessalonians verse 5:18, *"In every thing give thanks: for this is the will of God in Christ Jesus concerning you."* By being thankful, I access the strength and the power of His reality.

* The Bible clearly states that: *"The natural man cannot receive the things of God neither can he know them because they are spiritually discerned."* The entire premise and desire of many Bible translators is to make the whole thing understandable. And the Bible says; it's not understandable to the natural mind—it's spirit.

* I was really blessed, by my mother especially. She had me spend a lot of time while growing up memorizing Scripture. I'll tell you how God healed my memory after I destroyed it with LSD and Mescaline. I forgot everything I learned in school, but I could not forget Scripture. God used His Word to bring my memory back. And I feel so grateful for my mother, especially for spending all those hours and being diligent in having me memorize so much of the word. And after I got my memory back, I began memorizing more Scripture, and that is what restored it all. The Bible is very clear that the Word renews your mind. I tell people all the time that are suffering from Alzheimers or whatever to start memorizing the word. Get into the Psalms. Memorize the word. It'll get your mind back.

The memorized word comes to your mind at just the right time. What I've discovered, in my experience, is that the Holy Spirit is so faithful. If I'm diligent at hiding the word in my heart. Then at the time I need it—it just shows up.

There'll be times when people that are touring my gardens will ask me questions and the Holy Spirit brings to my mind the word. I wasn't even looking for it. I didn't even realize that it was there. It comes in spontaneous arrivals. I feel so thankful! I'm so blessed!

* Let me tell you how God brought the documentary that features the gardening practices He revealed to me into reality. I was in my orchard one day, having a conversation with God about everybody bugging me to write a book. I said to Him, "God, I'm not a woman. Women are multi-taskers. I am not. If I'm focused on writing a book, I'm not going to be able to take care of my garden and orchard. Can You help me?"

So, several weeks later, my wife hears about this home Bible study happening near us and says, "Paul, you otta go." And so we went. There was this guy who had come from Louisiana. So, I'm sharing in this group how God's been showing me how to grow things in the garden.

This guy comes up to me after the meeting and says, "Most of my family and friends are farmers. Can I come to your place and look at your garden? I might be interested. I'd like to see what you're doing." So, he came and toured the place with me. Then, he went back home and told his family and friends, "You've gotta document this. You gotta get this out there!"

* Then, Michael Barrett, the man who had the vision to make the film, hired two girls, Dana Richardson and Sarah Zentz, who had just gotten out of school. They had gone to school to become videographers. And they had never done anything like this before in their lives. Still, they made the film "Back to Eden." (It can be seen at https://www.backtoedenfilm.com)

The rest is God's story. We were completely blown away at the response the world has had to this film. None of us ever imagined the impact this film would have.

* It all goes back to God setting me free from drugs. He was convicting me about using. I could not give it up. I totally could not give it up! I told God, "The only way I can get free is if You take it away from me."

I was growing marijuana on my parent's place, down the hill below some trees where it couldn't be seen. I'm doing everything, man, to make this really grow well. Then, I harvest it, dry it, and invite my friends over. I roll this stuff up, and we're smoking it, and I'm as straight as an arrow. What a drag! All this work and nothing. All my friends are saying, "Where did you get this? This is the best stuff we've ever had!"

And I heard God inside my mind, "I took it." From that moment on, I was 100% free! It was so awesome! God was so good to me.

The thing I observed about smoking marijuana is, you sit there stoned and have these amazing ideas about how you're going to change the world. But you don't do anything. There's no motivation. It only destroys motivation.

For me, the experience of being set free was an amazing deliverance. It was just so awesome!

* The Bible says, *"If anyone be in Christ, he is a new creation. Old things are passed away. All things are new."* I love that. That's my reality.

* I want to walk in the light and be honest. *"If you walk in the light, as He is in the light, you will have fellowship with one another, and the blood of Jesus Christ will cleanse you from all sin."*

Those words are so powerful. *"If you walk in the light as He is in the light, you will have fellowship with one another."* It totally creates a freedom in relationships. It's so awesome.

Also, all the issues we have will be taken care of by the blood of Jesus. It brings such gladness! How could it get any better?

* People talk about flying when they get to heaven. The reality of what I'm seeing is; flying is way too slow. It says in First John that, *"We will be like Jesus."*

When Jesus arose from the grave, He traveled at the speed of thought. That's how He got around. And that's how we're gonna move. It's gonna be incredible! We saw Philip demonstrate this. He was in the middle of a major crusade; then, he just shows up on this wilderness road to meet a eunuch. He baptizes him, and then just appears back where he was—at the speed of thought!

Also, Jesus didn't walk through walls. He just appeared. He just showed up. Walls weren't an issue.

* Another thing that really speaks to me is when people say, "When I get to heaven, I'm going to ask about things." I don't believe that. The word says, *"We will know as we are known."* We are going to be completely in the light. Nothing will be unknown to us. My mind can't even conceive that. But that is what the word says.

"We will know as we are known."

Chapter Notes and Discussion Topics

Notes

How did this chapter affect you? And why?

Did you gain any new perspectives or perceptions?

What changed in you after reading this chapter?

How can you use this knowledge to help improve your relationships with God, yourself, and others?

Chapter Three

The Nourished Soul Gardening Guide for:

Growing Garden Fresh MADFATs

"Trust in the Lord with all your heart and lean not on your own understanding;
in all your ways submit to him, and he will make your paths straight.
Do not be wise in your own eyes; fear the Lord and shun evil.
This will bring health to your body and nourishment to your bones." Proverbs 3:5-8 NIV

When God created Adam, all of humanity was in him. He, and his offspring, were designed to live an eternal, perfect existence. From that one man came Eve and subsequently every other human being. So, you were in Adam along with the rest of us. He was the original seed of humanity. He was perfect, healthy, happy, well-nourished, vibrant, and without blemish or defect. God placed Adam, the seed of all humanity, in the Garden of Eden. *"Then the LORD God took the man and put him in the garden of Eden to tend and keep it."* Genesis 2:15 NKJV

You were there, in Adam. You were made to be perfect in every way.

God created Eve from the rib of Adam.

And the LORD God caused a deep sleep to fall on Adam, and he slept; and He took one of his ribs, and closed up the flesh in its place. Then the rib which the LORD God had taken from man He made into a woman, and He brought her to the man. Gen: 2:21-22 NKJV

Together, the two violated the one law God had instituted. They ate the forbidden fruit.

> *Then the serpent said to the woman, 'You will not surely die. For God knows that in the day you eat of it your eyes will be opened, and you will be like God, knowing good and evil.' So when the woman saw that the tree was good for food, that it was pleasant to the eyes, and a tree desirable to make one wise, she took of its fruit and ate. She also gave to her husband with her, and he ate.* Genesis 3:4-6 NKJV

They became corrupted. Their seed was damaged. Their characters became flawed. They would pass their flawed character on to their progeny—you. It's not your fault that you were born the way you are.

God knew this would happen, for He knows the end from the beginning of every story. Therefore, from the foundation of this world, God instituted a plan to remedy the flawed seed of humankind and put you back in the Garden—perfect. The Remedy came in the form of the Son of Man and the Son of God. His name is Jesus Christ.

> *Blessed be the God and Father of our Lord Jesus Christ, who has blessed us with every spiritual blessing in the heavenly places in Christ, just as He chose us in Him before the foundation of the world, that we would be holy and blameless before Him.* Ephesians 1:3-4 NASB

Jesus is the new Seed Who overcame the flaw and is the Way back to Eden. He is the second Adam.

> *If there is a natural body, there is also a spiritual body. So it is written: "The first man Adam became a living being; the last Adam, a life-giving spirit. The spiritual did not come first, but the natural, and after that the spiritual. The first man was of the dust of the earth; the second man is of heaven. As was the earthly man, so are those who are of the earth; and as is the heavenly man, so also are those who are of heaven. And just as we have borne the image of the earthly man, so shall we bear the image of the heavenly man.* 1 Corinthians 15:44-49 NIV

You can unite the seed of your humanity to His unflawed essence by acknowledging His gift and accepting Him as your personal Redeemer. To do this, you must be born again. It is a spiritual rebirth. This new birth is not a birth of flesh like coming from your mother's womb. Instead, it is a rebirth of your spiritual being.

> *Jesus answered and said to him, "Most assuredly, I say to you, unless one is born again, he cannot see the kingdom of God."Nicodemus said to Him, "How can a man be born when he is old? Can he enter a second time into his mother's womb and be born?"Jesus answered, "Most assuredly, I say to you, unless one is born of water and the Spirit, he cannot enter the kingdom of God. That which is born of the flesh is flesh, and that which is born of the Spirit is spirit.* John 3-6 NKJV

This spiritual rebirth is a seed planted in you by the grace of God and nourished by your faith in its reality. It is as real as your heartbeat and the air you breathe. It is the breath of new life. This seed sprouts hope in you. The hope of being restored to the eternal, perfect existence humanity was created to enjoy. God has promised this to you. It is yours. The seed of faith in His unlimited Remedy is in you. Nourishing that seed by allowing God to restore you will enable Eden-like fruit to become the produce of your heart, mind, and soul. The core of this fruit is love—God's love

Because of His enduring love for you, the Remedy God has provided can enable you to overcome the flawed character you inherited. *"For you know that God paid a ransom to save you from the empty life you inherited from your ancestors. And it was not paid with mere gold or silver, which lose their value. It was the precious blood of Christ, the sinless, spotless Lamb of God."* [1 Peter 1:18-19 NLT]

Jesus came not only to redeem you but to regenerate you. Therefore, you can be transformed by the renewing of your mind and enjoy the fruit of His Spirit—love, joy, peace, patience, kindness, goodness, faithfulness, gentleness, and self-control. I believe God does this is by sprouting, nurturing, nourishing, and growing *Garden Fresh* motives, affections, desires, feelings, actions, and thoughts in the garden of your mind.

Do you possess the wisdom to be renewed? If not, ask the Father. He will grant it to you—generously! *"If any of you lacks wisdom, you should ask God, who gives generously to all without finding fault, and it will be given to you."* [James 1:5 NIV]

Have you tried to mend your broken soul? Have you sought prosperity, health, and happiness? Have you attempted to fill that gaping, confused hole in your soul? Will you ever be well and joyful? Are you frustrated? Do you often flounder in your struggle against negative, embedded habit loops? Are you ready to experience the full richness, peace, and beautiful joys of freedom that God has promised you?

Many people can't seem to walk away from negativity. Many people start down the path toward a new life only to stall and wonder why they can't or won't let go of the weeds of rebellion.

Some people don't truly wish to be renewed. Their old ways are comfortable and familiar. Who wants to take time away from their addictions, from their other gods, from chasing after worldly goods, television, Facebook, or surfing the internet anyway?

Some people want others to change instead. Some folks believe that happiness is knowing who to blame for their problems, trials, and failures. However, many people don't realize that their problems, trials, and failures are often their greatest blessings? There is an old saying: *"A struggling vine makes the best wine."* [Author Unkown] James discusses this:

> *Count it all joy, my brothers, when you meet trials of various kinds, for you know that the testing of your faith produces steadfastness. And let steadfastness have its full effect, that you may be perfect and complete, lacking in nothing. If any of you lacks wisdom, let him ask God, who gives generously to all without reproach, and it will be given him. But let him ask in faith, with no doubting, for the one who doubts is like a wave of the sea that is driven and tossed by the wind. For that person must not suppose that he will receive anything from the Lord; he is a double-minded man, unstable in all his ways.* [James 1:2-8 ESV]

Are there joys to be found in the trials of this life? Yes, if they are used productively. Does God wish for you to grow from and through the struggles of being human? Yes! Can God and you use the pain in your life to propel you forward! Yes! Is there valuable knowledge to be drawn from each and every storm, drought, and blight of life? Yes! Does God wish to enlighten and refresh your MADFATs through it all? Yes!

Do you dare seek His ways? Is it time for you to be free? Are you willing to allow Him to renew your mind and transform your life? Does God have the power to recreate you? Without a doubt!

God does not make invalid statements. He promised, *"If anyone is in Christ, he is a new creation; the old has gone, the new has come!"* [1 Corinthians 5:17 NIV]

Is this your reality? Are you in Christ? Are you new? Has the old gone away?

You most certainly can be made new. The promise of new life can be yours. As God inspires your *MADFATs*, you and He together will clarify and enrich your *Nourished Soul.*

Your *MADFATs* will progressively resemble these:
* Motives—God's soul-enriching love and care breathe His ways into all my motives.
* Affections—God's loving-kindness warms my affections for Him, myself, and others.
* Desires—God's enduring faithfulness energizes my desires to know, obey, and honor Him.
* Feelings—God's soothing fruit of love, joy, peace, and patience seasons all my feelings.
* Actions—God's life-supporting laws of love mother my improving actions.
* Thoughts—God's tender love shepherds my thoughts with captivating wisdom.

Motives: Things that cause a person to act in a certain way, do a certain thing, etc, incentive—the goals or objects of a person's actions.

What are the new motivating forces you wish to empower your actions? Remember, you are seeking progressively improving, positive, uplifting, heaven-inspired motives. So, with that thought in mind, what motives do you believe should be driving you?

As a citizen of heaven, it would naturally follow that your motivations should be similar to those of the Son of God and the Son of man—Jesus Christ. In examining His life, it becomes crystal clear that the motivating forces behind His every act and word are invariably defined as soul-enriching love and care.

Motives will vary from person to person. They can also vary within yourself depending upon your spiritual, emotional, mental, and physical state. Regardless of your state of being, as a human, your motives will nearly always be self-absorbed without the heart-turning power implanted by the Holy Spirit. Only His power can banish self-seeking. Zeal for the glory of God and His cause rather than self cannot be self-generated. The Holy Spirit of God must provide this implanted motive. Jesus promises His Holy Spirit—if you ask.

> *So I say to you, ask, and it will be given to you; seek, and you will find; knock, and it will be opened to you. For everyone who asks receives, and he who seeks finds, and to him who knocks it will be opened. If a son asks for bread from any father among you, will he give him a stone? Or if he asks for a fish, will he give him a serpent instead of a fish? Or if he asks for an egg, will he offer him a scorpion? If you then, being evil, know how to give good gifts to your children, how much more will your heavenly Father give the Holy Spirit to those who ask Him!*
> Matthew 11:9-13 NKJV

When your motives have shifted from selfishness and pretense to loving and caring for others, you will know that the Holy Spirit has indeed been working on rewiring you.

Motives of soul-enriching love and care from God's Spirit will assist in dissolving two of the most devastating and corrupted character flaws inherited by each human soul—self-centeredness and fear. Don't fool yourself—*"All a person's ways seem pure to them, but motives are weighed by the Lord."* Proverbs 16:2 NIV

Only you and God can determine what your true motives are and how, together, you will strive to move yours into alignment with His.

Seeking glory for God through the soul-enriching love and care of yourself and others are beautiful motives to camp your life's patterns around. You can launch safely from these spiritual ports of call and seek new horizons as well as subtle variations on their themes. As you do this, God will breathe His enlightened brand of soul-enriching love and care into all your motives.

Jesus explained how to recognize His disciples: *"A new command I give you: Love one another. As I have loved you, so you must love one another. By this everyone will know that you are my disciples, if you love one another."* John 13:34-35 NIV

God's soul-enriching love and care breathe His ways into all my motives.

<u>*Affections:*</u> A fond attachment, devotion, or love. Someone or something you are attracted to.

What and who should you love? What are going to be your new attachments, devotions, and loves? What are the new affections you should cherish?

Remember, you are seeking progressively improving, positive, uplifting, heaven-inspired affections. With that thought in mind, what affections do you wish to rule your heart? Your affections should spring from your relationship with God. As you walk ever closer with Him and spend time in His presence, your affections will naturally change. You will love what He loves. You will seek what He seeks. You will be devoted to what He is devoted to.

What or who is God devoted to? What or who does He love? To whom is He attached? Scripture reveals that God is faithfully attached to, devoted to, and loves; Jesus, His Holy Spirit, and His created beings. God is love. You too, will become love as He renovates your heart. God's loving-kindness will warm your affections for Him, yourself, and others. The following pertinent scriptures demonstrate the focus of God's loves, attachments, and devotions. Jesus declared:

> *As the Father has loved me, so have I loved you. Now remain in my love. If you keep my commands, you will remain in my love, just as I have kept my Father's commands and remain in his love. I have told you this so that my joy may be in you and that your joy may be complete. My command is this: Love each other as I have loved you. Greater love has no one than this: to lay down one's life for one's friends.* John 15:9-13 NIV

And He said that the first and greatest commandment was to:

> *Love the Lord your God with all your heart and with all your soul and with all your mind and with all your strength. The second is this: 'Love your neighbor as yourself.' There is no commandment greater than these.* Matthew 12:30 NIV

Jesus will always seek to direct you toward the deepest essence of His laws of love and liberty; loving God, yourself, and others. When God's loving-kindness warms your affections, you will discover captivating delights in loving Him, yourself, and others in real and practical ways. You will realize that His Spirit is indeed—refreshing your soul. You will fulfill the law of love. It is written:

> *"Let no debt remain outstanding, except the continuing debt to love one another, for whoever loves others has fulfilled the law."* Romans 13:8 NIV

> *"For in Christ Jesus neither circumcision nor uncircumcision has any value. The only thing that counts is faith expressing itself through love."* Galatians 5:6 NIV

As your affections are transformed, you will discover a joy that few humans ever experience. You, my friend, will be free. You will become warmly affectionate toward God, yourself, and others.

To be attached and devoted to the things of this world often brings bondage to your soul. You can't keep them anyway. Why spend your life chasing them? Give up trying to gain the world. It won't last. Seek that which cannot be lost—loving-kindness toward God, yourself, and others.

God's loving-kindness warms my affections for Him, myself, and others.

Desires: Wish or long for, crave, want, a longing or craving, as for something that brings you satisfaction or enjoyment.

What and who should you eagerly desire? What are going to be your wants, cravings, and longings? What new desires should you long for? Remember, you are seeking progressively improving, positive, uplifting, heaven-inspired desires. So, with that thought in mind, what desires do you wish to rule your heart?

Your aspirations, yearnings, hungers, and inclinations will pull you toward what you focus on. You go where you focus. Consider this verse from the Psalm of Asaph as he sings to God:

I was so foolish and ignorant—I must have seemed like a senseless animal to you. Yet I still belong to you; you hold my right hand. You guide me with your counsel, leading me to a glorious destiny. Whom have I in heaven but you? I desire you more than anything on earth. Psalm 73:22-25 NLT

Are you there? Do you desire God more than anything on earth? Where is your daily focus? When you make a wish list, is improving your relationship with Him at the top? Jesus said that the greatest commandment was to love God with all your heart, mind, soul, and strength—was that for God's benefit or yours? He also said: *"And this is eternal life, that they may know You, the only true God, and Jesus Christ whom You have sent."* John 17:3 NKJV

If you are reading this book, my guess is that you have heard the call to eternal life. How do you get that? According to Jesus: *"this is eternal life, that they may know You, the only true God, and Jesus Christ whom You have sent."*

So put knowing, obeying, and honoring God on an ever-deepening level at the top of your list of new desires.

As you grow closer to Him and watch Him work in your life, it will become very obvious that He is faithful—even when you're not. It is written: *"If we die with him, we will also live with him; if we endure hardship, we will reign with him. If we deny him, he will deny us; if we are unfaithful, he remains faithful, for he cannot deny who he is."* 2 Timothy 2:11 NLT

He will faithfully strengthen and guard you from the evil one, guide you through this broken world, provide an escape from temptation, and brighten your days with fresh mercy each morning. He is faithful! It is written:

"No temptation has overtaken you except such as is common to man; but God is faithful, who will not allow you to be tempted beyond what you are able, but with the temptation will also make the way of escape, that you may be able to bear it." 1 Corinthians 10:13 NKJV

"But the Lord is faithful; he will strengthen you and guard you from the evil one." 2 Thes. 3:3 NLT

"The faithful love of the LORD never ends! His mercies never cease. Great is his faithfulness; his mercies begin afresh each morning." Lamentations 3:22-23 NLT

Experiencing the enduring faithfulness of God will energize your desires to know, obey, and honor Him. The soul-enriching love you share will grow. All other desires will fade to insignificance. You will rise with the morning and delight in the Lord's fresh mercies. It is in walking with and coming to know Him, as He truly is, that will make your excitement grow. All else will follow. Delight in knowing, obeying, and honoring God, and He will give you your heart's desires. King David wrote:

Trust in the Lord and do good. Then you will live safely in the land and prosper. Take delight in the Lord, and he will give you your heart's desires. Psalm 37:3-4 NLT

God's enduring faithfulness energizes my desires to know, obey, and honor Him.

Feelings: Emotions or emotional perceptions or attitudes; capacity for emotion, especially compassion.

Let's take a glimpse at some of the emotional tangles your complex store of feelings might whip up. These include the broad strokes of love, tenderness, warmth, anger, awe, patience, resentment, fear, hope, sorrow, serenity, anxiousness, grief, gratitude, kindness, self-pity, inspiration, lust, pride, surprise, greed, envy, confidence, depression, cheerfulness, passion, sympathy, enthusiasm, guilt, euphoria, empathy, concern, amusement, loneliness, contentment, joy, peace, and more.

You, my friend, are a wonder-filled and complicated creation! By allowing the Spirit's fruit of love, joy, peace, and patience to quiet your immense and often wandering flock of feelings, you will enjoy a soothing tranquility.

Remember, you are seeking progressively improving, positive, uplifting, heaven-inspired feelings. With that thought in mind, what feelings do you wish to rule your heart?

Your feelings are most likely the basis of nearly all your decisions. Right or wrong, it is true. Most people don't make decisions rationally. Most people make decisions emotionally. This is a key to why Jesus taught in parables. He wished to help people see the light through an emotional context and make decisions that would lead them to understand His mission and accept Him as their Savior.

He told stories about real-life situations that people had emotional attachments to. He didn't argue His points with a lot of pertinent facts, reasons, and logical data. He told a story. People understood His message readily and were often touched emotionally.

His teaching style was even prophesied:

"Jesus spoke all these things to the crowd in parables; he did not say anything to them without using a parable. So was fulfilled what was spoken through the prophet: 'I will open my mouth in parables, I will utter things hidden since the creation of the world.'" Matthew 13:34-35 NIV

God is love. Love is a dramatically vital emotion. It may be the most crucial, hungered-for feeling in the entire universe. Since God is love—God is emotional. Are all emotions good for you? No. Two of the most damaging emotional states are unhealthy, destructive fear and guilt.

A key element in God's strategy of moving you away from unhealthy, unproductive fear and guilt involves planting and nourishing the positive, spiritual fruit of love, joy, peace, and patience into your mind. If you nurture them, they will grow.

When you allow His Spirit's soothing fruit to season all your feelings, you will experience ever-advancing harmony with God's intent and design for you as His cherished child. So help Him plant the fruits of the kingdom of heaven in the garden of your mind. They will surely blossom, producing sweet, delicious harvests for all to enjoy. Jesus discussed this phenomenon in parables:

> *The kingdom of heaven is like a mustard seed, which a man took and planted in his field. Though it is the smallest of all seeds, yet when it grows, it is the largest of garden plants and becomes a tree, so that the birds come and perch in its branches. He told them still another parable: "The kingdom of heaven is like yeast that a woman took and mixed into about sixty pounds of flour until it worked all through the dough.* Matthew 13:31-33 NIV

The vital neural pathways of love, joy, peace, and patience that God and you will plant and nourish in your mind may begin as small seeds, but if nurtured and kneaded, they will grow into dominant plants in the garden of your soul and work all through it until your mind is filled with the Bread of life. These fruits of the Spirit will calm your anxious moments. They reside at the heart of your renewal. All other feelings will be brought under their authority.

Love is the foundation and power that upholds and sustains God's entire creation. During your *Nourished Soul's* healing and restorative journey into love-based living, the emotion of love will direct and leaven all others. Negative feelings will be dissolved by your brain as you discontinue using them. God will lift you above self-centered, fear-based patterns into His transcendent, freeing light. As He does this, His soothing fruit of love, joy, peace, and patience will tastefully season all of your feelings. That, my friend, is a sweet place from which to enjoy life.

God's soothing fruit of love, joy, peace, and patience seasons all my feelings.

<u>*Actions:*</u> Things done or performed. Acts that you consciously will and that may be characterized by physical or mental activity—conduct.

What are the new actions that will characterize you as a citizen of heaven? Remember, you are seeking progressively improving, positive, uplifting, heaven-inspired actions. With that thought in mind, what actions do you wish to reveal your true spirit?

When your motives, affections, desires, feelings, and thoughts are inspired and influenced by God's Spirit of power, love, and self-control, your actions will transcend the boundaries of a self-centered, fear-based existence. As the renewing of your mind transforms you, your behavior will become refined. God's life-supporting laws of love will mother your improving actions. You will be a light in the world.

> *You are the light of the world. A town built on a hill cannot be hidden. Neither do people light a lamp and put it under a bowl. Instead they put it on its stand, and it gives light to everyone in the house. In the same way, let your light shine before others, that they may see your good deeds and glorify your Father in heaven.* Matthew 5:14-16 NIV

Don't forget; this is not a self-help book designed to correct your behaviors. This book is about dying to self and selfishness and living to bring loving honor to God and loving care to yourself and others. When these become the overwhelming inclinations of your heart—your being will naturally reflect Him—the Father of useful, love-based actions.

You may wish to strive to emulate the attitude of James:

> *What good is it, dear brothers and sisters, if you say you have faith but don't show it by your actions? Can that kind of faith save anyone? Suppose you see a brother or sister who has no food or clothing, and you say, "Good-bye and have a good day; stay warm and eat well"—but then you don't give that person any food or clothing. What good does that do?*
>
> *So you see, faith by itself isn't enough. Unless it produces good deeds, it is dead and useless.*
>
> *Now someone may argue, "Some people have faith; others have good deeds." But I say, "How can you show me your faith if you don't have good deeds? I will show you my faith by my good deeds.* James 2:14-18 NLT

Consider the parable of Jesus regarding the final judgment and the separation of the sheep from the goats.

> *But when the Son of Man comes in his glory, and all the angels with him, then he will sit upon his glorious throne. All the nations will be gathered in his presence, and he will separate the people as a shepherd separates the sheep from the goats. He will place the sheep at his right hand and the goats at his left.*
>
> *Then the King will say to those on his right, 'Come, you who are blessed by my Father, inherit the Kingdom prepared for you from the creation of the world. For I was hungry, and you fed me. I was thirsty, and you gave me a drink. I was a stranger, and you invited me into your home. I was naked, and you gave me clothing. I was sick, and you cared for me. I was in prison, and you visited me.'*
>
> *Then these righteous ones will reply, 'Lord, when did we ever see you hungry and feed you? Or thirsty and give you something to drink? Or a stranger and show you hospitality? Or naked and give you clothing? When did we ever see you sick or in prison and visit you?'*
>
> *And the King will say, 'I tell you the truth, when you did it to one of the least of these my brothers and sisters, you were doing it to me!* Matthew 25:31-40 NLT

It is God's great love in you that elevates your compassion for the hungry, the thirsty, the naked, the stranger, the ill, as well as those in prison, and moves you to action. God will create within you empathy for and a drive to love and care for this world's other broken and highly valuable souls.

Overcoming negative character traits in your life is more readily accomplished by focusing your energy on benefiting others in need. You can enjoy the endless benefits of a generous heart. You can walk the surest path into that happy realm by dying to self through actions that involve laying down your narcissistic life in the service of others.

Jesus instructs: *"My command is this: Love each other as I have loved you. Greater love has no one than this: to lay down one's life for one's friends."* John 15:12-13 NIV

God's life-supporting laws of love are all about loving, caring, honorable relationships. As He writes His laws on your heart and mind, self-seeking will vanish. Your actions will demonstrate and dispense your faith. You will help and heal the world.

God's life-supporting laws of love mother my improving actions.

Thoughts: Thinking, reasoning, imagining, etc. A consideration or reflection, meditation, contemplation, or recollection.

Your thought life is the centerpiece of your *Nourished Soul.* Here is where the battles for your soul rage. What should your new thinking, reasoning, and imagining patterns be? Remember, you are seeking progressively improving, positive, uplifting, heaven-inspired thoughts. So, with that thought in mind, what new thought habits do you wish to rule your heart?

Consider this: Thoughts parent actions. You take no action that isn't directed by your thoughts.

Your struggles against the darkness occur within your thought life. Interestingly, resisting the evil one is more likely to be a matter of closeness to God and submission to His ways than it is a matter of personal power to resist the dark side.

Scripture opens the way: *"Therefore submit to God. Resist the devil and he will flee from you. Draw near to God and He will draw near to you."* James 4:7-8 NKJV

Knowing God, as He really is, will awaken in you an eager desire to submit to His loving care and draw near to Him. Then, resisting the darkness will unfold naturally. You will lose the sick need to trade your heavenly treasures for earthly trash.

You were born with an inherited system of neural pathways. The culture of self-centeredness and fear you were raised in has also infected your brain with well-cultivated patterns of thought that are decidedly in opposition to God's original design for the human race.

Your neural pathways will be rewired by God as you allow and assist Him in doing so. He will breathe His ways into your soul. He will bring into existence new, empowering, Spirit-filled neural habits that may not currently populate your mind. As you enjoy their fruit, you will progressively experience the joyous delights found in focusing on them. Your fundamental nature is going to shift. Dark neural patterns will fade away from lack of use as God's tender love shepherds your thoughts with captivating wisdom.

You have control of the thoughts that play on the main screen in your mind. You can choose to change them at will. It is the Spirit of God that plants in you the desire to think good thoughts and avoid the ones that promote darkness. He will captivate your thoughts.

It is written:

> *"We demolish arguments and every pretension that sets itself up against the knowledge of God, and we take captive every thought to make it obedient to Christ."* 2 Corinthians 10:5 NIV

You currently have between twelve and sixty thousand thoughts per day. These are usually repeats of the same thoughts you have nearly every day.

As God restores your soul, your thoughts will become beautifully true to His ideals, noble in their goals, right in their perspectives, pure in their content, lovely in their aspirations, admirable in their meditations, excellent in their ability to bear light and praiseworthy in their resulting actions.

God and you, together, will rewire your thinking habits.

Seek His wisdom and guidance. If you lack wisdom, ask Him, and you shall receive an abundance. *"If any of you lacks wisdom, you should ask God, who gives generously to all without finding fault, and it will be given to you."* James 1:5 NIV

Your mind is a complex neural-river system of free-flowing as well as focused thoughts. The stream of your life flows from the rich valleys of your mind into and through the echoing ripples of the thoughts it generates. Flood your soul with the joyful, life-generating waters flowing lavishly from the wells of salvation. *"With joy, you will draw water from the wells of salvation."* Isaiah 12:3 NIV

Advance. Strive to move forward in nurturing your *Nourished Soul.* Use every advantage to walk patiently with the Spirit of God, as together you focus on building your new neural pathways.

Keep wisdom before you; comprehend its true worth—hunger for wisdom's treasures. Assist the Holy Spirit as He strives to bring your thought patterns into the realm of light.

I, wisdom, dwell together with prudence; I possess knowledge and discretion.
To fear the LORD is to hate evil; I hate pride and arrogance, evil behavior and perverse speech.
Counsel and sound judgment are mine; I have insight, I have power.
By me kings reign and rulers issue decrees that are just; by me princes govern, and nobles—all who rule on earth.
I love those who love me, and those who seek me find me.
With me are riches and honor, enduring wealth and prosperity.
My fruit is better than fine gold; what I yield surpasses choice silver.
I walk in the way of righteousness, along the paths of justice, bestowing a rich inheritance on those who love me and making their treasuries full. Proverbs 8:12-23 NIV

Seek wisdom fervently, my friend. Its rewards are eternally worthy.

Your walk through this life does not need to be burdened. You can be set free from thought-based prisons. You need not fall; you need not fail; you need not suffer hopelessly. God's tender love will shepherd your thoughts with captivating wisdom.

There is a Way to freedom—not the simple freedom of a trouble-free life, but something more profound, richer, and more astonishing than anything you might have ever imagined. It is the freedom that weighs nothing but fills everything. *"So if the Son sets you free, you are truly free."* John 8:36 NLT

Amazing changes are coming your way. Your thought patterns will rise above the sewage of a fear-encrusted existence and glow with the light of love. Your inner life will be satisfied and enriched beyond all comprehension. Victory over the dark rebellion will increase as your weapons are sharpened. You will experience first-hand what Paul wrote:

The weapons we fight with are not the weapons of the world. On the contrary, they have divine power to demolish strongholds. We demolish arguments and every pretension that sets itself up against the knowledge of God, and we take captive every thought to make it obedient to Christ. 2 Corinthians 10: 4-5 NIV

A fundamental factor in refreshing your soul is the perpetual planting, nourishing, and fertilizing of heaven's seeds of love, joy, peace, and patience. Each day, as you spend time in scripture and focus on that day's *Nourished Soul Gardening Guide*, you will be germinating, sprouting, and growing the *Garden Fresh MADFATs* that God's Holy Spirit is implanting in you. As a result, you will move forward with His captivating wisdom, guidance, and power.

God's tender love shepherds my thoughts with captivating wisdom.

Mr. Paul's Insights, Inspirations, and Experiences Chapter Three

(As each Chapter neared completion, Mr. Paul would review it. Then, we would discuss it. I recorded our post review discussions. What follows are poignant and interesting excerpts from his recorded comments.)

* As you refer to the garden of Eden, I always come up with this major challenge I've had for years and years about the tree of knowledge of good and evil. From my perspective, God's character as revealed in James Chapter One: God cannot be tempted with evil, neither does he tempt anyone else with evil. The idea that He set man up to sin really contradicts His character. And the other reason I feel that God could not have created it—it had mixture., (good and evil). Everything God creates is totally pure. He has no mixture. So, those two issues really challenge my wanting to accept that He created the tree of knowledge of good and evil.
When God created the universe, He did it through His spoken word. But when it came to the creation of the human race, the whole thing changed. He physically came to the earth and physically picked up dust to form the body of man and breathed into him the breath of life. The next thing He did physically, He planted a garden for him. You see, that makes a significant statement. Everything else, as magnificent as it was, was created by word. But, when it came to the human race, it was hands-on. It was a different thing altogether. It was a significant demonstration.

* I feel that satan attended the conversation when God gave dominion over the earth to Adam. When he heard the words, *"Let him have dominion over everything we made."* It clicked. All of a sudden, he thought, "There's a god position. I'm gonna get it. I couldn't take His; I'm gonna get this one." And he designed a system to take the godhead away from Adam. I believe that the tree of the knowledge of good and evil was a genetically modified organism.

God, on His walk with Adam and Eve one day, said: "See that tree over there? That's not good for you; it's been altered. It's been changed. Don't eat it." He was only watching out for them. He was not setting them up to sin. The tree He warned them about wasn't good. Again, just think about His character. He doesn't tempt man to sin, and that tree was set up to tempt man to sin. And He doesn't have mixture. Everything He creates is pure. But, that tree had mixture. (good and evil). It doesn't align with His character. And I really believe that satan set that up to take the godhead away from Adam. He saw that opportunity and thought. "I get one more chance to be a god." And he took it. He took it away from Adam because God created Adam to be the god of this world, not satan.

When the New Jerusalem comes down from heaven, it will be just like the Garden of Eden. The tree of life is there. But the tree of the knowledge of good and evil is not there. I don't believe it was there in the beginning.

* This chapter references James Chapter 1, where James advises us that when we ask God for something, we should ask in faith. *"For He who doubts should not suppose that he will receive anything from the Lord."* I think that is such a huge principle a person needs to get. This is why satan always casts unbelief and doubt because he knows the word. And it says so clearly there that if you doubt, you should not expect anything from God. That's why in Hebrews, it says: *"Without faith, it is impossible to please God."* Faith is the only way to access God. When you have doubt and unbelief, you can completely cancel out anything from God. This is such a powerful reality that many people don't even think about. We need to get how critical it is to remain in faith. For when we are in doubt, God will often have nothing to do with it. And that's huge!

We've all had doubts because the enemy knows how effective they are. He puts those doubts in our minds. They are not from us. We don't think them up. He gives them to us. Because he knows the power of doubt, he knows that when we go there, we cancel out our connection with God. He's not stupid.

Faith is so powerful. Faith comes by hearing the word. When you hear the word, faith rises up, you believe, and say, "Yes! That makes sense. That's the truth!"

(I asked Mr. Paul if he was comfortable sharing more of his personal life with us. He said, "Sure, ask whatever you like." So, I asked how he and his wife Carol met.)

When I got back from Viet Nam, Carol's brother and my brother were really like major trouble makers. They always got in fights at school and were just real trouble makers.

When I got home, my brother said to Carol, "My brother just got back from Viet Nam; why don't you go out with him?" So she did, as a favor to him. And she didn't like me at all. Because I had just gotten back from Viet Nam and was like most guys coming back from there. I was not normal. So, it didn't go anywhere.

So, several years later, she asked one of our friends from high school, "What ever happened to that guy Paul Gautschi?" They told her, "Oh, he's going to Bible school right now." She had just gotten saved through the Jesus movement in California lead by Chuck Smith. When she heard I was in Bible school, she said, "Wow!" And started to write to me.

I was working in a camp in Wisconsin, and when I came home, I started connecting with her. And

I really pursued her. She didn't like it at all. But, man, I really made an effort. I was bringing her roses, making food for her; I was totally on it. And I won!

Both Carol and I have one sibling, but together we have seven children. She is not into gardening like me. She loves the produce but doesn't love to garden. She loves picking it. She really enjoys picking it.

(When you left California for Washington, was Carol on board with that move?)

It's really interesting how the Word gives us instructions. It says, *"A man should leave his father and mother and cleave to his wife."* It doesn't say that a wife should leave her father and mother; it says the man should. And I think the reason is this: If a man stays around his family, he gets carried. He never develops the responsibility of becoming a caregiver and taking care of his family because he's being helped.

I was finding that my mother is really strong and Carol is really strong. There was a lot of conflict. My mom was trying to tell us how to run our household, and Carol said, "No way." I knew it was best for our relationships to move away.

(Did you guys go back to visit much?)

Oh, it was awesome. God was so cool in what He did for us. We would go back every Christmas to be with our families. What was so awesome about that, I used to work for this doctor down there who had acreage above the Rose Bowl. He loved what I did with his trees as a professional arborist. He said, "When you come to California, tell me how long you want to be here, and I'll set you up with work." And he would set me up with all these doctors to work on their trees.

What was so nice about that is in January, it's so nice in California, and it's not nice here in Washington. And, I would make more in California in a month than I would make in Washington in a year. It was so cool. My kids would go to Disneyland cause Carol's mom's cousin was a buyer for them and would get us tickets. It was just such an incredible experience for years. We went down there every winter. It was so ideal. Also, the people we sold our house to would go on vacation about that time and would have us stay in the house to protect the place while they were gone. It was so awesome! All the details just came together. It was so nice!

Chapter Notes and Discussion Topics

Notes ___

How did this chapter affect you? And why? ___

Did you gain any new perspectives or perceptions? ___

What changed in you after reading this chapter? ___

How can you use this knowledge to help improve your relationships with God, yourself, and others?

Chapter Four

The Nourished Soul Gardening Guide for:

The Good Soil Promise

"Not by might nor by power, but by my Spirit,' says the Lord Almighty." Zechariah 4:6 NIV

Listen then to what the parable of the sower means: When anyone hears the message about the kingdom and does not understand it, the evil one comes and snatches away what was sown in their heart. This is the seed sown along the path. The seed falling on rocky ground refers to someone who hears the word and at once receives it with joy. But since they have no root, they last only a short time. When trouble or persecution comes because of the word, they quickly fall away. The seed falling among the thorns refers to someone who hears the word, but the worries of this life and the deceitfulness of wealth choke the word, making it unfruitful. But the seed falling on good soil refers to someone who hears the word and understands it. This is the one who produces a crop, yielding a hundred, sixty or thirty times what was sown. Matthew 13: 18-25 NIV

So, how does a person enjoy the promise of being the "good soil" so they hear and understand the message about the kingdom of God? To begin, one must be born again:

Jesus answered, "Most assuredly, I say to you, unless one is born of water and the Spirit, he cannot enter the kingdom of God. That which is born of the flesh is flesh, and that which is born of the Spirit is spirit." John 3:5-6 NKJV

You were born in the flesh through no choice of your own. Being born of the Spirit, however, involves a free will choice. I believe that the Spirit of God calls all souls homeward. But we must willingly allow Him to woo us. Being born again, as Jesus revealed, is a spiritual birth that involves the seeds of God's Spirit being planted in your heart, mind, and soul. This spiritual rebirth experience is an ongoing process that expands limitlessly as one matures in their walk with Him. It is the love walk with Jesus that inspires the desire to seek the richest soil of God's Spirit.

If you love me, you will obey what I command. And I will ask the Father, and he will give you another Counselor to be with you forever—the Spirit of truth. The world cannot accept him, because it neither sees him nor knows him. But you know him, for he lives with you and will be in you. *John 14:15-17 NIV*

As a result of the Spirit of God dwelling in you, you will be freely given the ability to discern heavenly, spiritual things that the spirit and wisdom of the world cannot comprehend.

For what man knows the things of a man except the spirit of the man which is in him? Even so no one knows the things of God except the Spirit of God. Now we have received, not the spirit of the world, but the Spirit who is from God, that we might know the things that have been freely given to us by God. These things we also speak, not in words which man's wisdom teaches but which the Holy Spirit teaches, comparing spiritual things with spiritual. But the natural man does not receive the things of the Spirit of God, for they are foolishness to him; nor can he know them, because they are spiritually discerned. 1 Corinthians 11-14 NKJV

The power to hear and understand the spiritual things that will transform you into the soil of the Spirit, "the good soil," comes from the Spirit of God. Jesus promises you the Holy Spirit if you ask. He said:

So I say to you, ask, and it will be given to you; seek, and you will find; knock, and it will be opened to you. For everyone who asks receives, and he who seeks finds, and to him who knocks it will be opened. If a son asks for bread from any father among you, will he give him a stone? Or if he asks for a fish, will he give him a serpent instead of a fish? Or if he asks for an egg, will he offer him a scorpion? If you then, being evil, know how to give good gifts to your children, how much more will your heavenly Father give the Holy Spirit to those who ask Him! Luke 11:9-13 NKJV

As a human, you may have some success in manipulating your feelings, actions, and thoughts (FATs). Even so, you will have little, if any, success in transforming your motives, affections, and desires. (MADs). Motives, affections, and desires are spiritually born. As such, they require the appropriate spiritual nourishment and nurture. They thrive on the forces of darkness or light. You choose the diet that sustains the force you wish to feed. Unfortunately, because you were born human, all your motives, affections, desires, feelings, actions, and thoughts are infected with self-centeredness and fear. They need to be rebirthed. God makes that possible.

> *Do not be overcome by evil, but overcome evil with good. I beseech you therefore, brethren, by the mercies of God, that you present your bodies a living sacrifice, holy, acceptable to God, which is your reasonable service. And do not be conformed to this world, but be transformed by the renewing of your mind, that you may prove what is that good and acceptable and perfect will of God.* Romans 11:21-12:2 NKJV

Being transformed by the renewing of your mind through the influence and power of God's Holy Spirit will turn a heart of stone into good soil.

Rarely, if ever, do human beings recover from or overcome any serious defect of character without the aid of God's power. In the book of Jeremiah, the question is asked: *"Can an Ethiopian change his skin or a leopard its spots? Neither can you do good who are accustomed to doing evil."* Jeremiah 13:23 NIV

Thus, the need for the indwelling presence of God's Holy Spirit.

You, my friend, have found yourself in a tough place—planet earth. You are behind enemy lines and have been infected with an eternally terminal disease—rebellious, self-centeredness.

Born of this disease are a seemingly endless variety of fears. Self-centeredness and its consequent fear-based unease can corrupt your every waking moment and may also venture into your dreams. If you would like to understand how ferociously fear has infested the world in which you live, simply examine a current list of phobias. There are hundreds of them, ranging from ablutophobia—fear of washing or bathing, all the way to zoophobia—fear of animals.

God knows your situation. He wishes to quiet your fears with His love. He longs to save, restore, and rejoice over you. *"The Lord your God in your midst, the Mighty One, will save; He will rejoice over you with gladness, He will quiet you with His love, He will rejoice over you with singing."* Zephaniah 3:17 NKJV

One of the main reasons people spend their lives in fear is that we all know we will eventually die. Without the hope of eternal life beyond this brief earthly existence, fear of death is always lurking, constantly nagging at us. But God uproots the weeds of the fear of death through faith in Jesus, for He has conquered death for us all.

> *For God has not given us a spirit of fear, but of power and of love and of a sound mind. Therefore do not be ashamed of the testimony of our Lord, nor of me His prisoner, but share with me in the sufferings for the gospel according to the power of God, who has saved us and called us with a holy calling, not according to our works, but according to His own purpose and grace which was given to us in Christ Jesus before time began, but has now been revealed by the appearing of our Savior Jesus Christ, who has abolished death and brought life and immortality to light through the gospel, to which I was appointed a preacher, an apostle, and a teacher of the Gentiles.* 2 Timothy 1:8-11 NKJV

The Spirit is sown in us, by God, as a deposit guaranteeing eternal life.

> *In Him you also trusted, after you heard the word of truth, the gospel of your salvation; in whom also, having believed, you were sealed with the Holy Spirit of promise, who is the guarantee of our inheritance until the redemption of the purchased possession, to the praise of His glory.* Ephesians 1:13-14 NKJV

God emptied the treasury of heaven in an effort to ransom, rescue, and restore you. He is a perfect Father. He is compassionate and gracious. He is with you during the good, the bad, and the ugly times of your life. The very best gift He can offer you is His own Spirit to dwell in you. His Spirit does not make you shy or timid but will empower you, open you to love, and aid you in controlling your self-centered, fearful nature. *"For the Spirit God gave us does not make us timid, but gives us power, love and self-control."* 2 Timothy 1:7 NIV

The Spirit of the Lord brings freedom and transforms you back into His image with ever-increasing glory.

> *Now the Lord is the Spirit, and where the Spirit of the Lord is, there is freedom. And we all, who with unveiled faces contemplate the Lord's glory, are being transformed into his image with ever-increasing glory, which comes from the Lord, who is the Spirit.* 1 Corinthians 3:17-18 NIV

Do all humans suffer from addiction? Do you?

Currently, there are nearly forty different types of 12 Step addiction recovery groups. There is a different type of recovery group for every addiction, from AA—Alcoholics Anonymous to WA—Workaholics Anonymous. Regardless of which group you attend, the first issue you are confronted with is personal powerlessness. The first of the Twelve Steps states that we are powerless over (our addiction), and our lives have become unmanageable.

There may be so many different types of addictions infesting humanity because we are born disconnected from God. This leaves a void within us that seeks connection. Unless the connection with Him is live, we often strive to fill that void with whatever distracts us. Through the millennia, many misconnected, searching souls have used indulgence in sensual pleasures, especially sexual pleasures and behaviors involving drugs, alcohol, food, power, work, money, and other addictive elements to numb a lonely heart and distract them from that hollow-inside-feeling. These pleasures often leave you empty, imprisoned, and addicted. It is God's indwelling Spirit that you need. With Him, your deepest hunger is satisfied. With Him, you are imbued with refreshing fullness.

> *Do not get drunk on wine, which leads to debauchery. Instead, be filled with the Spirit, speaking to one another with psalms, hymns, and songs from the Spirit.* Ephesians 5:18-19 NIV

Recovery from any addiction is a gift from God. Recovery is brought about by a renewing of the mind through the influence and power of God's Holy Spirit. Whether we are addicted or not, we all need God's Spiritual power to become the Good Soil that produces a heavenly harvest.

The gift of God's Holy Spirit was delivered as an essential promise before the disciples of Jesus could begin scattering the seeds of the gospel around the world.

Shortly before He was taken up to heaven, Jesus gave this command to them:

> *Do not leave Jerusalem, but wait for the gift my Father promised, which you have heard me speak about. For John baptized with water, but in a few days you will be baptized with the Holy Spirit.* Acts 1:4-5 NIV

Being immersed in water baptism is an experiential delight symbolic of joining Christ in His death and resurrection. Being immersed in the Spirit is also an experiential delight.

The fruit of the Spirit is experienced in the life of the vessel wherein He dwells—love, joy, peace, patience, kindness, goodness, faithfulness, gentleness, and self-control. It is this fruit that your searching soul craves—these satisfy your true hungers.

In addition to His fruit, God's Spirit bestows upon you unique gifts that manifest Himself through you for the common good. The gifts of the Spirit vary from person to person.

We have different gifts, according to the grace given to each of us. If your gift is prophesying, then prophesy in accordance with your faith; if it is serving, then serve; if it is teaching, then teach; if it is to encourage, then give encouragement; if it is giving, then give generously; if it is to lead, do it diligently; if it is to show mercy, do it cheerfully. 1 Corinthians 12: 6-8 NIV

Now to each one the manifestation of the Spirit is given for the common good. To one there is given through the Spirit a message of wisdom, to another a message of knowledge by means of the same Spirit, to another faith by the same Spirit, to another gifts of healing by that one Spirit, to another miraculous powers, to another prophecy, to another distinguishing between spirits, to another speaking in different kinds of tongues, and to still another the interpretation of tongues. All these are the work of one and the same Spirit, and he distributes them to each one, just as he determines." 1 Corinthians 12:7-11 NIV

"Just as He determines." It is on Him—all of it. You wouldn't even be drawn to God without His Spirit calling you, so—don't just go to church—be the church. Use your gifts.

It is often the pain produced by seeking to distract an over-burdened emptiness with the wrong choices that creates in you a willingness to listen to the call of the Spirit and enjoy sharing His gifts. Some will avoid the call. Some will miss the uplifting joys of doing what they ought to do because they want to. Some are weary and altogether weighed down from trying to keep pace with this constantly changing, broken world.

Jesus invites us all to come. *"Come to Me, all who are weary and heavy-laden, and I will give you rest. Take My yoke upon you and learn from Me, for I am gentle and humble in heart, and you will find rest for your souls."* Matthew 11:28-29 NASB

Come home. Find rest for your weary, heavy-laden soul. Sing the Spirits song! Be addiction free! Be reborn! Rebirth occurs in your soul, by the power of the Holy Spirit, but it never happens without your cooperation. God's Spirit is in you; His power is yours and enables you to use the gifts He bestows. Restoration to the foundation of love and care as the motivating principles of your life will only occur when you allow God's Spirit to dwell in you and express Himself through you.

How on earth does one do that? What does that mean anyway?

No human fully understands the process of exactly how God and His Spirit arrive and work in us. Many things about God are either misunderstood, completely wrong, or purposely lied about. His ways are beyond our comprehension. In this life, whether you understand it or not, what God desires, will be achieved. He said:

For my thoughts are not your thoughts, neither are your ways my ways, declares the LORD.

As the heavens are higher than the earth, so are my ways higher than your ways and my thoughts than your thoughts.

As the rain and the snow come down from heaven, and do not return to it without watering the earth and making it bud and flourish, so that it yields seed for the sower and bread for the eater, so is my word that goes out from my mouth: It will not return to me empty, but will accomplish what I desire and achieve the purpose for which I sent it. Isaiah 55: 8-11 NIV

Can you explain how electricity works? You may not completely understand it. This lack of understanding doesn't stop you from utilizing its power. When the power is on, you have faith that flipping the switch will bring the light. Faith is key to releasing the Spirit's power, love, and self-control into your soul. *"Now faith is the assurance of things hoped for, the conviction of things not seen."* Hebrews 11:1 NASB

Where does one get faith? From God's Spirit. It comes through His word. *"So then faith comes by hearing, and hearing by the word of God."* Romans 10:17 NKJV

Faith comes through exposure to His written, manifested, created, and shared word.

<u>The written word:</u> *"All Scripture is God-breathed and is useful for teaching, rebuking, correcting and training in righteousness, so that the servant of God may be thoroughly equipped for every good work."* 2 Timothy 3:16-17 NIV

<u>The manifested Word—God's Son, Jesus:</u> *"In the beginning was the Word, and the Word was with God, and the Word was God. He was in the beginning with God. All things were made through Him, and without Him nothing was made that was made. In Him was life, and the life was the light of men."* John 1:1-4 NKJV

<u>The spoken words of creation:</u> *"Then God said, "Let there be light"; and there was light." "For since the creation of the world God's invisible qualities—his eternal power and divine nature—have been clearly seen, being understood from what has been made, so that people are without excuse."* Genesis 1:3 NASB & Romans 1:20 NIV

<u>The Shared word:</u> *"Go therefore and make disciples of all the nations, baptizing them in the name of the Father and of the Son and of the Holy Spirit, teaching them to observe all things that I have commanded you; and lo, I am with you always, even to the end of the age."* Matthew 28:19-20 NKJV

Open yourself to God's word—it is everywhere! Gather it in—then give it away through your Holy Spirit endowed gifts.

Willingness to surrender your heart of rebellion and obey in love are also gifts of God's Spirit—pray for these benefits. Be humble. Find faith. It has worked for countless others—it will work for you. You may not be able to explain precisely how the Spirit of God works—however, you should still ask Him, in faith, to bestow upon you His benefits of power, love, and self-control as well as His fruit of love, joy, peace, patience, kindness, goodness, faithfulness, and gentleness.

All have witnessed His power first hand. For all have experienced Him working in their lives and see Him working in the lives of others. It is doubtful that you would be reading this book without His prompting. By accessing the power and light that come from the Holy Spirit and filling your heart, mind, soul, and imagination with the word of God, you are empowered to displace the darkness. You are enabled to replace fearful, guilt-laden, rebellious thoughts and life choices with those that reflect God's perfect character. As this experience becomes the basis of your life's journey, you will realize the immense, consuming power of your allies. In the book of Romans, Paul reveals your victory in the battle that rages over your soul. He writes:

> *If God is for us, who can be against us? He who did not spare his own Son, but gave him up for us all—how will he not also, along with him, graciously give us all things? Who will bring any charge against those whom God has chosen? It is God who justifies. Who is he that condemns?*
>
> *Christ Jesus, who died—more than that, who was raised to life—is at the right hand of God and is also interceding for us. Who shall separate us from the love of Christ? Shall trouble or hardship or persecution or famine or nakedness or danger or sword? ... No, in all these things we are more than conquerors through him who loved us.*
>
> *For I am convinced that neither death nor life, neither angels nor demons, neither the*

present nor the future, nor any powers, neither height nor depth, nor anything else in all creation, will be able to separate us from the love of God that is in Christ Jesus our Lord. Romans 8: 31-39 NIV

God is so very gracious to provide us with such rock-solid confidence and hope.

It is God's divine power that will give you everything you need. With this thought in mind, take a serious look at the first chapter in Second Peter. As you do, you will come to a fuller understanding of the victory that is yours. You will become ever more productive and effective in your knowledge of our Lord Jesus Christ. The wisdom and insight contained in the first few verses of Chapter One of Peter's second book are astounding! Here, Peter reveals deep truths of victory and promise that you will experience as you are restored. The promises contained in the following verses are foundational to your restorative process. Peter writes:

His divine power has given us everything we need for life and godliness through our knowledge of him who called us by his own glory and goodness. Through these he has given us his very great and precious promises, so that through them you may participate in the divine nature and escape the corruption in the world caused by evil desires.

For this very reason, make every effort to add to your faith goodness; and to goodness, knowledge; and to knowledge, self-control; and to self-control, perseverance; and to perseverance, godliness; and to godliness, brotherly kindness; and to brotherly kindness, love. For if you possess these qualities in increasing measure, they will keep you from being ineffective and unproductive in your knowledge of our Lord Jesus Christ. But if anyone does not have them, he is nearsighted and blind, and has forgotten that he has been cleansed from his past sins.

Therefore, my brothers, be all the more eager to make your calling and election sure. For if you do these things, you will never fall, and you will receive a rich welcome into the eternal kingdom of our Lord and Savior Jesus Christ. 2 Peter 1:3-11 NIV

Wow! Those are incredibly hope-filled promises.

It is God's divine power that gives you everything you need for life and godliness. Godliness!

Have you ever reached out for godliness? The desire for this state of being is a gift from above. This comes to you through your knowledge of Him. One definition of the word knowledge is familiarity. The more familiar you are with God, as He truly is, the more you will be drawn to Him. He is love, and He is light.

He has called you "by His own glory and goodness." When your picture of God is true, you cannot help but be drawn into His everlasting presence. He is glorious and valuable beyond any earthly treasure. He wants you in His life, now and forevermore. He longs to treat you like the royal child you are. Surrender to His Spirit's power, and He will lift you above misery and defeat.

Through God's glory and goodness, He has given you His very great and precious promises. You may rise above self-centered, fear-based living and the survival-of-the-fittest mentality of the evil one and delve deeply into the fearless home of love—even as you walk through the valley of the shadow of death. *"Yea, though I walk through the valley of the shadow of death, I will fear no evil; for You are with me; Your rod and Your staff, they comfort me."* Psalm 23:4 NKJV

Nothing and no one can separate you from the love of God—except you. He has provided for your complete redemption and restoration. Accept that you are accepted. Make Him your King!

God sacrificed Himself in the form of His Son to open the door of eternal life for you. And He offers Himself in the form of His Spirit to achieve victory over dark desires and carry you through the valley of the shadow of death that *is* this broken world. Rejoice, my friend, rejoice!

Self-centeredness and its ever-empty striving of fear cannot be satisfied. Self-centeredness always desperately needs more. The Spirit's indwelling heart of love and care will always fill you to overflowing and satisfy your heart's deepest desires.

It is the Spirit's task to restore you and your task to be available for Him. You may do this by seeking His power and insights through Scripture and creation and by allowing Him to guide your inner search as He directly reveals to you the light that will subdue the dark places in your heart.

Having the Holy Spirit of God dwelling within your heart is the only way to be the good soil and become increasingly effective and productive in your knowledge of our Lord Jesus Christ.

God's Spirit is your guide, comforter, and counselor on earth. He provides the power across the bridge that Jesus restored by living an unblemished, perfect, human life and bearing the burden of human suffering caused by rebellion. Jesus laid down His life for you and picked it up again as He rose from the grave to grant you victory through faith in His unfathomable, selfless sacrifice.

Jesus has healed the broken connection between heaven and earth.

Adam and Eve chose to admit into their domain the rebellious nature that would rip apart the sacred fabric of their offspring's characters. But Jesus has healed the great wound. You are born broken and powerless to repair yourself. Jesus Christ, the Great Physician, has provided everything you need for life and godliness.

The Spirit of God sees the future clearly. He can see around corners. He knows the end from the beginning. Seek His presence in your daily walk. Allow His fruit to bloom and produce fresh, succulent treats in the empowering moments of your earthly travels. Seek Him. He proclaims: *"... you will seek Me and find Me, when you search for Me with all your heart."* Jerimiah 29:13 NKJV

Are you eager to make your calling and election sure? If not, your mind may still be clogged with sewage from the lies of the enemy. Let God write His words on the tablet of your heart. He proclaims: *"I will put my law in their minds and write it on their hearts. I will be their God, and they will be my people."* Jeremiah 31:33 NIV

God's law is the perfect, restoring the art of love. *"The law of the Lord is perfect, restoring the soul; the testimony of the Lord is sure, making wise the simple."* Psalm 19:7 NKJV

Let the Holy Spirit's good soil of power, love, and self-control nourish the roots and fruits of your soul. In doing so, you will be refreshed and refreshing. Open your heart to Him, and He will enable you to access the full richness of His nutrient-dense spiritual sustenance.

You are His royal child. You are a citizen of His kingdom that will never, ever end. Love has triumphed over fear. Good is victorious over evil. God has been vindicated. He has given you everything you need for life and godliness. He wills to empower you with humble strength.

Jesus has all power. He freely offers His power to you through the indwelling presence and influence of His Holy Spirit. He will never leave you. It is written:

> *And Jesus came and spake unto them, saying, All power is given unto me in heaven and in earth. Go ye therefore, and teach all nations, baptizing them in the name of the Father, and of the Son, and of the Holy Ghost: Teaching them to observe all things whatsoever I have commanded you: and, lo, I am with you always, even unto the end of the world. Amen.*
> Matthew 28:18-20 KJV

All power is given to Jesus. He is very good at sharing. He has promised to share His soul-nourishing Spirit of power, love, and self-control with you. So ask Him. Then, reveal His

Spirit's transforming influence to the universe by being the good soil and producing crops that are succulent with His fruit of love, joy, peace, patience, kindness, goodness, faithfulness, gentleness, and self-control. Each day, invite His Spirit into the center of your mind's garden and allow Him to dominate your *Nourished Soul,* and you will enjoy the good soil promise.

"Those who are dominated by the sinful nature think about sinful things, but those who are controlled by the Holy Spirit think about things that please the Spirit. So letting your sinful nature control your mind leads to death. But letting the Spirit control your mind leads to life and peace. For the sinful nature is always hostile to God. It never did obey God's laws, and it never will. That's why those who are still under the control of their sinful nature can never please God. But you are not controlled by your sinful nature. You are controlled by the Spirit if you have the Spirit of God living in you." Romans 8:5-9 NLT

"Finally, be strong in the Lord and in his mighty power. Put on the full armor of God, so that you can take your stand against the devil's schemes. For our struggle is not against flesh and blood, but against the rulers, against the authorities, against the powers of this dark world and against the spiritual forces of evil in the heavenly realms." Ephesians 6:10 NIV

The Holy Spirit's soil of power, love, and self-control nourishes the roots and fruits of my soul.

Mr. Paul's Insights, Inspirations, and Experiences Chapter Four

(As each Chapter neared completion, Mr. Paul would review it. Then, we would discuss it. I recorded our post review discussions. What follows are poignant and interesting excerpts from his recorded comments.)

* The statement is made in this chapter: *"It is God's indwelling Spirit that you need. With Him, your deepest hunger is satisfied. With Him, you are imbued with refreshing fullness."* When I read that, what came to mind was the Rolling Stones song, *"I Can't Get No Satisfaction."* Their song title should have been. *"I Can't Get No Satisfaction Apart From God."* Cause that's the reality. We were created with a God-shaped vacuum inside of us that nothing but Him can fill. That's by design.

* Also, in this chapter is stated: Jesus invites us all to come. *"Come to Me, all who are weary and heavy-laden, and I will give you rest. Take My yoke upon you and learn from Me, for I am gentle and humble in heart, and you will find rest for your souls."* I really love the term, *"Take My yoke upon you,"* because it's an agricultural term. That is what they used to do the tilling to destroy the ground. I love how Jesus says: *"Come learn of Me. I don't do things like you do. My yoke is easy. My burden is light."* That is such a beautiful picture of the reality. I used to work so hard to fail. I tilled and did all this damaging work for years and years and never realized how futile and counterproductive it was.

* I saw how satan immediately influenced Adam to do that destructive work. Outside the Garden was the first time man began the destructive work of tilling the soil. This practice was from the influence of the devil. Cause he didn't do that in the Garden. Tilling the soil is so counterproductive. The thing that always amazes me is that we are supposed to be intelligent beings, and we should be seeing this. The Scripture that comes to mind says, *"How the god of this world has blinded the eyes of them lest, the light of the gospel of the glory of Christ, who is the image of God, should shine on them."* You know satan blinds our eyes, and we don't see. We keep doing these stupid things. However, I do get people who come to my place all the time who are really wanting to change things. A woman came yesterday who was moving to a ten thousand acre cattle farm in Argentina. We had the most amazing visit. I really tried to give her respect. She seemed to have been blessed by being here and seeing how Back to Eden Gardening works. It was great.

* I love the Scripture you quoted about the written word: *"All Scripture is God-breathed and is useful for teaching, rebuking, correcting and training in righteousness, so that the servant of God may be thoroughly equipped for every good work."* That means; doing things right. I love that! God's word teaches us how to do things right. It's such an awesome reality.

* You also quoted John 1:1-4 *"In the beginning was the Word, and the Word was with God, and the Word was God. He was in the beginning with God. All things were made through Him, and without Him nothing was made that was made. In Him was life, and the life was the light of men."* The translation you quoted says that all things were made *through* Him. But the King James Version states that, *"All things were made by Him."* I think that is a much more significant word. Everything was made by Him. He did it all. It was His word that created. It wasn't through Him; it was by Him. He did it all. The completed work.

*You quoted the verse, *"For God has not given us a spirit of fear, but of power and of love and of a sound mind."* I think that is so significant. Fear is not an emotion; it is a spirit. And it has the same power in the negative as faith has in the positive. It is something that we should give no place to—ever because it is really a destructive, damaging spirit. It is so awesome that the word says that, *"Without faith, it is impossible to please God."* Faith is so essential in our relationship with God. Can't be without it.

*You know how Scripture says, *"In the end times, knowledge will increase."* There has never been a time in history when we had access to so much knowledge. Ever! The availability of information is incredible.

* I asked Mr. Paul if any of his children were still living nearby, he replied. "I have one son who lives here in our guest house. Another son and his wife live in town. One lives in Portland. Some live in Idaho, and one is in Germany."

* I asked him if any of them garden like he does. He said, "I always answer that question with this question. 'Once you've had real, live food, would you accept a counterfeit?' My children grew up eating good food. They're not going to eat junk. They know better."

Chapter Notes and Discussion Topics

Notes

How did this chapter affect you? And why?

Did you gain any new perspectives or perceptions?

What changed in you after reading this chapter?

How can you use this knowledge to help improve your relationships with God, yourself, and others?

Chapter Five

The Nourished Soul Gardening Guide for:

Amazing Grace and the Touchstones

"For of His fullness we have all received, and grace upon grace. For the Law was given through Moses; grace and truth were realized through Jesus Christ." John 1:16-17 NASB

God's Amazing Grace Corrects All My Mistakes

Rejoicing in the full realization of God's amazing grace will become the atmosphere that surrounds you. You will savor a refreshing metamorphosis as you break through the sludge of rebellious, self-centeredness into the Son-light of your *Nourished Soul.*

God's grace will advance and sustain all aspects of your state-of-the-art restoration and revitalizing hope. It is His unmerited, unblemished grace that freely bestows upon you His perfect love and liberating power, as well as His eternal salvation. Incredible!

God's grace cannot be earned. It cannot be purchased. It cannot be taken away. It cannot be stolen. It cannot be destroyed. It cannot be diminished. It is yours without cost. It is yours without payment. It is yours without effort. It is undeniably yours. But, is God's grace free?

Yes and no. Yes, God's grace is freely granted to you. And no, God's grace is not free. It cost Him an incalculable expense. He emptied the treasures of heaven to grant you His grace.

He came Himself willingly in the form of His Son to bear the consequences of sin. Throughout eternity, He will bear the scars of His torture on the cross. He gave so much for us all. Thank you, our King—Jesus!

It is because Jesus has healed the separating wounds caused by rebellion that God's benevolent, inexhaustible, saving grace is freely granted to you. It is by His grace that you are reborn and reunited with His overflowing heart of empowering love. His amazing grace corrects all your mistakes! It is written:

> *"For everyone has sinned; we all fall short of God's glorious standard. Yet God, in his grace, freely makes us right in his sight. He did this through Christ Jesus when he freed us from the penalty for our sins. For God presented Jesus as the sacrifice for sin. People are made right with God when they believe that Jesus sacrificed his life, shedding his blood. This sacrifice shows that God was being fair when he held back and did not punish those who sinned in times past, for he was looking ahead and including them in what he would do in this present time. God did this to demonstrate his righteousness, for he himself is fair and just, and he makes sinners right in his sight when they believe in Jesus."* Romans 3:23-26 NLT

By God's grace, you are now freely made right in His sight through your faith in Jesus. The great opportunity you are presented with throughout the remainder of your time on earth is to grow amidst your weaknesses, insults, hardships, persecutions, and difficulties. Consider Paul's perspectives on life's struggles in light of God's all-sufficient grace:

> *Therefore, in order to keep me from becoming conceited, I was given a thorn in my flesh, a messenger of Satan, to torment me. Three times I pleaded with the Lord to take it away from me. But he said to me, "My grace is sufficient for you, for my power is made perfect in weakness." Therefore I will boast all the more gladly about my weaknesses, so that Christ's power may rest on me. That is why, for Christ's sake, I delight in weaknesses, in insults, in hardships, in persecutions, in difficulties. For when I am weak, then I am strong.*
> 2 Corinthians 12:7-10 NIV

Weaknesses, insults, hardships, persecutions, and difficulties are gifts that will hopefully enhance your journey into the light of God's all-sufficient grace. His power is made perfect in weakness.

Seek gratitude amidst the struggles of life. Pain is a motor that can move you. Utilize life's struggles, trials, and temptations to move you into the center of God's grace and as a trigger to release showers of His empowering light. God's unquenchable grace will encircle and rejuvenate your trusting, yielding heart.

Use pain to lift you into His magnificent presence. As you come face to face with the realities of His unbounded grace and what it cost Him to deliver it to you, you will realize your true worth in Christ. You, my friend, are valuable beyond all of your abilities to comprehend treasure. Your worth exceeds all the wealth this world contains. Realize it! Especially when you don't feel it.

When you feel defeated, and life seems like one giant, painful struggle, understand this—your love-encased soul stands perfected, confirmed, strengthened, and established in the all-sufficient energies of God's measureless, absolute grace. It is written: *"After you have suffered for a little while, the God of all grace, who called you to His eternal glory in Christ, will Himself perfect, confirm, strengthen and establish you."* 1 Peter 5:10 NASB

God's promises are yours by grace—through faith. Start each day on the solid ground of His abundant grace.

Your faith and hope are built upon the bedrock of God's amazing grace revealed through Christ. *"In him we have redemption through his blood, the forgiveness of sins, in accordance with the riches of God's grace that he lavished on us with all wisdom and understanding."* Ephesians 1:7-8 NIV

Rest in complete assurance of God's love-based grace. Know this—it is by His unmerited grace that He renews your mind and transforms your fearful, self-centered soul. His saving grace will draw you away from self-centeredness and fear and confirm within you a flourishing heart of love and blessings. This He grants without merit on your part. If you deserved His grace because of your wonderfulness, it wouldn't be grace.

Regardless of your tangled, bewildering difficulties, despite your core rebellions and the heart-expanding struggles that bless your journey—His grace is all-sufficient. It is evident that God allows pain and difficulties to enhance your growth. They are often found to be the pathway to growth in many of life's crucial arenas. Rejoice when they come and use them as stepping stones upward. Few souls grow without struggle. Jacob became Israel after struggling with God. *"And He said, 'Your name shall no longer be called Jacob, but Israel; for you have struggled with God and with men, and have prevailed.'"* Genesis 32:28 NKJV

Pain and struggle are paramount to your growth and fruitfulness. They may prove to be your most grace-laden assets. Struggle reveals grace. Vital grace. The grace of our Lord Jesus is so vital that; of all the topics covered in the Holy Bible, His grace was chosen as the very last topic, of the very last sentence, in the very last book—The Revelation of Jesus Christ. *"The grace of our Lord Jesus Christ be with you all. Amen."* Revelation 22:21 NKJV

Don't focus on the problem when struggles arise. Instead, seek the lessons to be learned and the blessings to share. Know that struggle is often the forerunner to blessings that are packed full of God's grace.

Fire cleanses. Fire eliminates the dross of life and focuses your attention. Can you pass the test of faith while in the fires of life? Yes, you can; with your gracious God by your side, as your Guide.

You will know peace amidst the flames. You will enter the grace-filled realm of blessings found in the essential wisdom intrinsic to struggle and pain and thrive through it all. You will prove that struggle can be a gateway to mature joy. See God's grace in each challenge of your life. Don't get down when troubles come—rather, look up! Your blessings are near.

Jesus came to re-open the gates of Eden. You will walk through them on your journey homeward. He restores your heart, mind, and soul as you focus on Him. You are no longer bound to rebellion and darkness. It is in focusing on and developing a relationship with Jesus that you will come to appreciate His grace and reinforce the desire to be reborn and reunited with His freeing heart of empowering love. When you know Him, truly know Him, your heart will be compelled to crave restoration. Spending time getting to know Him and growing in your understanding and realization of His unmerited, unblemished grace will enrich His Spirit's ability to empower and transform you. You will comprehend and experience God's amazing grace and enjoy the refreshing and propitious nourishment of the Touchstones. You will be infused with wisdom and proclaim:

* *God's amazing grace corrects all my mistakes.*
* *Touchstone #1: God's willing meekness inspires my humility.*
* *Touchstone #2: God loves me tenderly.*
* *Touchstone #3: God strives to recreate, redeem, and enrich me.*

God's amazing grace is the solid foundation upon which He restores your soul. Humility, love, and faith are the *Touchstones* against which the quality of your restoration will be tested.

Touchstone #1—God's Willing Meekness Inspires My Humility

A *Touchstone* is a stone that was used to test the purity of gold and silver. The key *Touchstone* of humility will be used to test the purity of your metal as you seek to allow God's Spirit to renew your mind and transform your life. Pride is the destructive, separating character flaw that launched satan's rebellion against God's wondrous, love-based kingdom. Humility is the antidote.

Remember this: *"Your ego is not your amigo."* Author Unknown

Humble yourself before God. Realize that it is only through His power that you were born a physical being. It is only by His power that you live and grow as a restored, spiritual being.

You alone cannot do this. You are powerless to overcome rebellious self-centeredness. The selfish heart owns the property of pride. Humility is the key to wisdom. *"When pride comes, then comes disgrace, but with humility comes wisdom."* Proverbs 11:2 NIV

The ongoing surrender of rebellious self-centeredness and fear precedes the restoration of a broken soul. It is along the path of humility that the selfish, fearful heart is transformed.

The prophet Micah instructs you concerning what God requires of you. *"He has showed you, O man, what is good. And what does the LORD require of you? To act justly and to love mercy and to walk humbly with your God."* Micah 6:8 NIV

God, in all His forms: Father, Son, and Spirit, is the Creator and King of the universe. He is cloaked in royal majesty, glory, unfathomable power, and unfaltering authority. Even so, He is loving, compassionate, humble, and kind. If the King walks humbly, should not His subjects?

Jesus led the Way up the path of humility when He stepped down from the throne of heaven and dwelt among us in the flesh. He then willingly gave up His life as He bore the consequence of rebellion on behalf of the entire human race—including you. He calls you: *"Come to me, all you who are weary and burdened, and I will give you rest. Take my yoke upon you and learn from me, for I am gentle and humble in heart, and you will find rest for your souls. For my yoke is easy and my burden is light."* Matthew 11: 28-30 NIV

Awakening to the knowledge of God's willing meekness may inspire your own humility. Humility is the opposite of pride and arrogance; it is meekness, but not self-loathing.

In relation to other human beings, you are no better and no worse—you are—different. We all share many, if not most, of the same characteristics and struggles, but the volume and degree of each can vary. Always be humble and kind. Have compassion for yourself and others—God does.

All souls have unique strengths and weaknesses and are born into unique circumstances. Each life has great value and specific purposes in God's kingdom. Each soul is cherished by our Father God. You ought to hold yourself and others in high esteem without being prideful.

Seeking humility involves discovering the truth about who you are in your standing with God and others. God sustains all life. He makes it rain on the rebellious as well as the obedient. You are not to judge. You don't know what God will use to turn a soul toward the light. Humility may require you to accept the painful, wrongful, terrible events that occur in this dark world. Humility may require you to live without understanding why. Trust is the key.

Pride is rigid. Humility bends with the will of God. Humbly surrender your will and your life to Him. Humbly give Him all glory. Some pertinent texts include:

> *I tell you the truth, unless you change and become like little children, you will never enter the kingdom of heaven. Therefore, whoever humbles himself like this child is the greatest in kingdom of heaven.* Matthew 18:4 NIV

Humility is the fear of the Lord; its wages are riches and honor and life. Proverbs 22:4 NIV

All of you, clothe yourselves with humility toward one another, because "God opposes the proud but gives grace to the humble." Humble yourselves, therefore, under God's mighty hand, that he may lift you in due time. Cast all your anxiety on him because he cares for you. 1 Peter 5:5 NIV

Practicing humility will create an honorable and attractive character within you. As you do this, the processes of neurogenesis and neuroplasticity will enable your brain to build and reinforce surrendered neural pathways of enriched meekness. Your brain will be rewired toward this increasingly positive state of being. Self-centered fear is the home of pride. God-centered and other-centered love and care is the home of humility. Always be humble and kind.

Surrender rebellious, self-centeredness, and fear to Him, for He loves you tenderly and hopes to free you from their terrible, consuming burdens. When you walk in love, self-centeredness fades.

Practicing humility will stretch your *Nourished Soul's* roots deep into the fertile soil of freeing, godly motives, affections, desires, feelings, actions, and thoughts.

As you purposely visualize and practice humility's speech, actions, and attitudes, freeing neural pathways will form and be retained in your new life patterns. Love, joy, peace, and patience will bloom beautifully through you and grace each soul you touch. This may often call for much thoughtful prayer and a closing of your mouth.

Touchstone #2—God Loves Me Tenderly

A childhood song teaches a foundational and vital message concerning God's love for you: *"Jesus loves me. This I know, for the Bible tells me so."* God loves you and tells you so throughout His written Word. He whispers His love for you in every scene of His wonder-filled, inspiring creation. All Scripture, all direct contact with God, and all creation declare that God is love.

The message of God's soul-enriching love is found written upon every carefully designed and deliciously scented flower. Its sureness stretches invitingly across every green, lush meadow. You will hear it in the cheerful bird's song and smell it in the clean air of a pine-freshened breeze. The sun's light delivers it, and the stars proclaim it—God is love!

He is a perfect Father and provides the health-affirming joys found in His written word and in His creation to make His children happy. Let's review a sampling of poignant Scriptural proclamations declaring the immensity of God's unrelenting, all-encompassing love for you:

Then the LORD came down in the cloud and stood there with him and proclaimed his name, the LORD. And he passed in front of Moses, proclaiming, The LORD, the LORD, the compassionate and gracious God, slow to anger, abounding in love and faithfulness, maintaining love to thousands, and forgiving wickedness, rebellion and sin. Exodus 34:5-7 NIV

The LORD appeared to us in the past, saying: "I have loved you with an everlasting love; I have drawn you with loving-kindness." Jeremiah 31:3 NIV

Your love, O LORD, reaches to the heavens, your faithfulness to the skies. Your righteousness is like the mighty mountains, your justice like the great deep.
O LORD, you preserve both man and beast. How priceless is your unfailing love! Both high and low among men find refuge in the shadow of your wings. Psalm 36:5 -7 NIV

Because of the LORD's great love we are not consumed, for his compassions never fail. They are new every morning; great is your faithfulness. I say to myself, "The LORD is my portion; therefore I will wait for him." The LORD is good to those whose hope is in him, to the one who seeks him. Lamentations 3:22–25 NIV

How great is the love the Father has lavished on us, that we should be called children of God! And that is what we are! 1 John 3:1 NIV

I trust in God's unfailing love for ever and ever. Psalm 52:8 NIV

And I pray that you, being rooted and established in love, may have power, together with all the saints, to grasp how wide and long and high and deep is the love of Christ, and to know this love that surpasses knowledge—that you may be filled to the measure of all the fullness of God. Ephesians 3:17-19 NIV

God's love for you is beyond your comprehension. Think about how low He stooped to rescue you. He stepped down from the throne of heaven and became a servant of man.

His love for you, His hope that you are reborn, and His desire for you to be restored to His image and likeness are calling you to bask in His Spirit's tender presence and to be renewed as you walk in His transforming love.

You are a beloved member of the family of God. No longer does the enemy have control of you. You are victorious—in Christ. This God grants freely because of His grace and His unflinching love for you. He emptied the treasury of heaven to ransom you from the enemy's dark realm. The most astonishing revelation of God's love was exposed as He, in the form of His Son, lived an unblemished life as an example for you to follow. Then He offered His perfect life on a hill far away, on an old rugged cross, your Creator chose to offer His all for you. It was love—defined. It is written:

For God so loved the world that he gave his one and only Son, that whoever believes in him shall not perish but have eternal life. For God did not send his Son into the world to condemn the world, but to save the world through him. John 3:16-17 NIV

Invest time each day seeking God's loving presence. You can practice His presence regardless of how your day is going. You may find doing this especially helpful when life comes upon you in difficult and trying ways. At any time, you can quiet your being, take some deep breaths and immerse your soul in the restorative pool of His great joy and soothing love.

As you realize and experience God's steady presence, negativity will flee from you.

Coming to know God's love brings you into a better understanding of who you really are and fills you with humble realizations of your true and pure worthiness and purpose.

You will comprehend His unfailing love in increasing measure as you seek Him with all your heart. Meditation can be a profoundly beneficial practice. Calm your soul daily. In this relaxed state, focus your soul on God's infinite love and your gratitude for all His blessings. Seek elevated, beneficial emotions each moment. Be uplifted and uplifting. *"A cheerful heart is good medicine, but a crushed spirit dries up the bones."* Proverbs 17:22 NIV

When you allow His re-creative, powerful affections toward you to fill you with new revelations of His loving care, your *Nourished Soul* will breathe His healing love, tender mercy, and kind compassion into the world around you. You will know peace amidst the storm.

Touchstone #3

God Strives to Recreate, Redeem, and Enrich Me

Now faith is the substance of things hoped for, the evidence of things not seen. Hebrews 11:1 NKJV

Faith is the substance of things hoped for, the evidence of things not seen. Fear is the opposite of faith. Fear is the substance of things not desired. The enemy of souls is a destroyer, not a creator. He can only tempt you to pervert and destroy what God has created. It is his desire to steal, kill, and destroy the works of God, including you.

Faith is a power-filled gift granted to you by your Father God. It makes sense that He hopes you will use this most precious and powerful gift to manifest the riches of His kingdom in your life and in the lives of those you touch.

The enemy obviously hopes you will distort the gift of faith by living in fear. The power of faith reveals itself from inside you. You are the stage upon which faith is displayed. *"The Kingdom of God is inside you."* Luke 17:21 KJV

You are the channel of the positive or negative forces of faith or fear in and for your life and the lives of those you influence. You can freely access either.

Faith or fear. The choice is yours. If your faith is focused on God's uplifting hope, then good things will become evident. If fear is the dominant force in your mind, then negativity will surround you, spiritual starvation will enfold you, and darkness will subtly overpower you.

The choice is yours. Where is your focus? Who do you trust? Even when apparently bad things happen in your world, you may choose to have faith that God can bring good out of them.

> *"And we know that God causes all things to work together for good to those who love God, to those who are called according to His purpose."* Romans 8:28 NASB

Focus the eyes of your heart on Him, on His Kingdom, and His righteousness, and He will provide for all your needs.

> *"So don't worry about these things, saying, 'What will we eat? What will we drink? What will we wear?' These things dominate the thoughts of unbelievers, but your heavenly Father already knows all your needs. Seek the Kingdom of God above all else, and live righteously, and he will give you everything you need."* Matthew 6:31-33 NLT

Don't worry. Have faith. God provides for your needs. Faith in God can even heal your body. Recall the true tale of the woman in Mark chapter five who placed her faith in the healing power of Jesus. She believed that if she just touched His robe, she would be healed of a twelve-year affliction. Her faith was rewarded, and after her healing, Jesus said to her: *"Daughter, your faith has made you well; go in peace and be healed of your affliction."* Mark 5:34 NKJV

Your faith can make you well. Faith opens the door to the incredible power of God.

Let's review how you obtain faith? Or, if you have faith, how do you increase it?

Once you have faith, is it only to be used for your own selfish desires; or to benefit others as well? Ponder the following verses:

Fix your eyes on Jesus—The Author and finisher of your faith. Hebrews 12:2 NKJV

So then faith comes by hearing, and hearing by the word of God. Romans 10:17 NKJV

He purified their hearts by faith. Acts 15:9 NIV

For it is by grace you have been saved, through faith—and this not from yourselves, it is the gift of God—not by works, so that no one can boast. For we are God's workmanship, created in Christ Jesus to do good works, which God prepared in advance for us to do. Ephesians 2:8-10 NIV

What good is it, my brothers, if a man claims to have faith but has no deeds? Can such faith save him? Suppose a brother or sister is without clothes and daily food. If one of you says to him, "Go, I wish you well; keep warm and well fed," but does nothing about his physical needs, what good is it? In the same way, faith by itself, if not accompanied by action, is dead ... Show me your faith without deeds, and I will show you my faith by what I do. James 2:14:18 NIV

Let's weave these thoughts together—Fix your eyes on Jesus, the Author and finisher of your faith—your faith comes by hearing the word of God—He purifies your heart by faith—you are saved by grace, through faith—you were created in Christ to do good works which God prepared in advance for you to do—you demonstrate your living faith by what you do for others.

Faith is both belief and action—it is belief in action.

As your God-inspired faith grows, your love for others will be increasingly revealed through your caring actions. And as your God-inspired caring actions increase, your capacity for love and faith will grow. It starts with God, flows through you to others, and enriches you as you give it away.

Free-flowing faith, love, and care—they will become a swelling circle of enchanting delights that nourish your re-creation in ever-increasing cascades of joy.

Following God's ways in faith, love, and care may very well allow access to spiritual, mental, physical, and financial health. Allow His Spirit to inspire and empower you to progressively demonstrate your faith by way of utilizing His systems for success.

God's systems for success appear to flow in this order;

First—Acknowledge God as the owner and giver of all: *"The earth is the LORD'S, and all it contains, the world, and those who dwell in it." – "Every good gift and every perfect gift is from above, and comes down from the Father of lights, with whom there is no variation or shadow of turning"* Psalm 24:1 NASB & James 1:17 NKJV

Second—Ask with other-focused motives. *"You ask and do not receive, because you ask with wrong motives, so that you may spend it on your pleasures."* James 4:3 NASB

Third—Pass His gifts along to others. As you give, you receive: *"Give, and you will receive. Your gift will return to you in full—pressed down, shaken together to make room for more, running over, and poured into your lap. The amount you give will determine the amount you get back."* Luke 6:38 NLT

You are the pipeline through which God's riches are to flow. Everything is His. As you pass His riches along—you are enriched.

Scripture reveals this undeniable truth: *"The generous will prosper; those who refresh others will themselves be refreshed." "The generous will themselves be blessed, for they share their food with the poor."* Proverbs 11:25 NLT & Proverbs 22:9 NIV

Enjoying and sharing God's love, care, and all His generous gifts with others is the goal. When you slow the flow through fear-filled, selfish motives, the blessings are diminished for all.

Consider the Dead Sea. Do you know why it's dead? It's dead because nothing flows out of it. Don't be a dead soul that only takes and never gives. Be a living stream, refreshing the world around you. Sharing your worldly goods, as well as your faith, love, and care, will dissolve self-centeredness. You will find great pleasure in giving of yourself and your God-endowed assets to benefit others, for when you give, you will receive. Exercise your faith through generous love.

Be restored on the firm foundation of faith expressing itself through love. *"For in Christ Jesus neither circumcision nor uncircumcision has any value. The only thing that counts is faith expressing itself through love."* Galatians 5:6 NIV

Faith is a giving thing. Love is a giving thing. Caring is a giving thing. As you give these, you will receive them. Jesus calls you to love and care for your neighbor as yourself. You will find it much more beneficial for all when you care for yourself from other-centered motives. God enables this foundational shift away from self. As He repurposes your motives, you will find that you are increasingly moved to love and care for yourself to be better able to love and care for others. This is a wonder-filled and freeing state of existence.

The motivating force behind your new economy will be giving rather than getting. You will seek to bless rather than be blessed. Living in this state of unburdened love will release a heaven-sourced flood of soul-satisfying refreshment for all involved. It will open gateways into the awareness of God's Spirit working through you. This awe-inspiring metamorphosis will help build your solid faith in God's unfailing provisions. *"The LORD is trustworthy in all he promises and faithful in all he does."* Psalm 145:13 NIV

God will transform your basic instincts and cause your fundamental nature to spring from a new perspective. You will enjoy a vibrant, living faith and trust in all He is, arranges, and allows. God does it all through Christ. *"And my God will supply every need of yours according to his riches in glory in Christ Jesus."* Philippians 4:19 ESV

Christ Jesus attracts your heart to His by His unselfish, undying love. He draws you, cleanses you, gives you a new heart, puts His Spirit of power, love, and self-control in you, strengthens you, enriches you, prepares work for you to do in advance, and grants you eternal life. Beautiful!

As you continue to exercise and practice your faith through God-centered and other-centered love and care, it will grow, and you will come to relish an ever-expanding joy in your soul.

You need not want for anything. You need not live in lack. Life is difficult. But God is all-powerful. He will lead you out of fear and into faith in His bountiful, generous, all-encompassing love and care. He will care for your every need, if you rightly relate yourself to Him. Everything is His—everything! Every breath of air, every living cell, every heartbeat—nothing exists without His sustaining power. *"The earth is the LORD's, and everything in it. The world and all its people belong to him."* Psalm 23:1 NLT

You don't actually own anything in this world. Everything and everyone belong to God. You are a steward of what is His. Man does not possess the ability to create one original, living molecule. They are all born of God. You should strive to be the best steward that He will enable you to be. Wealth is real, but it is not yours.

You will find the most profound blessings as you seek to bring God's wealth into the stream of life and use it to benefit yourself and others as it may relate to His causes. You will realize encouraging peace in recognizing that when material blessings do come into your possession, it is God Who enables those transactions. *"But remember the Lord your God, for it is he who gives you the ability to produce wealth, and so confirms his covenant, which he swore to your ancestors, as it is today."* Deuteronomy 8:18 NIV

God has a system for success for everything He creates. He has revealed the pathways to blessings in His Word. The clearest way through the maze of life is to follow His directions—commandments. If you desire to be happy, healthy, and hopeful, seek His direction, guidance, and counsel. *"Seek the Kingdom of God above all else, and live righteously, and he will give you everything you need."* Matthew 6:33-34 NIV

God has actually asked you to test His system for achieving sustainable prosperity. Only once, but He does ask. The test is found in the book of Malachi. It has to do with you either cheating Him or recognizing the reality of His ownership and how you appreciate His gifts by returning a portion of them. He will use that portion to benefit others.

God declares:

> *"Should people cheat God? Yet you have cheated me!*
>
> *"But you ask, 'What do you mean? When did we ever cheat you?'*
>
> *"You have cheated me of the tithes and offerings due to me. You are under a curse, for your whole nation has been cheating me. Bring all the tithes into the storehouse so there will be enough food in my Temple. If you do," says the LORD of Heaven's Armies, "I will open the windows of heaven for you. I will pour out a blessing so great you won't have enough room to take it in! Try it! Put me to the test! Your crops will be abundant, for I will guard them from insects and disease. Your grapes will not fall from the vine before they are ripe," says the LORD of Heaven's Armies. "Then all nations will call you blessed, for your land will be such a delight," says the LORD of Heaven's Armies."* Malachi 3:8-12 NLT

I have continually tested this promise of God for decades. It has never failed.

Does it mean that I have never seen hard days or been blessed with trials and temptations? No, of course not. We are all entrusted with the ability to learn His ways as His light illuminates the abundant potential intrinsic to the struggles of life on earth. Jesus died, but He rose again—you can too! Even though the mortal body you currently reside in is broken, often ill, and slowly fading away, your spirit is being renewed day by day!

> *Therefore we do not lose heart. Though outwardly we are wasting away, yet inwardly we are being renewed day by day. For our light and momentary troubles are achieving for us an eternal glory that far outweighs them all. So we fix our eyes not on what is seen, but on what is unseen. For what is seen is temporary, but what is unseen is eternal.* 2 Corinthians 4:16-18 NIV

Does your faith grasp the reality of the unseen? If not—dig a little deeper. Uncover the riches of abiding faith, hope, and love. Rejoice in the midst of life's trials. Surrender to God's Spirit as your guide, benefactor, and counselor. Don't short yourself. God is a God of limitless expansion. He has created you in His image and likeness. He wants you to prosper in every aspect of life. *"Beloved, I pray that in all respects you may prosper and be in good health, just as your soul prospers."* 3 John 2:2 NASB

He has provided everything you need for life, prosperity, and godliness through His systems for success. Allow Him to write His laws of love and liberty on your heart and in your mind.

Carefully follow His ways, and you will prosper in everything you do.

Prosperity is often interpreted as financial wealth. The word prosperity is defined as; a successful, flourishing, or thriving condition, especially in financial respects; good fortune.

God will enrich you in appropriate ways and times. Conditions often dictate the release of His rewards. There are great benefits to following His ways. It is written:

> *"Carefully follow the terms of this covenant, so that you may prosper in everything you do."* Deuteronomy 29:9 NIV

> *"The Lord will grant you abundant prosperity – in the fruit of your womb, the young of your livestock and the crops of your ground – in the land he swore to your ancestors to give you. The Lord will open the heavens, the storehouse of his bounty, to send rain on your land in season and to bless all the work of your hands. You will lend to many nations but will borrow from none. The Lord will make you the head, not the tail. If you pay attention to the commands of the Lord your God I give you this day and carefully follow them, you will always be at the top, never at the bottom."* Deuteronomy 28:11-13 NIV

When God blesses you, use it rightly, and more abundance will be poured upon you. Use God's system for financial success—honor Him with the first fruits of your labor. Freely share the gifts He grants you. Invest in divine purposes and store your treasure in heaven. Understand that financial wealth is only a tool. True riches are more often found; in a close connection with God, in health, in family, in friends, in being trustworthy, in nature, and in love. Use what is given you to purposely care for yourself, others, and God's cause.

Access the power of God's Spirit to develop a godly character, for therein resides the truest wealth. Share what is granted you in faith—expressing itself as love. You are transformed by grace.

> *"For the grace of God has appeared, bringing salvation to all men, instructing us to deny ungodliness and worldly desires and to live sensibly, righteously and godly in the present age, looking for the blessed hope and the appearing of the glory of our great God and Savior, Christ Jesus, who gave Himself for us to redeem us from every lawless deed, and to purify for Himself a people for His own possession, zealous for good deeds."* *Titus 2:11-14 NASB*

God loves you! As you accept His love and the freely offered grace He grants you, you will come to a richer knowledge and understanding of His unmerited favor and a warming absorption of the *Touchstones.* You will know that:

God's amazing grace corrects all my mistakes.
God's willing meekness inspires my humility.
God loves me tenderly.
God strives to recreate, redeem, and enrich me.

Mr. Paul's Insights, Inspirations, and Experiences
Chapter Five

(As each Chapter neared completion, Mr. Paul would review it. Then, we would discuss it. I recorded our post review discussions. What follows are poignant and interesting excerpts from his recorded comments.)

This Chapter prompted me to share a testimony of a significant healing God did for me. It came to me as I was reading. He healed me because of His goodness.

I had a thing growing on my nose. It was a black thing that wouldn't come off. I had no injury there, yet I had this black growth. And I just kind of ignored it. Then, one day, I got a call from this guy who told me that he had a rental property with a big Douglas fir in front of it. He told me he was concerned that the strong winds we get may one day blow the top off of it and damage the house. He wanted me to give him an estimate for having the top removed.

So, I went over to his house and looked at it. The first thing I said was, "I would never top a tree. Because if you top a tree, the new growth will come off the side of the tree and will not be well attached, so when the wind blows, they will break off. It's just not an option. Your only alternatives are to either leave the tree alone or take it out. My opinion is that the tree is strong. It is in really good shape, and there are no broken branches which indicate that it has been holding up just fine in the wind. I don't think you have anything to worry about."

He looks at me and says, "I want to thank you for being really honest and talking yourself out of a job. But you're not okay. That black thing you have on your nose. That's a carcinoma. If you don't have it removed, it can grow into your brain and kill you. You know, I'm a dermatologist; I know what

I'm talking about. You need to call my office and make an appointment to have that removed."

I said, "Let me tell you something. I have a real hesitation about having you cut it because I think it will spread. And, I also know the Great Physician, Almighty God, and I'm gonna take it up with Him. Then I'll get back with you."

So, I went home, called him up, and made an appointment for three weeks later. And every night when I went to bed, I prayed, "God, I need healing. I don't want to go to this dermatologist; I don't want him cutting on it. Obviously, this thing is not safe. Would you please heal me?"

He gave me a premonition of healing.

My wife had this bottle of really potent vitamin E. It wasn't liquid; it was like car grease. Every night before I went to bed, I would rub it on this thing and pray.

So, time went on, the three weeks passed quickly, and I was praying every night and putting this vitamin E on. Then, on a Wednesday, the night before I was supposed to go to that Doctor, I told God, "Well, tomorrow's my appointment God. I sure would like to be healed. I don't want to go to that Doctor."

Thursday morning, I wake up and on my sheet is this black thing like a scab. I think, "What the heck is that?" And just brush it off. I get up and look in the mirror, and that thing isn't there anymore. I said, "God, You are amazing! You took it off right at the deadline!

I called the office and told the guy, "I'm not coming in. That thing came off. I'm good."

Several years later, my brother was in his office for some kind of treatment. Our last name is Gautschi, which is not a very common name. And the Doctor says, "Gautschi. Do you know a guy named Paul?"

My brother affirmed, "Yeah, he's my brother." The Doctor said, "He had a really serious carcinoma on his nose and was supposed to come in and have it removed, and he never did. Would you have him call me? I would like to have him come in so I can look at it. I'm really concerned that he didn't deal with it."

My brother said he would. So, I called the guy up and went to his office. It was so incredible to watch his expressions. I could tell that he didn't want to believe that I was healed. He's poking at it and looking at it. I still have a little indentation there. You could just tell that he didn't want to believe it. But it wasn't there. God removed it.

And I think it's so cool that God left a mark there on my nose. Because every time I look in the mirror and see that little indentation, I'm reminded of His healing.

This all reminds me of the story of Naaman in the Old Testament. He was a General in the Roman army. He had taken a young Jewish woman as a slave. She was in his house. Naaman had leprosy, and this young woman tells him, *"You know, there is a Prophet in Israel who knows God. He can heal you."*

He goes over to Elisha's house, and Elisha tells him to go and dip seven times in the Jordon River, and you will be healed. Naaman leaves really angry and says, *"Man, we've got much nicer rivers back home. What's up with this ugly Jordon River?"* And his companion says, *"If he had told you to do something great, you would have done it. This is not a big deal. Just do it. You've got nothing to lose."*

I love how the Scriptures describe it; when he dipped the seventh time in the Jordon, his skin was like that of a baby. What I like about what God did for Naaman is; for the rest of his life, he had to give testimony to God's healing. Cause wherever he went amongst his macho friends, they would taunt him, saying, "Hey Naaman, what's up with this baby skin." He couldn't hide this amazing declaration of his healing. A man his age doesn't have baby skin. It's obvious that this is unusual. And so, he had to constantly give testimony of God's healing. I love that!

God is good. He is so good.

Chapter Notes and Discussion Topics

Notes ____

How did this chapter affect you? And why? ____

Did you gain any new perspectives or perceptions? ____

What changed in you after reading this chapter? ____

How can you use this knowledge to help improve your relationships with God, yourself, and others?

Chapter Six

The Nourished Soul Gardening Guide for:

The Covering and the Way Up

Christ's Robe of Right Covers My Life

Mr. Paul Gautschi, the Patriarch and a steward of the Back to Eden Gardening movement explains with exuberance and wonder the gardening method that our Father God taught Him. He shares how life in the Garden of Eden was not backbreaking and sweaty work. Instead, the tending of God's garden was an enjoyable, lighthearted tending of luscious, life-enhancing trees, bushes, vines, herbs, grasses, and awe-inspiring flowers.

The tending of the Garden of Eden was an educational avocation of health and happiness that revealed the Father's love in every delicately designed and sweetly scented flower. Each new dawn escorted in another rain-free, beautiful day of tending and tasting the freshness and lush creativity of God. Adam and Eve walked and talked with God in the cool of the evenings and were likely educated about the precise laws that balanced the intricacies and inter-dependence of all life forms. Once a week, on the Sabbath, they rested completely in the gracious and lavish love of their Creator. Their daily avocation and their fondness for and devotion to one another and their Papa God was a source of ever-expanding joy and loving allegiance.

However, when Adam and Eve rebelled, it all came crashing down. The first physical manifestation of their dark choice was their awareness that they were naked.

Although there is no direct biblical reference to the two of them having a covering of light before the fall, many believe this was the case. A common explanation for this belief is the fact that they were created in the image and likeness of God, Who clothes Himself with light. *"O LORD my God, You are very great: you are clothed with honor and majesty, Who cover Yourself with light as with a garment, Who stretch out the heavens like a curtain."* Psalm 104:1-2 NKJV

Also, when Moses came down from Mount Sinai after seeing God, the radiant glory of God shined from him with such brightness that he had to cover his face because it shone so brightly it frightened others. *"So when Aaron and all the children of Israel saw Moses, behold, the skin of his face shone, and they were afraid to come near him."* Exodus 34:30 NKJV

Whatever happened after the rebellion of Adam and Eve, they soon realized that they were naked and needed to be covered, which they did with fig leaves. *"Then the eyes of both of them were opened, and they knew that they were naked; and they sewed fig leaves together and made themselves coverings."* Genesis 3:7 NKJV

In his prayerful search for growing enough food for his family with a well that only produced one half gallon of water per minute, Mr. Paul shared with me that God directed him to observe nature and all the thriving life forms that existed without man watering them. In the wild, God showed him how rich and healthy the soil was under the covering of many previous year's decomposing, fallen leaves, needles, and grasses. God taught him that a covering was essential for life to exist. He saw that all visible life forms have a covering. Man and animals have skin or fur, trees have bark, birds have feathers, and living soil has organic material from previous years and often a cover crop of some kind.

When Adam and Eve fell, there were other consequences, a part of which was being driven from the garden to till the land in order to produce food by the sweat of the brow. *"Therefore the LORD God sent him out of the garden of Eden to till the ground from which he was taken."* Genesis 3:23 NKJV

Tilling the ground to grow food rips the covering off the soil and brings death to microbial life. If you rip the covering off any life form, death follows. Tilling the soil has been the focus of gardening since the fall. As revealed to Mr. Paul, Back to Eden gardening is a no-till, enjoyable, low-labor, and productive way to grow nutrient-dense food in covered soil. The covering is a rich source of life. It nourishes and protects the microbial life in the soil's microbiome.

After their fall, Adam and Eve covered themselves and their shame and guilt with manmade garments. But God took the skins of sacrificed animals, and He covered them. *"And the LORD God made garments of skin for Adam and his wife, and clothed them."* Genesis 3:21 NASB

The right covering of sacrificed animals given to our original parents was provided for humanity by God and is undoubtedly symbolic of the righteous covering dispensed through the gracious sacrifice God Himself made on our behalf in the form of His Son, Jesus Christ.

In Scripture, garments or coverings are symbols of righteousness.

Isaiah declares these health and happiness affirming truths:

"I will greatly rejoice in the LORD,
My soul shall be joyful in my God;
For He has clothed me with the garments of salvation,
He has covered me with the robe of righteousness,
As a bridegroom decks himself with ornaments,
And as a bride adorns herself with her jewels.

For as the earth brings forth its bud,
As the garden causes the things that are sown in it to spring forth,
So the Lord GOD will cause righteousness and praise to spring forth before all the nations."
Isaiah 61:10-11 NKJV

Mr. Paul shared with me that in the Back to Eden gardening method, given to him by the Creator, he chooses to use arborist's wood chips to cover the soil in his orchard and garden. These wood chips serve to protect and feed the rich soil he now enjoys. And, for him, this garden covering is symbolic of Christ covering, nourishing, and protecting him.

The covering of Christ over your soul secures your heavenly destiny and protects the spiritual habitat and biome in the garden of your mind. The succulent waters that drip profusely from the soul-enriching love and care of Christ's essential covering not only absorb His heavenly rains but make available the light-based, spiritual nutrients that feed and refresh your *Nourished Soul.*

By grace, through faith, as you willingly accept the garments of Christ's righteousness to cover the shame and guilt you inherited from your ancestors, without adding any fig leaves of your own, your restoration is assured. Christ is your Covering as well as your Way up and out of the consequences of your inborn, fallen nature, for He is the Way, the Truth, and the Life. *"Jesus said to him, "I am the way, the truth, and the life. No one comes to the Father except through Me."* John 14:6 NKJV

The Way Up

Jesus answered, "I am the way and the truth and the life.
No one comes to the Father except through me. John 14:6 NIV

Jesus Is My Friend, My Savior, and My King

Jesus, my Friend, proclaimed: *"You are my friends if you do what I command. I no longer call you servants, because a servant does not know his master's business. Instead, I have called you friends, for everything that I learned from my Father I have made known to you."* *John 15:14-15 NIV*

Jesus, my Savior, inspired these words: *"If you openly declare that Jesus is Lord and believe in your heart that God raised him from the dead, you will be saved. For it is by believing in your heart that you are made right with God, and it is by openly declaring your faith that you are saved."* *Romans 10: 9-10 NLT*

Jesus, my King, answered, *"My kingdom is not of this world. If My kingdom were of this world, then My servants would be fighting so that I would not be handed over to the Jews; but as it is, My kingdom is not of this realm."* *John 18:36 NASB*

As my Friend, I greatly desire to be a faithful friend to Him and a reliable expression of His love. As my Savior, I openly declare that it is only through faith in His willing sacrifice that I am sanctified and saved. And, as my King, I humbly submit to His authority and love-based, supreme power.

Everything my empty heart has ever hungered for during my brief journey on earth, I have found in Him. I couldn't satisfy that deep longing in my soul with the things of this world. Because; the kingdom of Jesus is not of this realm. The realm of the Spirit is where my searching soul struck gold!

Does Jesus long to be your Friend? It is obvious that He does.

Before He was arrested and taken away from His twelve disciples, Jesus prayed three specific prayers—one for Himself, one for His twelve disciples, and one for all believers. Since most of us fall into the all believers category, let's take a look at that prayer:

> *I do not ask for these only, but also for those who will believe in me through their word, that they may all be one, just as you, Father, are in me, and I in you, that they also may be in us, so that the world may believe that you have sent me.*
>
> *The glory that you have given me I have given to them, that they may be one even as we are one, I in them and you in me, that they may become perfectly one, so that the world may know that you sent me and loved them even as you loved me.*
>
> *Father, I desire that they also, whom you have given me, may be with me where I am, to see my glory that you have given me because you loved me before the foundation of the world.*
>
> *O righteous Father, even though the world does not know you, I know you, and these know that you have sent me. I made known to them your name, and I will continue to make it known, that the love with which you have loved me may be in them, and I in them.* John 17:13-26 ESV

Through His every thought, motive, word, glance, and act, Jesus revealed the Father's wish that we know Him and Jesus and that we all be together—as one. It sounds like a desire for friendship, don't you agree?

So, how do you become friends with your Savior and King Jesus? He is not here in a physical body, so it is a different type of relationship—it's better. Whereas a human friend is only with you part of the time, Jesus is always present through His indwelling Spirit. Plus, He is not a broken, self-interested, fear-geared, needy mess, like some of us humans. Okay—all of us humans. Not only is He not a broken, self-interested, fear-geared, needy mess—He has all the power and authority in the universe. He is the Great Physician. Scripture discloses His longing to heal and restore you, to make you a joint heir with Him forever, and to be your closest Friend.

This world is passing away. The one Friend you definitely want on your side when your days are done is Jesus!

How have you built friendships in the past? What are some key ingredients that make a friendship? You can use many of the same relationship skills you use to develop earthly friendships in becoming friends with Jesus.

Here is a partial list of principles most people find important in building strong friendships.

You should; spend time together, keep your promises, be dependable, apologize when you've made a mistake, be honest, share on an intimate level, be loyal, be respectful, be a good listener, be helpful, be fun, be trustworthy, be there when needed, be thoughtful, be understanding, go beyond the call of duty and stay in touch no matter what.

Jesus is always there to walk beside you and relish your friendship. To relish is to delight in something or someone that satisfies your desires. Relishing your friendship with Jesus, your Savior, and your King is the sweetest possible way to spend any moment of any day.

As you realize that He is a steady, unflinching Friend Who will hold you together, fill you with peace, and guide you toward love, joy, and freedom, your deepest desires are richly satisfied. His friendship brings joy! Real joy – that jumping up in the air kind of joy! Just think about it. The Creator of the universe wishes to spend every second of every day with you personally!

He said: *"And surely I am with you always, to the very end of the age."* And: *"I will never leave you nor forsake you."* Matthew 28:20 NIV & Joshua 1:5 NIV

Jesus is always with you, speaking to your heart and encouraging you to be near Him. He convicts you of what is beneficial and what is not. He helps you, strengthens you, and upholds you with His righteous right hand. He will never depart from you or leave you stranded. He longs to build a deep, loving, and satisfying relationship with you, now and forever.

Consider how you spend your days in light of these crucial words from Jesus: *"Now this is eternal life: that they know you, the only true God, and Jesus Christ, whom you have sent."* John 17:3 NIV

Could it be that you are chasing after the wind with all of your busyness, worries, and concerns? Could it be that you are unsuccessfully striving hard to be good so you can make it to heaven? Could it be that darkness has overtaken your soul, and you can't grasp the way out? Could the answer truly be as simple as coming to know Jesus as your Friend, Savior, and King? It is yes, for me!

Of all the humans Jesus could have chosen to walk with Him on earth, He chose Peter. Peter was a flamboyant, self-involved, impetuous, broken soul. Yet, he walked with and came to know Jesus. He wrote:

> *May God give you more and more grace and peace as you grow in your knowledge of God and Jesus our Lord.*
>
> *By his divine power, God has given us everything we need for living a godly life. We have received all of this by coming to know him, the one who called us to himself by means of his marvelous glory and excellence.* 2 Peter 1:2-3 NLT

Jesus Himself declared the eternal value of knowing Him, learning God's will through Him, and subsequently living in the light of God's laws of love. He said:

> *Not everyone who says to Me, "Lord, Lord," shall enter the kingdom of heaven, but he who does the will of My Father in heaven. Many will say to Me in that day, "Lord, Lord, have we not prophesied in Your name, cast out demons in Your name, and done many wonders in Your name?" And then I will declare to them, "I never knew you; depart from Me, you who practice lawlessness!"* Matthew 7:21-23 NKJV

Please hear this! If you get nothing else from this book—get this! Jesus wants you to know Him—personally. This is why it is so essential to allow Him to restore you and clear away the things in your life that have been blocking you from the heart-warming, awe-inspiring joys of knowing Him. Relish His friendship. You won't regret it—ever.

Loving relationships are built on time spent together honoring, conversing with, and enjoying one another. Jesus calls you His friend. He will satisfy your deepest desires. Let your childlike, trusting heart come into direct contact with His. To do this will be your greatest gift!

Jesus came to reconnect you with the Father. What a privilege you have to be in His presence and rest in His everlasting, all-encompassing love, peace, and joy. He even asks the Father to give you His Spirit of truth to be in you as your constant connective advocate so you may know Him as your Friend.

If you love me, keep my commands. And I will ask the Father, and he will give you another advocate to help you and be with you forever—the Spirit of truth. The world cannot accept him, because it neither sees him nor knows him. But you know him, for he lives with you and will be in you. I will not leave you as orphans; I will come to you. John 14:15-18 NIV

From the heart of Scripture, echoes of deep love whisper the yearning desires of Jesus that you experience the joys of knowing Him, the Father, and the Spirit of truth. Invest yourself in His soul-filling, all-satisfying, pain-shattering love. As you relish His steady friendship, you will become well acquainted with His Spirit, for He will live in you.

Knowing Jesus, the Father, and the Spirit allows you to share yourself and your honest struggles with them. When you have a trusted friend, you often share your worst days with them, right?

When a close friend knows you, they know your moods, sense your needs, desire the best for you, and love you through it all. Jesus knows you. You can know Him. He is the most benevolent, faithful Friend you will ever have.

Jesus' communications certainly proclaim that He wants a top-of-the-list, unrivaled relationship with you. The eternal scars He wears in His hands, side, and feet bear witness to His deep desire to be your Friend. He calls you His friend, His treasured possession, His beloved, His saint, His temple, His coheir, His chosen one, His redeemed, and His bride. Wow! It's true—Jesus really loves you.

Be open, free, and unguarded as you walk and talk with Him. You can share your sweetest moments and highest passions as well as your darkest days and most painful heartbreak, confusion, frustration, and any other emotion with Him and still relish and enjoy His Friendship. Actually, this is imperative for building a solid relationship with Him. He does not exist only to grant your requests. He is your closest Friend and will share all of your joys, struggles, and sorrows. He is your Rock.

In the presence of Jesus, darkness flees. As you embrace His friendship and enjoy His all-satisfying presence, you will solidly build your relationship with Him. When you walk with Him, your dark motives, affections, desires, feelings, actions, and thoughts are upended. You will be filled to capacity with the all-encompassing light of His love. Your rebellious desires will fade as you remain in His presence. You will know that Christ's Robe of Right Covers the Seeds of your Renewing Life and He is your Friend, Savior, and love-based King!

Jesus Loves Well and Shows Me How

Jesus said: "Just as the Father has loved Me, I have also loved you; abide in My love." John 15:9 NASB

Love is the essence of life. Don't conform any longer to the pattern of this world. Be transformed by the renewing of your mind. Self-centeredness and fear are the patterns of this world. Love is the pattern of God's kingdom and the basis of His spiritual, mental, and physical laws.

You are called to love. You are called by love. Your heart's greatest desire is love. You are called to love God, yourself, and others as the fulfillment of God's commandments.

Jesus taught that your soul's highest attainment is love:

Love the Lord your God with all your heart and with all your soul and with all your mind. This is the first and greatest commandment. And the second is like it: Love your neighbor as yourself. All the Law and the Prophets hang on these two commandments. Matthew 22:37-40 NIV

As you experience God's love, you will naturally exhibit a healthy love for yourself and others.

When I say *"love for yourself,"* don't confuse this with self-centeredness. Many of the joyless, fearful, anxiety-creating, and unsuccessful experiences you endure in this life can be directly attributed to self-centeredness and fear.

Love is God-centered and other-centered. Love is free and freeing. Release yourself to its transcendent, otherworldly influence. Partake of the divine nature—be love-based. As you give love, you will receive love. This is the sure path to joyful days and a life that you will be passionate about.

It is your calling and extraordinary privilege as God's child to embody and manifest love. Let your heart soar above the exhausting battlefield of self-centeredness and fear and sail homeward in the heavenly atmosphere of love. Give, and you shall receive.

Why does Jesus alert you to love as the primary motivation and focus of your relationships with God, yourself, and others? Why is this one aspect of your existence so vital?

In the writings of John the Beloved, we find this valuable clue: *"Dear friends, let us love one another, for love comes from God. Everyone who loves has been born of God and knows God. Whoever does not love does not know God, because God is love."* 1 John 4:7-8 NIV

Humans were originally created in the image and likeness of God. Genesis 1:26 NIV

Human beings were designed as love-based, Holy Spirit-filled creatures. As you are transformed by the renewing of the garden of your mind and restored to your original design, *"in the image and likeness of God,"* the core motivations of your renewed heart will be to love.

Paul tells you that without love, nothing you do has value.

If I speak in the tongues of men and of angels, but have not love, I am only a resounding gong or a clanging cymbal. If I have the gift of prophecy and can fathom all mysteries and all knowledge, and if I have a faith that can move mountains, but have not love, I am nothing. If I give all I possess to the poor and surrender my body to the flames, but have not love, I gain nothing. 1 Corinthians 13:1-3 NIV

What is love? Is it just the elusive, flowery, goofy feeling you get when someone tickles your fancy? Love has many faces. God's definition of love is found in 1st Corinthians, where Paul continues his treatise on the value of your love. He writes:

Love is patient, love is kind, it does not envy, it does not boast, it is not proud, it is not rude, it is not self-seeking, it is not easily angered, it keeps no record of wrongs. Love does not delight in evil but rejoices with the truth. It always protects, always trusts, always hopes, always perseveres. Love never fails. *1 Corinthians 13:4-8 NIV*

How can you possess this kind of love—God's love? It comes to you and through you as you experience the indwelling presence and influence of His Spirit.

God's love in you is the delightful, delicious expression of the fruit of His Spirit. Love reveals the unambiguous presence of God in you.

The fruit of God's Spirit is: *"Love, joy, peace, patience, kindness, goodness, faithfulness, gentleness and self-control."* Galatians 5:22-23 NIV

Love heads the list of His precious fruit as it blossoms in your life.

None of the restoration you will experience as God rewires your mind will have any lasting value without His implanted love. Pray continually for the outpouring of God's Spirit through your life as He fills you with His love. Jesus promised you His Spirit—if you would ask.

Ask God for His Spirit—He will fill as much of your *Nourished Soul* as you allow Him to. The beauty of His Spirit's fruit will adorn your being. He will color your world with vital vibrancy. His delicious fruit will grow abundantly in the garden of plenty He will plant in your restored heart. Your life will become a lantern, bringing His light to the dark world around you. All whose lives intersect with yours will be brightened as you love. And guess who else benefits from your free-flowing love? That's right—you. Give, and you shall receive.

Giving is the basis of the greatest economy in the universe. It is a win-win-win style of advanced, unending, prolific prosperity. Jesus modeled it in every action and step of His walk on earth and explained it in some very penetrating, weighty, and wise words. He said:

> *If you love those who love you, what credit is that to you? Even sinners love those who love them. And if you do good to those who are good to you, what credit is that to you? Even sinners do that. And if you lend to those from whom you expect repayment, what credit is that to you? Even sinners lend to sinners, expecting to be repaid in full.*
>
> *But love your enemies, do good to them, and lend to them without expecting to get anything back. Then your reward will be great, and you will be children of the Most High, because he is kind to the ungrateful and wicked.*
>
> *Be merciful, just as your Father is merciful.*
>
> *Do not judge, and you will not be judged.*
>
> *Do not condemn, and you will not be condemned. Forgive, and you will be forgiven.*
>
> *Give, and it will be given to you. A good measure, pressed down, shaken together and running over, will be poured into your lap. For with the measure you use, it will be measured to you."* Luke 6:32-38 NIV

In the above verses, Jesus reveals the insider's secrets for peaceful living: Love your enemies and be good to them, be merciful as your Father God is merciful, don't judge, and you won't be judged, don't condemn, and you won't be condemned, forgive, and you will be forgiven, give, and it will be given to you. With the measure you use, it will be measured to you.

Especially give love. Give love even when you don't wish to. Even if the other is your enemy. The act of giving love encapsulates all your searching heart's desires. Every benefit you seek can be obtained by giving it away—especially love.

Some people seem harder to love than others, especially those you may deem your enemies. However, the benefits to you and to them may be more incredible than you can even imagine. Remember, you are called to love your enemies. Jesus instructed you to: *"Love your enemies! Pray for those who persecute you! In that way you will be acting as true children of your Father in heaven."* Matthew 5:44 NLT

Surely, the benefits associated with being free from the negativity and health-damaging aspects of dark, angry feelings far outweigh the gain you might believe you receive from carrying them around in the pit of your self-focused, rotten moods. When you allow your emotions to include resentment, animosity, bitterness, ill-will, malice, or other negatives such as these, you are giving control of your internal state of being to the darkness. These are all manifestations of self-centeredness and fear. Acceptance and forgiveness will set you free.

You cannot change others. You cannot change many of life's situations. But you can always allow God to free your soul of the need to judge and condemn others. Love is the power and purpose behind everything God is and does. When you experience and express His love, you enjoy the sweetest, most refreshing, and succulent fruit of His Spirit.

The process of transformation involves the deflation of self-centeredness as you become distinctly filled with God's Spirit. This restorative experience is ongoing. You will be perceptibly refreshed and allowed to reflect the essence of God. *"God is love."* 1 John 4:8

When self sits on the throne of your heart, love fails to be expressed; when Christ sits on the throne of your heart, love becomes your purpose.

Love carries its sweetness from God to you, from you to others, and back to God. It will never end and never fail. Love stretches out in all ways and in all directions—always.

God came to earth in the form of His Son, Jesus Christ, to demonstrate and reveal the essence of His character and purpose—self-sacrificing love.

Christ showed us true love in action as He humbled Himself. He willingly stepped down from His heavenly throne and submitted to being born a human. He was fully God and fully man. From this position, He didn't Lord His power over us. Instead, He became the servant of all. He ultimately sacrificed Himself on our behalf as He laid down His life and then picked it up again. He showed us the Way to victory over self-centeredness and fear—dying to self. Paul knew this state:

> *I have been crucified with Christ; and it is no longer I who live, but Christ lives in me; and the life which I now live in the flesh I live by faith in the Son of God, who loved me and gave Himself up for me.* Galatians 2:20 NASB

Jesus lifted all humanity above Himself and bore the consequence of birth into this fear-filled, self-centered rebellion against God's universal laws of love. He restored the severed strands of connective love.

There couldn't be a greater revelation of His true heart than what God has done in the form of His Son. He could not have possibly done more to remove the blinders from your eyes concerning the truth of His character and desires for you.

When you understand the depth of His great love for you, your natural response will be to love Him back. The most beneficial way for you to love Him is to allow Him to grant you freedom from a rebellious, self-centered, fear-dominated heart and obey what He asks. Jesus instructed His disciples:

> *As the Father has loved me, so have I loved you. Now remain in my love. If you keep my commands, you will remain in my love, just as I have kept my Father's commands and remain in his love. I have told you this so that my joy may be in you and that your joy may be complete.*
>
> *My command is this: Love each other as I have loved you. Greater love has no one than this: to lay down one's life for one's friends. You are my friends if you do what I command. I no longer call you servants, because a servant does not know his master's business. Instead, I have called you friends, for everything that I learned from my Father I have made known to you. You did not choose me, but I chose you and appointed you so that you might go and bear fruit—fruit that will last—and so that whatever you ask in my name the Father will give you. This is my command: Love each other.* John 15:9-17 NIV

What did He command? Love. This message was not for the disciples alone. They were to take what Jesus had taught them and share it with the world. They were to make disciples of all nations.

> After His resurrection: *"Jesus came and said to them, 'All authority in heaven and on earth has been given to me. Go therefore and make disciples of all nations, baptizing them in the name of the Father and of the Son and of the Holy Spirit, teaching them to observe all that I have commanded you. And behold, I am with you always, to the end of the age.'"* Matt 28:18-20 ESV

Realization of God's love leads to loving God; loving God leads to obedience; obedience leads to true freedom. When true freedom is realized, you will love God even more. Loving God, even more will lead to a heart filled with genuine, healthy love for yourself and others; loving God, yourself, and others leads to complete joy. Joy leads to love. This is God's way of life blessing life and love encouraging love. God demonstrates this phenomenon in how He waters this world and how His word accomplishes what He wills:

> *As the rain and the snow come down from heaven and do not return to it without watering the earth and making it bud and flourish, so that it yields seed for the sower and bread for the eater, so is my word that goes out from my mouth: It will not return to me empty, but will accomplish what I desire and achieve the purpose for which I sent it.* Isaiah 55:10-12 NIV

Love is like the pure water lifted above the sea and carried over the parched earth to refresh and enrich. The revitalizing rain waters fall to the earth, bringing life, then return to the sea where it is cleansed and sent back again. Love is the never-ending current of life surging from God to you, from you back to God and others. You are the channel through which the refreshing waters stream. The sea of love freely flows from heaven when you allow the vital droplets to rain upon those about you. God's love surges through you by the power of His Spirit. Participating in the circle of love will make your joy complete. To know and follow the Way up—love well.

Jesus Cares Well and Shows Me How

"The greatest among you will be your servant." *Matthew 23:11 NIV*

The definition of care is the provision of what is necessary for the health, welfare, maintenance, and protection of someone or something.

Jesus said:

> *Whoever wants to be my disciple must deny themselves and take up their cross and follow me. For whoever wants to save their life will lose it, but whoever loses their life for me will find it. What good will it be for someone to gain the whole world, yet forfeit their soul? Or what can anyone give in exchange for their soul? For the Son of Man is going to come in his Father's glory with his angels, and then he will reward each person according to what they have done.* Matthew 16:24-27 NIV

How does that sound? Does denying yourself, taking up your cross, and following Jesus in losing yourself as you care for the needs of others appeal to you? In getting to know and follow the Way up, can you care for His children? Can you be more concerned with the needs and protection of others than with your own? To a degree and in certain situations, you may answer yes to this. But, within yourself, you do not possess the power to transform your soul into an unfailingly self-sacrificing, light-bearing force for good. These motives must come from God's Spirit. It is He Who restores your core beliefs and inspires the motives, affections, and desires associated with a caring heart. You do care. I know you do. Just remember—that faculty is born of God. It is not self-generated.

Picking up a cross? Denying yourself? Giving up your life? These caring states don't come naturally to the heart-sick, rebellious, self-centered, survival-of-the-fittest, human dilemma you are likely trapped in—right?

You may have some semblance of success in altering and controlling your *(FATs)*—feelings, actions, and thoughts. However, the transitions to, and the restorations of pure, caring, heaven-inspired *(MADs)*—motives, affections, and desires, cannot be generated by self-will. These inspirations are born of the Holy Spirit. Regeneration of the soul is God's department.

You can, nonetheless, enable Him to do His work by creating an environment within you where His healing, restoring powers will be effective. You are the only being in the universe that can grant Him access to the garden of your mind and allow Him to nourish it.

Often these dramatic changes are more easily assimilated by a simple shift in perspective. Let's look at this denial-of-self-centeredness, cross-bearing from a brighter viewpoint.

What if choosing to care for others in the face of free moral agency was the most joyful home for the human soul?

Why not choose to live in a caring state of mind and allow God to consume your crippling, self-centered, fear-based existence? The enlightening book of Hebrews states that you are surrounded by a great cloud of witnesses who sacrificed self for their faith. Why not stand among that great cloud of witnesses. Why not be the light through which God may dispel the darkness. Why not see, and focus on the joy set before you beyond enduring *your* cross.

> *Therefore, since we are surrounded by such a great cloud of witnesses, let us throw off everything that hinders and the sin that so easily entangles. And let us run with perseverance the race marked out for us, fixing our eyes on Jesus, the pioneer and perfecter of faith. For the joy set before him he endured the cross, scorning its shame, and sat down at the right hand of the throne of God. Consider him who endured such opposition from sinners, so that you will not grow weary and lose heart.* Hebrews 12:1-3 NIV

For the joy set before Him—He endured the cross. Did the cross bring Him joy? Well, of course not. However, He saw beyond it. He saw you standing before Him on the other side of the cross—joyful, grateful, victorious, and free. His great heart of love could not bear the thought of eternity without you. He cares so deeply that He gave His all—for you!

Fix your eyes on Jesus. Consider Him. Throw off everything that hinders your connection with the powers of heaven and allow Him to set you free from the sin that easily entangles you.

Cross-bearing is a painful business. It cuts across the grain of deeply entrenched self-centeredness. Oh, but the joys, rewards, and blessings that accompany the complete willingness to lay down your life in caring for others—wow! Living in a caring, generous state could very well be your highest calling and most uplifting frame of mind.

The moments where you experience this reality are the moments that will take your breath away and lift you above the tragic noise of self-centeredness. Beautiful!

Don't allow the darkness to rob you of the heavenly gifts inherent in living a caring, generous life. God's system of being blessed through generosity is without equal in this world of self. *"One person gives freely, yet gains even more; another withholds unduly, but comes to poverty. A generous person will prosper; whoever refreshes others will be refreshed."* Proverbs 11:24-25 NIV

Self-centeredness is the great burden you bear. The self-centered, fear-based life is the one you will enjoy losing. *"For whoever wants to save their life will lose it, but whoever loses their life for me will find it."*

The world may contend with you in your transformation from self-centeredness to God-centeredness and other-centeredness. You may contend with yourself in this process as well. Self-centeredness will not go away quietly. The dark one does not want you to walk free in the light.

If you find that you are faint of heart at the prospect of taking this journey into unknown spiritual territory, pray for courage. Take heart and be of good cheer—your Leader has gone before you. He has overcome the world. You, too, may have peace amidst the disquieting, troublesome trials and sorrows of this world. Jesus declared:

> *I have told you all this so that you may have peace in me. Here on earth you will have many trials and sorrows. But take heart, because I have overcome the world.* *John 16:33 NLT*

Your beliefs feed your motives, affections, desires, feelings, actions, and thoughts. Your faith in Jesus assures your salvation and stimulates your unselfish, *Nourished Soul.* How you live your life is the fruit of your beliefs. God can inspire and rewire your beliefs.

Faith is the substance of things hoped for. Have faith in God's power to recreate you into the image and likeness of Himself and His Son, Jesus. Let Him remold self and fear into love and care.

After being sentenced to death, ridiculed, spit upon, and beaten, Jesus took up His cross and started walking toward the place of ultimate self-denial and sacrificial death of self-centeredness.

In following Him, you are invited to walk the same path. Jesus tells you that as His follower, you may be blessed with the same persecution that His prophets endured, but your reward awaits, and, no matter what, you will find hope in Him.

> *Blessed are you when people insult you, persecute you and falsely say all kinds of evil against you because of me. Rejoice and be glad, because great is your reward in heaven, for in the same way they persecuted the prophets who were before you.* *Matthew 5:10-12 NIV*

Jesus inspires you to rejoice and be glad when following Him. Regardless of what you face in this life, you can do it with joy in your heart and praise on your lips, for you know that in following Jesus your reward in heaven will be great.

Paul knew something about suffering for the cause of Christ, and he rejoiced to be counted worthy of this great trust. He advises you concerning the benefits of faith, hope, and suffering:

> *Therefore, since we have been justified through faith, we have peace with God through our Lord Jesus Christ, through whom we have gained access by faith into this grace in which we now stand. And we boast in the hope of the glory of God. Not only so, but we also glory in our sufferings, because we know that suffering produces perseverance; perseverance, character; and character, hope. And hope does not put us to shame, because God's love has been poured out into our hearts through the Holy Spirit, who has been given to us.* Romans 5:1-5 NIV

Jesus calls you to strive toward being trained for heaven. Using your gifts and talents in caring for the needs of others is a primary training ground. During your walk on earth, you may discover that your soul's most significant challenges may come during times of worldly prosperity. It is written: *"You say, 'I am rich; I have acquired wealth and do not need a thing.' But you do not realize that you are wretched, pitiful, poor, blind and naked."* Revelation 3:17 NIV

Riches, prosperity, and wealth are not the roots of all evil. However, the love of them is. A lifetime lavished with all the riches of this world pales in comparison to one moment in heaven. In suggesting that you pick up your cross and follow Him, Jesus has called you to deny yourself. But what does that mean? It is different for each of us and yet the same for all of us. Your cross is unique to you. But every cross has some common features. They all have to do with denying self-centeredness and living in a contented state of caring. This is good news.

When you answer God's call to become a citizen of heaven, the transformation from a self-centered to a God-centered and other-centered experience will be your most pleasant reality. Living inspired by a mindset of caring will illuminate every incandescent neural pathway in the love-watered garden of your mind. You will be free. The cataclysmic burdens of self-centeredness and fear will fall away. Your Lord invites you to:

> *Come to me, all you who are weary and burdened, and I will give you rest. Take my yoke upon you and learn from me, for I am gentle and humble in heart, and you will find rest for your souls. For my yoke is easy and my burden is light.* Matthew 11:28-30 NIV

Caring for others is a light-bearing load. As you pick up your cross and follow Jesus, you needn't worry, fear or fret about the future. Jesus and your Father in heaven know precisely what you need and will provide for you according to what they know will be the very best for you.

Jesus assures you:

> *So do not worry, saying, 'What shall we eat?' or 'What shall we drink?' or 'What shall we wear?' For the pagans run after all these things, and your heavenly Father knows that you need them. But seek first his kingdom and his righteousness, and all these things will be given to you as well. Therefore do not worry about tomorrow, for tomorrow will worry about itself. Each day has enough trouble of its own.* Matthew 6:31-34 NIV

He will guide you and provide for all your needs. God has a thousand ways to meet your needs that you are not even aware of. The way God seems to provide most often for your needs is to inspire, motivate, equip, and encourage you to work. God is productive. His creations are too.

Upon creating Adam, God set about giving him tasks to perform. God's kingdom is one of balance and order. It makes sense that the energies spent by the inhabitants of heaven are divided in healthy, refreshing ways, between worship, work, rest, and play. We should do the same.

Our world is out of balance: we worship our work, work at our play and play at our worship with no time to rest. Perhaps your focus, like that of many others, is misdirected. Are you obsessed with the things of this world? Remember the words of Jesus, *"What good will it be for someone to gain the whole world, yet forfeit their soul?"* Matthew 16:26 NIV

Seek first God's kingdom and His righteousness. Don't be out of balance. Be productive while taking time to worship, rest and play. Discover your calling. Realize your talents. Use the skills God bestows upon you for His glory and to benefit others. Don't be lazy, but don't forfeit your soul in the unyielding demands of the worldly drive for more, more, more.

Into each heart, God plants desires to do certain things, to accomplish great and simple tasks.

You should always seek His will in each and every choice. He has plans for you. You are here for a reason. Perhaps the most excellent way for you to deny yourself, pick up your cross and follow Him in caring for others is to do what He calls, inspires, and equips you to do.

The cross you bear to caring generosity may very well include the work God has prepared in advance for you to do. It may also prove to be your most fulfilling life experience.

Theodore Roosevelt said, *"Far and away, the best prize that life offers is the chance to work hard at work worth doing."* What are the tasks you have been created to perform?

You will find that much of God's will for your life is revealed in the Holy Scriptures. The directions found there are for each human being to follow in order to live the most Spirit-led, balanced, productive, healthy, and contented life possible in this broken world.

You should not only allow God to restore your soul but also invite Him to help you search your heart. Perhaps you need to go on a vision quest where you spend time alone with God in fasting and prayer as you seek His guidance for your life. Take a couple of days. Find a place in nature where there are no distractions and listen. Ask Him to enlighten and inspire you concerning the work He has prepared for you to do. Look into your soul. What excites you? If you could do anything, what would it be? What piques your interest? God has a purpose for your life.

Scripture states: *"For we are God's workmanship, created in Christ Jesus to do good works, which God prepared in advance for us to do."* Ephesians 2:10 NIV

In facing decisions about your life and what God has for you to do, you can nearly always make safe choices by asking these simple questions. In considering your life choices, simply invite His Spirit's guidance as you ask:

1.) Will this choice violate Biblical truth?
2.) Will this choice bring glory to God?
3.) Have I been called and equipped to do what is necessary to accomplish this?
4.) If I have been called but not equipped—how can I become equipped?

Nearly 70% of people are unhappy with their current occupation and define their job as the most significant stressor in their lives, even over financial and marriage issues.

Perhaps many are unhappy and over-stressed because they are not doing the work God prepared for them to do. Many never take the time to discover and explore what good works God prepared in advance for them to do.

You are not here by mistake. God has a plan and many different purposes for your life. You have many roles to play. The joy set before you often dwells on the other side of a cross you will bear for Him and others. Come to Him; humbly seek His will in each position you find yourself in. Take time to discover His plans for you. He has prepared good works for you to do. As you pursue your chosen work, please remember these Scriptural instructions:

> *Whatever you do, work at it with all your heart, as working for the Lord, not for human masters, since you know that you will receive an inheritance from the Lord as a reward. It is the Lord Christ you are serving.* Colossians 3:23-24 NIV

There He is again, wanting to reward you—sweet! Becoming more caring as you strive to know and follow Jesus will enrich your walk with Him. Remember, He is your Friend. He wants the very best for you. His Spirit will guide you into the paths that will enable you to pick up your cross and follow Him.

Is your cross the work that He has prepared in advance for you to do? Quite possibly. Jesus came to earth to perform specific tasks. Why would it be different for you? Seek His wisdom and guidance. He will grant it. And don't shy away when you know what you are called to do.

Remember the words of James: *"If any of you lacks wisdom, let him ask God, who gives generously to all without reproach, and it will be given him. But let him ask in faith, with no doubting, for the one who doubts is like a wave of the sea that is driven and tossed by the wind. For that person must not suppose that he will receive anything from the Lord; he is a double-minded man, unstable in all his ways.* James 1:5-8 ESV

Habitually seeking wisdom from God may prove to be the wisest skill you ever develop.

The wealthiest and wisest man exposed in Scripture had this to report concerning the benefits of wisdom:

Happy is the man who finds wisdom and the man who gains understanding;
For her proceeds are better than the profits of silver, and her gain than fine gold.
She is more precious than rubies, and all the things you may desire cannot compare with her.
Length of days is in her right hand, in her left hand riches and honor.
Her ways are ways of pleasantness, and all her paths are peace.
She is a tree of life to those who take hold of her, and happy are all who retain her. Proverbs 3:13-18 NKJV

To know and follow the Way up—Care well.

May Jesus grant you and yours—health, happiness, hope, wisdom, and work you are passionate about and inspired by.

As you come to know and follow Him – *The Covering and the Way Up*, you will be able to say whole-heartedly:

** Christ's Robe of Right Covers My Life.*
** Jesus is my Friend, my Savior, and my King.*
** Jesus loves well and shows me how.*
** Jesus cares well and shows me how.*

Mr. Paul's Insights, Inspirations, and Experiences
Chapter Six

As each Chapter neared completion, Mr. Paul would review it. Then, we would discuss it. I recorded our post review discussions. What follows are poignant and interesting excerpts from his recorded comments.

* Of all the Chapters I've read, this one has a significant anointing. I was just totally blessed reading it. I was like, wow! This is really, really special. I was saying amen through the whole thing. It was so good. This is my comment on the whole chapter; "This chapter is an uppercase AMEN!"

* It's amazing to be used by the Lord. I've had testimonies from people who have come to the Lord as a result of the Back to Eden Gardening film. One testimony was from a guy who was ready to commit suicide. He told me, "I was going to end it all, but I had this thought. 'I'm gonna go to Youtube one more time just to see what's there; then I'm outa here.'" He came across a video of one of my Back to Eden Gardening tours. As he watched it, he had this thought, "Wow, I can do this with my family!" Cause his family was falling apart at that time. And he shared how he totally repented, brought his family back together, and they all came to know the Lord. It was totally awesome. The video saved his life, and he and his family came to know God. I thought, "Wow, God. That is so cool."

* Being used by God is so sweet and fulfilling. Only God knows who or what will touch a soul for his kingdom. It's like the disciples of Jesus. They were all so unique. Peter was so out there, and John

was such a friend. He was the disciple whom Jesus loved. How significant. Jesus loved them all, but there was something special about John because he endeared himself to the Lord. Peter and John were used to reach different souls. It just depends on who they are and what they're going through. It's such a wide range.

* God can use us all.

Chapter Notes and Discussion Topics

Notes ______________________________

How did this chapter affect you? And why? ______________________________

Did you gain any new perspectives or perceptions? ______________________________

What changed in you after reading this chapter? ______________________________

How can you use this knowledge to help improve your relationships with God, yourself, and others?

Chapter Seven

The Nourished Soul Gardening Guide for:

Untangling the Night

Therefore, since we are surrounded by such a great cloud of witnesses, let us throw off everything that hinders and the sin that so easily entangles. And let us run with perseverance the race marked out for us, fixing our eyes on Jesus, the pioneer and perfecter of faith. Hebrews 12:1-2 NIV

The slimy fog of shame desecrates my bliss as the sour, putrid sponge of darkness sucks all joy into the cesspool of sin, rebellion, and disobedience.

My heart breaks as I willfully sever the cords of love that now dangle in the black evil taking possession of my appetites and passions.

I push aside the still small voice and rush toward the sin that so easily entangles me. I hate this place but love it too. Perplexed, I continue into the cold arms of death and allow the dark one to sway my soul. "God, please save me," I pray, as the evil desires in me push my torn heart away from the Source of power and peace. Tortured—I plunge off the ledge.

His voice, fainter now, whispers, *"If you keep my commands, you will remain in my love, just as I have kept my Father's commands and remain in his love. I have told you this so that my joy may be in you and that your joy may be complete."* John 15:10-11 NIV

The sweetness of God's enthralling presence vaporizes when I seek to violate His laws of love and liberty. Light and darkness cannot coexist. I'm the learning, precious child of God who suffers the angst of my rebellion. Darkness is never satisfied. Light dispels the darkness.

Why do I choose to pursue the dark one's vile lies again and again when I know they will leave me empty, lonely, ashamed, and heartsick? It's because I was born into a rebellious world. Rebellion rages in my soul as a default position. *"The heart is more deceitful than all else and is desperately sick; who can understand it?"* Jeremiah 17:9 NASB

I don't understand it. However, I do know this; it is supernatural for me to desire and to seek the light. This desire is born of God's Spirit.

Jesus is the pioneer and perfecter of my faith. The pain of leaving His friendly presence to trash my soul makes me run back into His waiting arms. The habitual desire to leave Him behind and wade in the septic darkness of evil fades as His enduring faithfulness steadily energizes my desires to know, obey, and honor Him.

Most humans were born with or have developed and reinforced destructive habits that feed the desires of darkness. Regardless of how demeaning and unwanted the thoughts and acts that produce the darkness may be, certain cues trigger routines that end in predictable, shameful, and guilt-laden rewards.

Inner cravings, also known as Motives, Affections, and Desires (MAD's), ignite the habit loop—Cue, Routine, Reward. The habit loop looks like this:

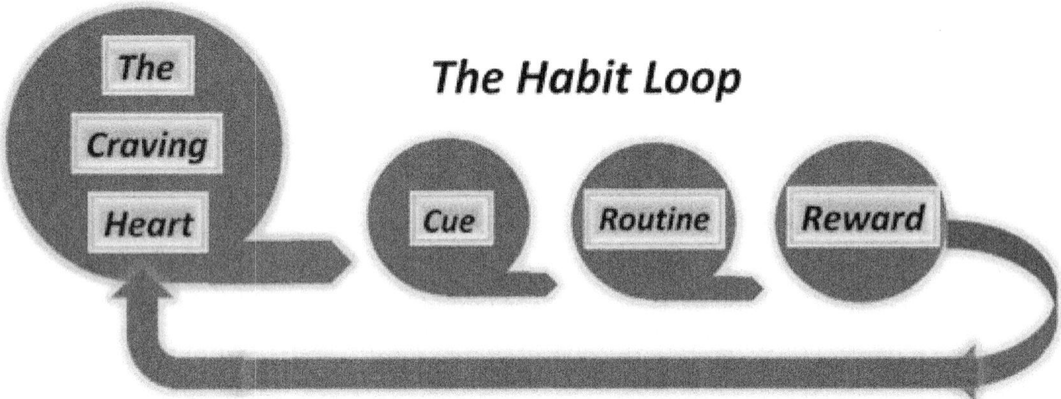

As you fix the eyes of your heart on Jesus, you will be transformed by the renewing of your mind. The dark habits that so easily entangle you will continue to slip further and further from your life's patterns. You will find that some dark habits require more patience and practice to replace than others. An example would be the habit of checking out the attractive beauty of others to feed sexual lust. As this habit progresses, many may find themselves lost in immoral affairs, pornography, or even ongoing sexual scenarios played out in their mind. These thoughts and actions often end in guilt and shame.

You can turn the power of any habit against itself by using old cues to trigger new routines. You can take the same cue—a sexually attractive person or sexual thought—but instead of using those cues to feed sexual lust, use them as a trigger to send your mind to another place—a new routine. Your old cues are a very effective way to trigger new routines such as prayer or praise or shifting your attention to something else like the memory of a special experience or the consuming joy of God's presence. EEE

It will take time, but through practice, this technique will dissolve your undesirable habits.

You can use your old cues to free you from the bonds of darkness and lift you to a higher plane. When an old cue begins pulling you into a dark routine, you can use that cue to focus the eyes of your heart on Jesus. Allow His warm presence to enfold you. You may get so lost in the enticing communion that transpires in those tender moments that the darkness simply slips away. It is beautiful! God will lift your soul into rewarding places that darkness never could.

But, what if you, like me, discover that sometimes the end rewards you seek *are* shame and guilt?

Without understanding why, we humans can crave the rewards of rebellion—shame and guilt. We are born into and habitually drawn into rebellion against the kingdom of God and His ways.

The titillating and powerful chemical rush that accompanies even the anticipation of many rebellious thoughts and acts is a large part of the habit loop—craving. Cravings can be specific or a general yearning for something—you're not sure what, but when all is quiet, you know something is missing. This may be why the world is so busy. We need to avoid that quiet, empty place.

These deeper cravings are most likely caused by unfulfilled God-hungers and the dimmed or lost connection with your Creator. You were born separated from the Source of all fulfillment.

It is peace that you need—God's peace.

Before He returned to our Father in heaven, Jesus promised you the gift of peace.

> *"I am leaving you with a gift—peace of mind and heart. And the peace I give is a gift the world cannot give. So don't be troubled or afraid."* John 14:27 NLT

God's gift of peace does not attend the thoughts and acts of darkness. Your deepest craving, even if you may not completely realize it, is likely to be the peace that comes from being right with God.

Adopting His habits will significantly enhance your ability to enjoy His promised peace. God revealed this promised peace and the effect produced by being in right standing with Him long ago through His prophet Isaiah: *"And the work of righteousness shall be peace; and the effect of righteousness quietness and assurance forever."* Isaiah 32:17 KJV

God offers you assured right standing with Him, by faith in the atoning work done by Him in the form of His Son—Jesus Christ. It is yours now!

Nearly any experience you find pleasurable can trigger an avalanche of cravings. Even certain fantasies involving dark thoughts or acts can cause your brain to release a cascade of feel-good, brain-produced drugs. Oh, baby! When you've completed your dark routine, shame and guilt activate the reward center in your brain. Ahhhh—home!

Can shame and guilt be a reward? Yes, shame and guilt can activate a reward cascade in your brain. Did you know that you cannot have an addiction without shame and guilt? If you search the internet for images of the addiction cycle, you will find that they will nearly all include shame or guilt or both.

The following chart is one such illustration:

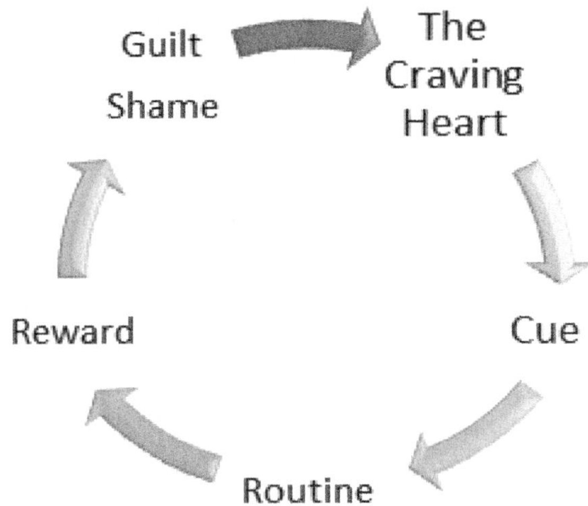

It's curious to note that shame and guilt, as well as pride, trigger similar neural circuits in your brain. The insula, amygdala, portions of the prefrontal cortex, and the nucleus accumbens are parts of the reward cascade in the brain and are activated during pleasurable experiences. Pride, shame, and guilt seem to activate these same areas of the brain. This could explain why we love to beat ourselves up—when we do, we engage our brains' reward circuits [DDD]

For many humans, self-criticism, shame, and guilt have become a kind of home base. Even though they are painful, they are familiar—like family.

Regardless of how unhealthy they may be—they are familiar. Your brain likes familiar patterns. That's why it creates habitual neural pathways. Your brain creates habitual neural pathways, so it doesn't have to think about every little thing. You can be productive, and your brain can be thinking about something else. These habits become familiar through repeated use. They are changed by repeatedly replacing them. Seek better rewards when old cues trigger you. Better rewards are available. Discovering and implanting better rewards by seeking and following God's Way is a recurring theme in this book. God asks you to follow His ways for your own good.

> *And now, Israel, what does the Lord your God require of you, but to fear the Lord your God, to walk in all His ways and to love Him, to serve the Lord your God with all your heart and with all your soul, and to keep the commandments of the Lord and His statutes which I command you today for your good?* Deuteronomy 10:12-13 NKJV

Before and during times of temptation to participate in dark cues, routines, and rewards, you may wish to throw off everything that hinders you and focus your spiritual, emotional, and mental energies on replacing them. You can use temptation to trigger God's light!

Some effective methods that provide Spirit-enriched nourishment to the roots and fruits of your soul and feed your growth as you synthesize the Son-light are:

1.) I Escape the Darkness by Remaining in God's Light
2.) Through Pain and God's Light, My MADFATs are Made Right
3.) Papa's Love PATERNs of Light Dissolve My Night

I Escape the Darkness by Remaining in God's Light

You, my friend, are a human. You were born rebellious and infected with the dis-ease of self-centeredness. From your first breath, you began your struggle toward and against God's sure laws of love, liberty, and light. Many of the fortuitous situations you find yourself in often come disguised as trouble and pain. But let's shine a new light upon these magnificent opportunities.

Let's refocus our perspectives and go right to the marrow of the golden bones that lay buried in the backyard of your challenging existence.

Your unique emergence into the universe is different from that of other intelligent beings mentioned in Scripture. These other intelligent beings (angels) seem to have been brought into existence in the clear light of God's kingdom and His laws of love and liberty.

When lucifer launched his evil, traitorous rebellion and kingdom of darkness, the bewildered angels either chose to remain in the light and thus, loyal to God or rebel and follow the sneaky snake satan into the deceptive, infecting darkness. But you—you were born in rebellion. You arrived behind enemy lines under the curse of transgression. What produce can you glean from this uncommon dilemma? What benefits can you enjoy? What will be laid in your gathering basket that others can't reach? What will the King do for you?

Is God into rewards? Is it selfish even to think this way—or is it simply the reality—a common event in the kingdom of light? Is it status quo in God's kingdom to be prosperous, cherished, rejoiced over, and rewarded? Yes! Don't most people enjoy rewarding their children in healthy ways?

You are God's child. He is a rewarder. As a perfect Father, wouldn't He want you to enjoy the rewards inherent in and intrinsic to His kingdom of love and light? Yes!

Jesus said to pray to your Father God for this: *"Your Kingdom come, your will be done, on earth as it is in heaven."* Is it possible that in the kingdom of heaven, rewards are a natural result of living under the laws of love and liberty? Could everything Jesus asks of you lead to a reward? Oh, yea! Now you're on to something. Now you're seeing the light!

Is it possible that doing right will always bear positive rewards? Yes!

Does doing wrong always lead to negativity and pain? In the end—Yes.

It is for the benefit of His creation that God does everything that He does. He can be no other way, for God is love.

Love gives, love sacrifices, love provides, love awards, love rewards, love perseveres, love protects, love hopes, love delivers, love grants, love bestows, love lavishes—it can be no other way. And get this—when love refreshes others, the giver receives more than is given. Love cannot be diminished by giving—it can only increase. This is the opportunity that has been hidden from you by the dark one. He desires to steal, kill and destroy you and your every blessing and advantage. Don't let him take your rightful inheritance. Fill your treasure chest at the throne of the Creator. Store up your treasures in heaven. Get your full reward. Follow God into the light.

You will escape the darkness by remaining in the light, for light dispels darkness. God's promises are yours. You can participate in His divine nature by remaining in Jesus—the light of the world.

He proclaims:

> *"Yes, I am the vine; you are the branches. Those who remain in me, and I in them, will produce much fruit. For apart from me you can do nothing."* John 15:5 NLT

> *"I am the light of the world. Whoever follows me will never walk in darkness, but will have the light of life."* John 8:12 NIV

What, exactly, is the light that is referred to so often in the Scriptures? The answer to this question is challenging because of the unlimited resources available through God's light. However, our research into this topic revealed some common threads. Light is goodness and truth. Conversely, darkness is evil and lies. Those definitions seem sufficient for our discussions.

As you move into the light of life, your entire being will be revitalized. The temptations that have so often dragged you into the pit will dissolve. Never forget—the Lord is at your right hand. He is your courage, security, and delightful inheritance. Unbounded blessings follow those whose light is the Lord.

Lord, you alone are my portion and my cup; you make my lot secure.
The boundary lines have fallen for me in pleasant places; surely I have a delightful inheritance.
I will praise the Lord, who counsels me; even at night my heart instructs me.
I keep my eyes always on the Lord. With him at my right hand, I will not be shaken. Psalm 16:5-8 NIV

Keep the eyes of your heart focused on Jesus—the light of the world—and you will not be shaken. Don't wait until temptations are overwhelming you. Move your being into the light before they strike. Take pre-emptive action. Prepare for the struggle before it is upon you. Train your brain. Wash it clean in the purifying light of love pulsing from the heart of God. Absorb goodness and truth from His word.

Allow His Spirit to displace the discomfort that attends temptation, fear, and dark urges. Instead, use them to transport your mind into God's light. The light that shines from His words vanquishes the darkness. *"The unfolding of your words gives light; it gives understanding to the simple. "* Psalm 119:130 NIV

Jesus leads the way. When the most severe temptations of the evil one came upon Him after He had fasted 40 days in the wilderness–He relied on God's Word for light to defeat the darkness.

The first temptation: To be ruled by hungers of the flesh.

"During that time the devil came and said to him, "If you are the Son of God, tell these stones to become loaves of bread." But Jesus told him, "No! The Scriptures say, 'People do not live by bread alone, but by every word that comes from the mouth of God.'" Matthew 4:3-4 NLT

The second temptation: To doubt God.

"Then the devil took him to the holy city, Jerusalem, to the highest point of the Temple, and said, "If you are the Son of God, jump off! For the Scriptures say, 'He will order his angels to protect you. And they will hold you up with their hands so you won't even hurt your foot on a stone.'" Jesus responded, "The Scriptures also say, 'You must not test the LORD your God.'" Matthew 4: 5-7 NLT

The third temptation: To treasure the things of this world and devotion to the darkness more than loyalty to God's kingdom.

"Next the devil took him to the peak of a very high mountain and showed him all the kingdoms of the world and their glory. "I will give it all to you," he said, "if you will kneel down and worship me." "Get out of here, Satan," Jesus told him. "For the Scriptures say, 'You must worship the LORD your God and serve only him.'" Then the devil went away, and angels came and took care of Jesus." Matthew 4:8-11 NLT

You face the same temptations—just not at the same extreme levels and in the same dire situation that Jesus did. They are all designed to shift your focus away from God's light and love. And, they are all founded upon the dark one's lies about God's character and trustworthiness. God is trustworthy! He will keep you in perfect peace as you fix your thoughts on Him and trust Him. *"You will keep in perfect peace all who trust in you, all whose thoughts are fixed on you!"* Isaiah 26:3 NLT

Jesus rebuffed Satan's temptations to submit to the flesh, to doubt God, and to seek worldly wealth above seeking God and His will. Had He surrendered to any of the dark one's temptations, He would not have qualified as the unblemished Lamb of God. These would have been fear-based, self-centered moves. Instead, He went to Scripture for light and power to dissolve the temptations of the dark one. He had spent time in the written word, time in creation, time in prayer, and time in sharing the light with others. He had invested much time and energy in sourcing the light of God found in these delivery systems.

He rebuked the dark one with the word of God found in Scripture. His responses are object lessons for us all—don't allow fleshly desires to control you—trust God no matter what—and seek Him above all else. First of all, submit to God. Then, resist the devil, and he will flee from you.

It is written: *"Therefore submit to God. Resist the devil and he will flee from you. Draw near to God and He will draw near to you."* James 4:7-8 NKJV

Jesus had done His homework. In His mind were planted the light-bearing neural pathways of selfless, other-centered love and obedience to the ways of heaven. He demonstrated to you that the power to submit to God and resist the devil comes from the Father of light.

Don't wait for temptations to come upon you. Take precautionary action. Strike first against the enemy of light. Walk your sacred pathway. Understand that you are unique.

As you continually plant Scripture in the garden of your mind, as you pray, as you witness God in nature, and as you share God's goodness and truth with others, He will shine His light into and through you in ways that are unique to you and your path. Within the borders of the revelations of God's light, found in these channels, there exists subtle pathways—differing variations and disseminations of light (goodness and truth).

Some light may exist that you do not see. Others may understand and see clearly what is foreign to your knowledge base and experience. We are all different. God knows this and creates pathways for you individually and for the human race corporately to follow.

Consider this—God created you and knows best how to communicate with you. He knows how to bring His love and His light to you personally. Your sacred pathway is likely to be different from that of others, but all God's pathways lead through Jesus.

> *Jesus said to him, "I am the way, the truth, and the life. No one comes to the Father except through Me."* John 14:1-6 NKJV

This statement, made by Jesus, appears to reveal that even if you don't know Who He is, you still connect with the Father through Him. Even if you never actually heard His name or were told of His sacrifice on your behalf during your time on earth—Jesus is still the Way for you to receive the light of God and traverse the limitless expanse of space and time to stand before His throne.

He alone is the Way. He alone bore the full weight of rebellion and healed the great wound. He is the ladder that Jacob saw in his vision. He *is* the Stairway to heaven.

He is the Way, the Truth, and the Life.

Your sacred pathways toward home travel through Him—whether you believe it or not. Every avenue, every sacred pathway toward your heavenly home, is open through Him.

Every soul is different. Therefore, the spiritual avenues that create an effective pathway to God for someone else may not be effective for you at all. Some people love to listen to a good sermon; others may feel trapped in a pew and find their spirit lifted by serving someone in need. Some connect with God well when out in the wild; others may dislike the woods. Some sense God's presence when alone and worship Him during those moments; others feel closer to Him through confronting an injustice. You must seek your effective, personal pathways. [FF]

You are likely to encounter God on many, if not all, true pathways, for He is everywhere. However, one or more will definitely make sense to you over the others. And this may change as you grow. Your individual path may vary from day to day and will likely change as you mature in the light.

You will move your being toward the light in different ways at different times. However, God will always be found in His creation, if you look. His light will always shine from His Word. Spend time with Him there for yourself. Study it on your own—regularly—with His Spirit as your guide. You will discover previously unseen light with each and every new search.

It will take time and practice, but be persistent and consistent as you spend your energies seeking the light of God through prayer, through the study and planting of His written word in the garden of your mind, through His creation, and through sharing His goodness and truth with others.

Invite and relish God's friendly presence wherever and whenever you seek the light. He will delight in directing you to the perfect paths for you to follow.

Anytime you are tempted, do not allow yourself to turn from God's presence, but move your being toward Him, into His cleansing light. If negative cues seem overpowering and draw you into the darkness, invite God along. Recognize His presence while participating in your negative habits. He is there anyway; you might as well acknowledge Him. This may help you to more fully realize His sure love. In the presence of God's light—darkness flees—unless you insist on keeping a hold on it. God will shine His light upon you but won't force it into you.

Strive to allow Him to replace negativity and darkness by filling your mind with new, enlightened *MADFATs*. Continue to crawl into the light. When participating in the deeds of darkness—expose them.

In the book of Ephesians, Paul tells you, *"For you were once darkness, but now you are light in the Lord. Live as children of light and find out what pleases the Lord. Have nothing to do with the fruitless deeds of darkness, but rather expose them."* Ephesians 5:8-11 NIV

Darkness fades when exposed to the light. Sin is vanquished in the presence of the Holy One. Dark motives, affections, desires, feelings, actions, and thoughts may come upon you at any time, especially if you have a brain filled with these types of neural pathways. However, as you use dark temptations to leverage the focus of your mind onto positive, uplifting neural pathways such as grace, love, and gratitude, the darkness will fade away. The light will cause the darkness to fade away.

Spiritual renewal is a pro-active, purpose-driven endeavor that will take time, commitment, and the power of God to accomplish. Your *Nourished Soul* will be well watered, enlightened, and refreshed on your journey as you absorb His warm rays of wisdom. These rays will sparkle as they fill your mind with the understanding that is spiritually discerned and clearly visible in His written Word.

Seek His light there. It is written:

> *Your word is a lamp for my feet, a light on my path.* Psalm 119:105 NIV

> *All Scripture is God-breathed and is useful for teaching, rebuking, correcting and training in righteousness, so that the servant of God may be thoroughly equipped for every good work.* 2 Timothy 3:16-17 NIV

Strive to expose the darkness in your soul to the light of God's Word.

The life and love of Christ are woven through the tapestry of Scripture as the foundational thread tying His heart to yours. Allow His Spirit to unveil the deep truths and light that radiate from Him. In Him resides the rich Son-light that will shatter the blackness of your human quandary.

> *In him was life, and that life was the light of men. The light shines in the darkness, but the darkness has not understood it.* John 1:4-5 NIV

God's children are often enabled to bloom love, hope, peace, patience, and forgiveness as they reflect His light through the good times and through the growth-enhancing challenges that are plentiful in our broken world.

The most profound realizations of the light and love of God may come to you through sharing it with others. As you help others find the Way, the Truth, and the Life, you will experience release from the darkness. It is in giving to others that you receive. Joy will radiate through your soul as you walk in other-centered bliss. God's light will shine through you to illuminate the path for others.

As a child of the light, God's radiance will draw you away from the deeds of darkness, purifying you and dressing you in the armor of light. Though the light and the life He offers is not understood by the darkness, He has revealed it to you.

The Son of God came to testify to the truth and to be the light that vanquishes the darkness. You can choose to move your being toward His light or to close your eyes to it. The darkness brings slavery and devastation to your being. The light of God dispels the darkness. That may be why the first words He spoke when creating this world were, *"Let there be light."* Genesis 1:3 NIV

Let there be light (goodness and truth) in you. Then share it.

> *This is the message we have heard from him and declare to you: God is light; in him there is no darkness at all. If we claim to have fellowship with him yet walk in the darkness, we lie and do not live by the truth. But if we walk in the light, as he is in the light, we have fellowship with one another, and the blood of Jesus, his Son, purifies us from all sin.* 1 John 1:5-7 NIV

> *The night is nearly over; the day is almost here. So let us put aside the deeds of darkness and put on the armor of light.* Romans 13:12 NIV

Through Pain and God's Light, My MADFATs Are Made Right

> *Consider it pure joy, my brothers and sisters, whenever you face trials of many kinds, because you know that the testing of your faith produces perseverance. Let perseverance finish its work so that you may be mature and complete, not lacking anything.* James 1:2-4 NIV

Before we discuss the great benefits of life's pains and temptations, let's pause to review what your *MADFATs* are. They are your: Motives, Affections, Desires, Feelings, Actions, and Thoughts.

Motives: incentives that cause a person to act in a certain way, do a certain thing, etc.
Affections: fond attachment, devotion, or love. Someone or something we are attracted to.
Desires: to wish or long for; crave. want. a longing or urge.
Feelings: an emotion or emotional perception or attitude.
Actions: something done or performed; act; deed.
Thoughts: the capacity or faculty of thinking, reasoning, and imagining.

Your *MADFATs*—define you. They are indicative of your core character and may very well reveal your destiny. Allow God to shine His purifying light upon them. Air them in the atmosphere of His perfecting love. You will seek Him and find Him when you seek Him with all your heart. Respond to His still, small voice that calls you. He will fuel the fire in your *Nourished Soul* and inspire you to wholeheartedly strive toward the development of a heaven-bound spirit.

Pain and temptations are often untapped gifts. Consider them pure joy! Use them to leverage your soul into God's light—His goodness and truth. Troubles are frequently the fertilizers that feed your restoration. Pain is commonly the admission price into the arena of spiritual growth. The ordinarily difficult to admit piece of this reality is; the temptations that seem to bring you pain, overpower you, and control you—come from inside you. It is written:

> *When tempted, no one should say, 'God is tempting me.' For God cannot be tempted by evil, nor does he tempt anyone; but each person is tempted when they are dragged away by their own evil desire and enticed. Then, after desire has conceived, it gives birth to sin; and sin, when it is full-grown, gives birth to death.* James 1:13-15 NIV

The temptations that drag you away are, often, the dark, previously planted, and reinforced patterns of thought that are stuck in your brain. They are patterns and ways of thinking and behaving that may have become automatic. As you continue to utilize them, they become stronger and expose your soul to ever-increasing loss.

If you never experienced pain from the opportunity living on earth bestows upon you and others you love, you might never seek a solution to your brokenness—God's light and love.

Life's painful struggles can be the bellows that breathe heat to forge the newly enlightened motives, affections, desires, feelings, actions, and thoughts that will be seared into your soul.

If you, like me, have had your heart broken by the pain derived from self-inflicted violations of God's laws of love and liberty, there is hope.

The fact that your conscience is still feeling pain when temptations overrule you and you fall into sin is an inspiring sign that you are being influenced by the Holy fires of God's Spirit.

Don't waste the pain. Capitalize on it. Use it! Let it propel you further into the light and away from the dark side.

Pain is essential to your survival. Ever put your hand on something very hot? You learned quickly not to do that—right? The same benefits of pain can be applied to emotional and spiritual pain—if you allow it. Pain can be the motor that either propels or derails you. You decide.

The pain produced by the negative effects of participating in the desires of darkness can help move you toward the light. Pain is meant to warn you. Use it to sharpen your resolve as you enjoy the refreshing wonders granted to the children of the light. You are meant to be a child of the light.

Embrace pain as a great learning tool. Allow it to move you toward the light. Allow yourself the right of forgiveness and use the difficulties that darkness creates to open channels of God's grace, light, and love.

Displace and replace the dark desires that drag, tempt, entice, and conceive death in your soul. Replace them with what you are really looking for—the lost connection with God and His Son Jesus Christ. Pain often provides the incentive you may need to shift your heart's desires toward Him. Use it well my friend.

God is knocking on the door of your soul. Don't spend your life apart from Him. Use all the experiences of this life to draw you ever closer to His great heart of love and soul-enriching light.

Understand and utilize pain. Enjoy your days as you deeply absorb the endless hope found in the promises of God, especially amidst the learning opportunities that trials, suffering, loss, and pain bring.

See beyond the mountain of distractions that trouble and temptation bring and enjoy God's enduring grace as He remakes you. The good news is that the pain-producing, evil desires that drag you off the path and entice you toward the temptations of darkness can be displaced and replaced. God has provided the Way!

> *No temptation has seized you except what is common to man. And God is faithful; he will not let you be tempted beyond what you can bear. But when you are tempted, he will also provide a way out so that you can stand up under it.* 1 Corinthians 10:13 NIV

God will not allow you to be tempted beyond what you can bear. Temptation is common to humanity; the power to dissolve it comes from God. All your temptations and spiritual struggles stem from your rebellious, human nature and dark, self-centeredness and fear. These established neural pathways lead you into participating in negative characteristics and the unholy yearnings of the world. This problem is rooted in the neural circuits of your brain.

Many of the dark, desolate neural circuits that empty your soul of light; you inherited from your ancestors. God ransomed you from this captivity. *"For you know that God paid a ransom to save you from the empty life you inherited from your ancestors."* 1 Peter 1:18 NLT

Seek God's direction, guidance, and counsel in planning your life. It is important to have a plan for each day that includes time spent in the light in ways that work for you. Make it your "light plan."

Many of us get into trouble with dark temptations when we are alone or in the company of those who enable us to walk in darkness.

When you are facing time alone or with others who can easily lead you off the path, it may be best to plan that time. Set up a "light plan" schedule and have an exit strategy. Broadcast your plan to others so they are aware. Do all of this with love and kindness as your guide while not allowing others to coerce or intimidate you. You are a royal child of the King of the universe. No one has the right to manipulate you.

Whether you are alone or in the company of others, create your "light plan" with healthy activities that you enjoy.

Who you are now is the result of your souls' passions, appetites, perceptions, and thinking patterns. You are free to choose to stay where you are, or you can choose to surrender to God and allow His Spirit to empower and restore you. He is the only true Source from which to seek the solution to rebellious self-centeredness, fear, and short-circuited *MADFATs*. Only under His Spirit's influence, power and direction will you be enabled to get them right.

Your Savior, Jesus Christ, is the solution. He is the healing water of life. You can trust in Him, Whose knowledge and wisdom is beyond your understanding. He knows your heart and mind better than you do. As you place your confidence in Him, you will not fear when heat comes; you will not worry in times of drought; you will never fail to bear fruit.

Paul captured the confusion of your human struggle in his letter to the church in Rome in the following verses:

> *So I find this law at work: When I want to do good, evil is right there with me. For in my inner being I delight in God's law; but I see another law at work in the members of my body, waging war against the law of my mind and making me a prisoner of the law of sin at work within my members. What a wretched man I am! Who will rescue me from this body of death? Thanks be to God—through Jesus Christ our Lord! So then, I myself in my mind am a slave to God's law, but in the sinful nature a slave to the law of sin.* Romans 7:21-25 NIV

If you do not make an effort to allow God to plant new, heaven-inspired neural pathways in your mind, you will remain a slave to the law of sin and stay in the same, sorry state. If nothing changes—nothing changes. Only you can open your heart and allow God to rewire your broken nature and the dark, self-centered, fearful neural pathways that are enshrined in your brain.

Temptations, fears, and dark urges nearly always pass in one of three ways:

1.) You indulge them. In which case, they are likely to come back stronger—increasing in frequency and urgency.
2.) You see them as triggers and transform them into motivating forces that move you into the light of God. When you do this, they come back weaker, less often, and less urgent, and eventually stop coming back at all—unless invited. When you stop accessing dark neural pathways, your brain begins to prune them back and eventually dissolves them.
3.) You die. Sometimes, as a result of your temptations, fears, and dark urges.

It is the second choice pattern you wish to focus on. If you shift your perspective on temptations, fears, and dark urges from something you must fight and resist to something you will use as leverage to lift you into the light, then you are operating in a spiritual realm that many never experience.

Remember always: *"The work of righteousness will be peace, and the effect of righteousness, quietness and assurance forever."* Isaiah 32:17 NKJV

Papa's Love PATERNs of Light Dissolve My Night

"You are all children of the light and children of the day.
We do not belong to the night or to the darkness." 1 Thessalonians 5:5 NIV

To dissolve is defined as: 1. to cause to pass into solution: 2. to cause to disappear or vanquish; dispel. 3. to bring to an end by or as if by breaking up; terminate.

Remember, the brain God gave you will dissolve unused neural circuits and patterns. It does this by generating a protein in your brain known as proBDNF. ProBDNF binds to unused neurons in your brain and eliminates them. But if a neural circuit is active and used, your brain will produce an enzyme that transforms proBDNF into BDNF (Brain Derived Neurotropic Factor). The presence of BDNF ensures the survival of the neurons in a circuit, and the more it is used, the stronger it is. [A]

This is the process by which your brain dissolves neural circuits that are not used. One of the easiest ways to stop using the destructive, dark neural circuits that reside in your brain is to replace them by focusing on the new ones God's Spirit and you will plant and nourish in the garden of your mind.

You can easily shift the focus of your thinking. The more often you leverage dark thoughts or cues to shift your mind's focus into the light, the more readily your brain will make this an automatic habit. You may not be able to control the transient thoughts that flow in and out of your mind, but you do have control over what plays on the main screen. Consider these instructions from Paul:

> *Do not be anxious about anything, but in every situation, by prayer and petition, with thanksgiving, present your requests to God. And the peace of God, which transcends all understanding, will guard your hearts and your minds in Christ Jesus.*
>
> *Finally, brothers and sisters, whatever is true, whatever is noble, whatever is right, whatever is pure, whatever is lovely, whatever is admirable—if anything is excellent or praiseworthy—think about such things.* Philippians 4:7-8 NIV

Paul is lifting the veil on what science has now discovered. By focusing our thankful prayers and petitions, as well as our thinking patterns, on whatever is good, the peace of God that transcends all understanding will guard our hearts and minds in Christ Jesus. He instructs us to think about whatever is True, Noble, Right, Pure, Lovely, Admirable, Excellent, and Praiseworthy.

I rearranged his list to read Pure, Lovely, Praiseworthy, Admirable, True, Excellent, Right, and Noble. Thus I created the acronym (P.L.P.A.T.E.R.Ns), which I then entitled *Papa's Love PATERNs of Light*. I like to refer to our Father God as Papa. *"Now we call him, "'Abba, Father.'" For his Spirit joins with our spirit to affirm that we are God's children."* Romans 8:16 NLT

The word Abba is commonly known to mean Papa. Calling our Father God by the name Papa warms His presence in our lives. I feel safe, accepted, and loved by Him when I call Him Papa. He is a perfect Father. Before and during times of temptation, you can melt those dark thoughts away by focusing your mind on *Papa's Love PATERNs of Light.*

Fear is the pattern of this world. Love is God's pattern.

Rather than struggling to beat the negativity planted in your brain, why not simply fill it with the light of God and beautiful, positive neural pathways?

Even before a negative, tempting, or destructive neural pathway fires and your thinking is drawn into it, simply invoke *Papa's Love PATERNs of Light*. The more you focus your mind on what is Pure, Lovely, Praiseworthy, Admirable, True, Excellent, Right, and Noble, the easier it will be for your brain to dissolve the dark, negative neural circuits that draw you away from the light.

Shifting my mind's focus to *Papa's Love PATERNs of Light* is a common path I seek frequently throughout my day, especially when tempted by the dark side. The following affirming declarations are some that Papa and I are making real, permanent, and actualized neural pathways in my brain. I repeat them often throughout the day. They encapsulate the essence of this book's challenge and are supernaturally granted by God's Spirit. It is He Who empowers your will and mine.

I open my entire being to God's Spirit and envision Him enriching me with these capabilities: I declare out loud, so my heart, mind, and soul can hear it, that:

> *"I will to be calm, I will to be free, I will to be healthy, happy, and wholly devoted to Thee. All that is goodness and truth I will to be mine. I willingly allow God's light to fill me."*

I also use the acronym for *Papa's Love PATERNs of Light* like this: Jesus is the only being that fulfills all of the attributes on the list. So, I often envision Him standing before me. I look directly at

Him, consider His perfect character and His all-consuming presence. I say to Him:

"Jesus you are:
***P**ure and unblemished,*
***L**ovely as a needed touch,*
***P**raiseworthy as Creator of all,*
***A**dmirable as my life-saving Friend,*
***T**rue as a rainbow's promise,*
***E**xcellent and merciful,*
***R**ight in all you do, and*
***N**oble as my eternal King."*

The goodness and truth that radiate from Him dispel the darkness. Invite Him into the depth of your temptations—He knows and is the Way up.

I refer to the two aforementioned declarations often and have them well memorized. They are permanent fixtures in my mind's garden. In addition to these declarations, I have another one I really love and declare often throughout my day. It is also a meditation I use at night as I am falling asleep.

While visiting with Mr. Paul, he told me that he experienced a period of severe depression for years after his return from the Viet Nam war. People were trying to get him on medication, but he refused and instead relied upon the word of God to heal his emotional state. Specifically, he found healing in the counsel found in 2 Corinthians. *"Casting down imaginations, and every high thing that exalteth itself against the knowledge of God, and bringing into captivity every thought to the obedience of Christ;"* [2 Corinthians 10:5 KJV]

Mr. Paul focused on bringing every thought captive to the obedience of Christ. Jesus never asks us to be depressed. His desire for our emotional well-being is to be full of joy! *"These things have I spoken unto you, that my joy might remain in you, and that your joy might be full."* [John 15:11 KJV]

Mr. Paul did overcome depression through the power in God's word and is one of the most joyful souls I have ever encountered. His testimony inspired me to incorporate the same verses into my life to help overcome challenges I have faced for many years. And guess what? It works. But, it does take practice. At least for me. It is another tool I have incorporated to shift my mind's focus from darkness to light. And from sadness to joy!

The affirming meditation Papa God and I designed started with the verse mentioned by Mr. Paul and grew from there. I call it my *Scripture Soup.* I speak directly to Jesus and say out it loud, so my brain can hear it unless others are around; in that case, I speak it to my mind.

I take every thought captive and make it obedient to You, my Friend, Jesus. For You counsel me and nurture me to grow in faithfulness, cheerfulness, kindness, generosity, healing friendships, complete joy, and freeing love.
Your peace transcends all understanding and guards my heart and mind in You, my Savior, Jesus.
You are the Author and Perfector of my faith.
Your peace enfolds my soul in a cocoon of Your gracious and lavish love and rewards my entire being with garden-fresh thoughts that are pure, loving, praiseworthy, admirable, true, excellent, righteous, and noble.
I do love You, my King, Jesus, with all my heart, all my mind, all my soul, and all my strength. And my neighbor as myself.
Because I am your tenderly loved and obedient follower, I am super-blessed, love-based,

mercy-wrapped, happily healthy, and eternally free.
All that is goodness and truth is mine. Let there be light in me.

I allow these soul-enriching affirmations to saturate every cell in my body and plant their virtues in every corner of the garden of my mind. I declare these truths regularly. Practice makes perfect. Sometimes I express them quickly in desperate moments; at other times, I savor them for long periods and repeat them like a mantra. I breathe in their simple yet powerful, elegant beauty and peace. I enjoy the pure light of their noble aspects and revel in the Master Artist's touch. Beautiful!

Often I just use a portion of one of these affirming declarations or even just a few words depending on what my mind is trying to feed me. For example, if sad or angry, I might just repeat the words, "love, cheerfulness, and generosity," to remind me that Jesus did inform me that I will have trouble in this world but to be of good cheer. Sadness and anger are self-centered emotions. I don't deny them. However, I've learned that they are not all that productive if I hang on to them for very long. A good way out of their grasp is to be loving and generous toward someone else.

When tempted by some negative thought, I often repeat: *"I take every thought captive and make it obedient to You, my Friend, Jesus. For You counsel me and nurture me to grow in faithfulness, cheerfulness, kindness, generosity, healing friendships, complete joy, and freeing love."*

You can certainly design and redesign your own faith-filed, affirming declarations, prayers, and Scripture Soups and repeat them often. Your mind tends to believe what it is fed the most. Let it feast upon the light. The weeds of negative, destructive, self-defeating neural pathways that are planted in your mind's garden are troublesome because you have nurtured and practiced them repeatedly. Your brain will dissolve them and they will die once you stop using them. When they come to mind, use them as triggers to launch new thought patterns. You can use temptation to harvest the fruit of the Spirit and His promise of power, love, and self-control.

The input your soul receives is your choice. You are what you eat—in all aspects of life, especially in the realm of the Spirit. If you feed your soul a steady diet of negative images and information, you will reap their damaging effects upon your character and destiny. However, If you feed your soul uplifting, heaven-inspired images and information, you will reap the positive benefits and hope that accrue by allowing God's Spirit access to and influence over your mind's focus. Paul explains this reality in the book of Romans:

> *"Those who are dominated by the sinful nature think about sinful things, but those who are controlled by the Holy Spirit think about things that please the Spirit. So letting your sinful nature control your mind leads to death. But letting the Spirit control your mind leads to life and peace. For the sinful nature is always hostile to God. It never did obey God's laws, and it never will. That's why those who are still under the control of their sinful nature can never please God. But you are not controlled by your sinful nature. You are controlled by the Spirit if you have the Spirit of God living in you."* Romans 8:5-9 NLT

Allow God's Spirit to dominate your thought life. Remain in Christ. In Him—your soul is safe. Rejoice in Him during your transformation into pure and excellent thought patterns. Praise Him, for though you are born into a corrupt world, you are not of this world. When you are in Christ, you are a new creation. You are His. Allow Him continuous access to your soul. Present your requests by prayer and petition, with thanksgiving, and the peace of God, which transcends all understanding, will guard your heart and mind in Him.

God will rewire your thinking as you seek *Papa's Love PATERNs of Light* to dissolve your night.

Dark manifestations of the broken human nature are evidence that the ultimate, inward spiritual battle rages on. The ultimate battle is the battle for dominion over the human heart. This battle requires different types of weapons from those the world uses. They are not weapons of destruction; they are weapons of restoration.

> *For though we walk in the flesh, we do not war according to the flesh. For the weapons of our warfare are not carnal but mighty in God for pulling down strongholds, casting down arguments and every high thing that exalts itself against the knowledge of God, bringing every thought into captivity to the obedience of Christ.* 2 Corinthians 10:3-5 NKJV

God's Spirit frees you from acting on every sinful thought. He empowers you to be obedient to Christ. No longer must you live as a slave in service to your fallen nature. You have been freed to obey and serve Christ. Your renewed mind will seek the ways of life. Willing obedience to God's ways opens wide the entrance to true freedom, true love, true joy, true peace, and the true you.

When temptation is really upon me, and I have allowed the darkness to ignite unhealthy thoughts and desires, I try to play the tape through to remember the predictable heart-breaking consequences waiting at the end of my rebellion. At times I fall. But, more often these days, I find myself remembering that I am already freed by God's amazing grace. I am now seeking to walk in accord with His Spirit. If I pay attention, I can sense Him marshaling His forces to raise my awareness and pull me out of the pit. He is always uplifting.

When I am focused on Him and Who He is, rebellion is certainly more difficult to engage in; not impossible, but certainly less attractive. Sin's rewards always fade. God's rewards always grow.

Envision this as your destiny: vigorously surrendering control of your heart, mind, soul, and strength to God's Spirit of love. Sweet! With your permission and willingness, He will fill the garden of your mind with beautiful, life-bearing, joyful neural pathways as He rewires your *MADFATs.*

Praying the promises of our Papa God gives us a considerable advantage amidst the struggle. This is one of my favorite prayers when tempted: *"Be confident of this, that he who began a good work in you will carry it on to completion until the day of Christ Jesus."* Philippians 1:6 NIV

Focus your mind on things that please the Spirit. Utilize *Papa's Love PATERNs of Ligh*t and allow your brain to dissolve all that isn't Pure, Lovely, Praiseworthy, Admirable, True, Excellent, Right, and Noble.

Pray the promises of God back to Him. Claim them as yours. God doesn't forget His promises. Claim His promises that touch you most deeply. Notice that nearly all of God's promises are subject to following His ways, usually love-based obedience and faith.

By the power of the Holy Spirit and God's on-board system for dissolving dark neural habits, put to death your rebellious nature and allow the Spirit of God to govern your mind and fill you with health, happiness, love, joy, and peace.

Untangle the night and use temptation to trigger God's light with these instruments.

1.) I Escape the Darkness by Remaining in God's Light
2.) Through Pain and God's Light, My MADFATs are Made Right
3.) Papa's Love PATERNs of Light Dissolve My Night

Mr. Paul's Insights, Inspirations, and Experiences Chapter Seven

As each Chapter neared completion, Mr. Paul would review it. Then, we would discuss it. I recorded our post review discussions. What follows are poignant and interesting excerpts from his recorded comments.

* In this chapter, you refer to that verse in 2 Corinthians: *"Bring into captivity every thought to the obedience of Christ."* Every time I come across that verse, I'm reminded of my deliverance from a significantly traumatic time in my life. As I mentioned earlier in my comments, Scripture is what God used to help me get totally free from depression. It was powerful. It took a while, but it worked.

It's that concept of bringing every thought into captivity to the obedience of Christ. It changes everything. Immediately if you have a wrong thought come, you bring it back to the word and get it corrected. It was a tenacious effort. It took some time, but I totally overcame depression with the word of God.

I was depressed for quite a few years after returning from the war in Viet Nam. It was Post Traumatic Stress Disorder and went on for years and years. It was a very, very difficult time. My wife really dislikes the use of drugs, but she wanted me to get on them because I was really hard to live with. My older daughter kept telling her that she should leave me cause life wasn't good. It was a pretty tough time. But, Yay God and His word! I overcame and got delivered.

It happened by practicing that Scripture; *"Bring every thought captive to the obedience of*

Christ." You see, your thoughts create your reality. "As a man thinks in his heart, so is he." I had to really get ahold of that. When any negative, depressing thought came, I just completely turned it around with the word of God.

It was like exercise. Like the Scripture says: *"Work out your own salvation."* It was a major workout but, I was delivered and overcame. Yay, God and His word!

I love the Bible. It is an incredible owner's manual. It teaches us how to live.

Chapter Notes and Discussion Topics

Notes ______

How did this chapter affect you? And why? ______

Did you gain any new perspectives or perceptions? ______

What changed in you after reading this chapter? ______

How can you use this knowledge to help improve your relationships with God, yourself, and others?

Chapter Eight

The Nourished Soul Gardening Guide for:

IOU Love

"Let no debt remain outstanding, except the continuing debt to love one another, for whoever loves others has fulfilled the law." Romans 13:8 NIV

Why does the bible claim that we owe a debt of love? Why love yourself and others? Why love your life? Why love God? Why be obedient to His laws of love? Because—the richness of His empowering kingdom is wrapped in the delicious delights and benefits enjoyed by the soul who obeys God's call to love. Love fulfills the law.

As you spend yourself in loving service and obedience to God's intentions and designs, He will live in you. Consider this verse penned by John, a close disciple of Jesus:

> *This is love: not that we loved God, but that he loved us and sent his Son as an atoning sacrifice for our sins. Dear friends, since God so loved us, we also ought to love one another. No one has ever seen God; but if we love one another, God lives in us and his love is made complete in us.* 1 John 4:10-12 NIV

The natural response to love is love. God is love. Love is the purest, most powerfully motivating force in the universe. But love isn't love till you give it away.

Oscar Hammerstein wrote: *"A bell is not a bell till you ring it. A song is not a song till you sing it. Love in your heart isn't put there to stay. Love isn't love till you give it away."* [GG]

This is the message that resounds throughout God's Word: *"Love in your heart isn't put there to stay. Love isn't love till you give it away."*

The Holy Scriptures have much to say about love. Let's touch on some vital verses describing various aspects of love and how you should respond to its manifestations. You will become increasingly enriched and blessed as the love-based fruits of God's sweet Spirit feed your *Nourished Soul.* Don't rush through these verses. Pause between them, breathe deeply of their hope and enjoy the beauty of their enlightening truth.

> *Behold what manner of love the Father has bestowed on us, that we should be called children of God!* [1 John 3:1 NKJV]

> *We love because he first loved us. Whoever claims to love God yet hates a brother or sister is a liar. For whoever does not love their brother and sister, whom they have seen, cannot love God, whom they have not seen. And he has given us this command: Anyone who loves God must also love their brother and sister.* [1 John 4:19-21 NIV]

> *God is love. Whoever lives in love lives in God, and God in them. This is how love is made complete among us so that we will have confidence on the day of judgment: In this world we are like Jesus. There is no fear in love. But perfect love drives out fear, because fear has to do with punishment. The one who fears is not made perfect in love.* [1 John 4:16-18 NIV]

You can love God by obeying His commands.

When asked which was the greatest commandment:

> *Jesus replied: "'Love the Lord your God with all your heart and with all your soul and with all your mind.' This is the first and greatest commandment. And the second is like it: 'Love your neighbor as yourself.' All the Law and the Prophets hang on these two commandments.'"*
> Matthew 22:37-40 NIV

Why did Jesus sum up all the law and the prophets—in two short sentences? He was being asked which of the Ten Commandments was the greatest, yet, He responded by telling the Pharisees who were trying to trap Him, to love God, themselves, and others. If you review the Ten Commandments, you will discover that the first four are meant to influence and enhance your love relationship with God. The last six are meant to influence and enhance your love relationships with others. All ten are meant to influence and enhance your inner relationship with love as you express it upwardly toward God, outwardly toward others, and internally toward yourself. Love is the foundation of God's universe and the motivating force behind His laws of love.

Jesus was sent by the Father not only to redeem you but to enlighten you. He left this earth with a resounding, crucial message—love one another.

Before He was separated from His disciples, He tried to comfort them. Most of His comfort came via instructions—instructions concerning the deeper realities. He spoke these words to His disciples. If you are His disciple, they are meant for you too.

He said:

As the Father has loved me, so have I loved you. Now remain in my love. If you keep my commands, you will remain in my love, just as I have kept my Father's commands and remain in his love. I have told you this so that my joy may be in you and that your joy may be complete. My command is this: Love each other as I have loved you. Greater love has no one than this: to lay down one's life for one's friends. You are my friends if you do what I command. I no longer call you servants, because a servant does not know his master's business. Instead, I have called you friends, for everything that I learned from my Father I have made known to you. You did not choose me, but I chose you and appointed you so that you might go and bear fruit—fruit that will last—and so that whatever you ask in my name the Father will give you. This is my command: Love each other. John 15:1-17 NIV

God is very clear. His commandments are—love. This is the deeper revelation. This is the core message of all God's laws of love. *"Let no debt remain outstanding, except the continuing debt to love one another, for whoever loves others has fulfilled the law."* Romans 13:8 NIV

Why is obedience to God so important? Obedience to His commands, as related to your life, is a revelation. It reveals your heart's stance toward Him and all His children—including yourself.

It's all about love. Look around you. Listen. Notice what the core desire of nearly every heart is—love. The economies of the world might not function at all without this one ingredient—love.

How many people get up and go to work each and every day as an expression of their love for others by caring for their needs? How many people have surrendered their lives to the cause of love? How many people exercise, diet, work, save, invest, plan, sacrifice, sweat, spend, breathe, surrender all, live in, and endure pain for that elusive, fragile, necessary experience of love? Probably; all of us. I'll bet that you have dedicated a large percentage of your life to love. Is there a better way to spend it? No. Love is likely to be the most vital, rewarding, risky, and worthwhile adventure of your life.

So very delicious are the sweet tastes of love!

The book of Proverbs declares, *"Whoever pursues righteousness and love finds life, prosperity and honor."* Proverbs 21:21 NIV

Have you ever felt completely unloved? That is a sad, bad day. Hope fades, and life seems somehow emptier when you don't feel that anyone at all loves you. But this is never true. While you may go through dry spells regarding the love of a mate, friends, or family, you will never be without God's unconditional love.

First Corinthians 13, often referred to as the "Love Chapter," ends with these words, *"And now these three remain: faith, hope and love. But the greatest of these is love."* 1 Corinthians 13:13 NIV

As you absorb the contents of this book, it is most often God's type of unconditional love we wish to focus primarily on. This type of love is the most freeing love, for it asks for nothing in return. Sharing love, like God shares love, is its own reward.

How does one get love? If it is so vital, where does one go to get it?

It is interesting to learn that the most readily available source of love is inside you. Love is not only out there trying to get in. Love is also inside you, trying to get out.

Consider this exchange between Jesus and some questioning Pharisees, *"Now when He was asked by the Pharisees when the kingdom of God would come, He answered them and said, "The kingdom of God does not come with observation; nor will they say, 'See here!' or 'See there!' For indeed, the kingdom of God is within you."* Luke 17:20-21 NIV

The kingdom of God is within you! God is love. Love is in you. It is the core of your being.

As a redeemed, restored citizen of God's kingdom, you too are called to love. Love flowing through you is the single most crucial, decisive, and fundamental imperative of your existence.

In the grand scheme of life, all that you do without love is futile. Demonstrations of love through you reveal God's indispensable essence moving in you. Paul wrote:

> *If I speak with the tongues of men and of angels, but do not have love, I have become a noisy gong or a clanging cymbal. If I have the gift of prophecy, and know all mysteries and all knowledge; and if I have all faith, so as to remove mountains, but do not have love, I am nothing. And if I give all my possessions to feed the poor, and if I surrender my body to be burned, but do not have love, it profits me nothing.* 1 Corinthians 13: 1-3 NKJV

Throughout the remainder of this *Nourished Soul Gardening Guide—IOU Love*—I hope to illuminate specific remedies that will help implant in your mind a plethora of the Holy Spirit's soul-enriching, love-based neural pathways. Once implanted, nourished, and well-practiced, they will chase away the darkness and bring to your life phenomenally refreshing avenues of love.

These beautiful remedies will revive consistent goodness and gentleness in the manner in which you express your refreshed temperament to God, yourself, and others. Through focusing your mind on them, God's Spirit will renovate all relationship practices that devalue your interactions with and the perceptions of those other humans who inhabit your world.

The Spirit's inventiveness will enrapture you as He redirects your relationship patterns into many unspoiled regions of love. These exist just beyond the shadowy and dark contemplations that may have infiltrated your soul.

The Spirit of God will sweep away the strongholds of animosity holding sway over your relationships and enliven your neural circuits with resilient thought waves of tenderness. You will no longer be robbed of your inheritance of the incredible capacity to fully enjoy and share what you most need to share—love.

Your *Nourished Soul* will drown out the cacophony of crippling noise of the evil one and free you to breathe love into every situation and soul you encounter.

Harmony with the Spirit's melody of affection will reverberate through all communications emanating from you and bridge the chasms of separateness that can derail your ability to peacefully connect with others. Kindness, compassion, sensitivity, warmth, and benevolence will flow freely from your Spirit-enriched soul and permeate your every breath. Hurting hearts will be drawn to you.

Your joy in sharing God's love will know no bounds. You will invigorate and not crumble. Many will be inspired to seek what you have found.

You will be a witness to the competent direction of your Master Gardener—Jesus.

As your new mind considers and your renewed soul communicates with God, yourself, and others, you will discover that your inspiring, Holy Spirit-implanted, love-based neural pathways will alleviate the obnoxious, heart-damaging patterns of judging, criticizing, and harming God, yourself, and others. Instead, you will become an untangled, freed, and liberated channel of love.

Your newly dominant aspirations will guide you automatically toward these love-based remedies.

God untangles my mind to understand and forgive.
God frees my heart to love and encourage.
God liberates my soul to help and heal.

God Untangles My Mind to Understand and Forgive

Dysfunctional; is the current buzzword for broken people, families, and organizations that are not whole and healthy. The primary problem with each of these is—people. People are the problem. We are all broken and not functioning as designed.

You are one of the billions of broken souls who currently inhabit planet earth. We all have something in common besides being broken—none of us chose to be here.

As Henry Ward Beecher said, *"God asks no man whether he will accept life. That is not the choice. You must take it. The only choice is how."*

Each of us simply showed up one day, slowly grew into consciousness, and began our journey. This broken world is not your fault. You, like all of us, have inherited negative neural pathways. You were born bent toward rebellious self-centeredness and fear.

You are also extremely influenced by the society and culture you are born in, raised in, and live in. You learn by example. You may have learned by example to blame God for the negative acts of the dark side. You may have learned by example and practice to judge nearly everyone and everything. You are not to blame. You are simply broken, like everyone else.

Humans have developed a bias toward negativity and often assign more weight to negative experiences than positive or neutral ones, even if the negative experience is deemed inconsequential.

You were born into a world of negativity. Just watch the news, read a newspaper or listen to almost anyone talk for a few minutes about someone else. The central focus is often negativity in the form of judging. You are not to blame for the negative, self-focused neural pathways you were born with or learned by example from your environment. You are, however, responsible for allowing God to rewire your mind and restore your soul.

Your patterns can be healed through God's power and your willingness to refocus your considerations. You go where you focus. What is your focus when you consider or talk about others? Do you judge others, or do you understand and forgive them for being born human? In judging others for their weaknesses, you forget that they belong to God. We are all His children, whom He loves. Scripture warns about the dangers of judging others:

> *Do not judge others, and you will not be judged. For you will be treated as you treat others. The standard you use in judging is the standard by which you will be judged.*
> Matthew 7:1-2 NLT

As God's Holy Spirit rewires your *MADFATs*, you will be imbued with His consistent fruit. Your considerations and attitudes toward God, yourself, and others will be filled with love, joy, peace, patience, kindness, goodness, faithfulness, gentleness, and self-control.

Each child of God has a unique personality and is born into a unique set of circumstances. No child of God gets to choose how, when, or where they are born. And every child of His born on this magnificent globe called earth is born broken. You are one of the broken souls.

You are not to blame. It is not your fault. Instead—it is your gift. You may use your brokenness and struggles as witness to God's restorative powers and reveal to others His goodness and mercy.

Ernest Hemingway wrote: *"The world breaks everyone and afterward many are strong at the broken places."* [II]

The healing of your broken places often makes you stronger. As you experience God's restoring power over your brokenness, you will become a more vital witness to the world concerning His ability to renew, rewire and restore human souls.

The traditional Japanese art of *"Kintsugi"* is a metaphor for turning the brokenness in our lives into strengths and assets. In Japan, when a cherished vase or clay pot is broken, rather than throwing it away, precious metals such as gold and silver are employed to repair, restore and even strengthen the brokenness. Thus turning shattered fragments into whole, healed works of art.

Scripture declares: *"And yet, O LORD, you are our Father. We are the clay, and you are the potter. We all are formed by your hand."* Isaiah 64:8 NASB

God is the potter. You are a cherished clay pot that is broken. His endless grace, healing powers, blessings, love, understanding, and forgiveness will restore your broken parts and transform them into valuable assets drawing attention to His tenderhearted Remedy—Jesus.

Your life is God's gift to you. Your gift to Him is what you choose to do with it. Use your broken places as valuable assets, restored by God and healed by His grace, to benefit those who may witness His reviving abilities in your life.

We are all broken and in need of restoration. As others witness your healed brokenness, your understanding, and forgiveness, your love, and care, they too may be put back together.

This planet can be a confusing, dangerous, and, at times, painful place. However, every broken experience can be turned into a positive asset. *"And we know that God causes everything to work together for the good of those who love God and are called according to his purpose for them."* Romans 8:28 NLT

Your time here will be more enjoyable if you don't focus on the dark side of human existence. Our world is full of negativity. But it is also full of beauty, joy, peace, and love. Every cloud has a silver lining.

What do you see when you look at the world around you? If what you see is negative, try looking with new eyes—eyes of understanding and acceptance toward this broken yet beautiful world. Eyes that understand and forgive yourself and others.

God made His children beautiful. We are all garnished with His image and likeness. We may have wilted mightily under the heat of the dark one's affliction, but we are still God's beautiful, tenderly loved children. The trust God has placed in you by allowing you to be born on earth will prove to be one of your greatest gifts through all eternity. Don't forget it. You have been granted one of the most beneficial opportunities of all time. You get to be a human! You are also allowed to move past the inborn tendency of focusing on the trouble displayed in many moments of life. Strive to focus on the good in every moment of time and every person you meet.

When you view God's world through the lens of goodness and love, you are allowed to move beyond your current state through the power and insight bestowed upon you by the Holy Spirit. You can operate on a higher spiritual plane.

> *"The person without the Spirit does not accept the things that come from the Spirit of God but considers them foolishness, and cannot understand them because they are discerned only through the Spirit."* 1 Corinthians 2:14 NIV

Spiritual things are spiritually discerned. Seek the Holy Spirit's presence and enlightenment, and you will clearly see what is really happening on this troubled planet. You will clearly understand the battle for all souls. Yours included.

Amazing; are the bright possibilities for you to learn from your human condition.

Throughout the endless ages, you will know what few ever will. You will know the experiences of rebirth. You will be lifted from the brokenness. You will learn from Jesus the keys to overcoming and growing amidst this planet's challenges. You can be like Jesus. You can be completely understanding and forgiving. You can accept this world as it is.

Be diligent in seeking His Spirit's presence and power to move past the negativity that inhabits your soul. Jesus came to earth as God among us; to redeem our race, dispute the lies of the dark one, reveal the true character of God, and demonstrate for us—the Way up. He revealed to you what your attitudes toward this human experience should be.

May you discover and adopt the attitudes of Christ Jesus toward this world, toward God, yourself, and others.

> *May the God who gives endurance and encouragement give you the same attitude of mind toward each other that Christ Jesus had, so that with one mind and one voice you may glorify the God and Father of our Lord Jesus Christ. Accept one another, then, just as Christ accepted you, in order to bring praise to God.* Romans 15:5-7 NIV

One of today's most quoted and demonstrative prayers may help you understand that you can see through the lies of the dark one and blow away the enshrouding mist that attempts to cloud the events of daily life on this beautiful, life-generating, love-designed world.

This famous prayer was originally written by St. Francis of Assisi. It reads:

> *Lord, make me an instrument of Thy peace; where there is hatred, let me sow love;*
> *where there is injury, pardon; where there is doubt, faith; where there is despair, hope;*
> *where there is darkness, light; and where there is sadness, joy.*
> *O Divine Master, grant that I may not so much seek to be consoled as to console;*
> *to be understood, as to understand; to be loved, as to love;*
> *for it is in giving that we receive, it is in pardoning that we are pardoned,*
> *and it is in dying that we are born to eternal life. Amen* JJ

Rather than focusing your heart, soul, mind, and strength on the negative aspects of God's broken children and judging them, seek to console others rather than be consoled, to understand rather than be understood, and to love rather than be loved. It is in giving these that you will receive them. It is in pardoning others that you are pardoned. Rather than judge—understand and forgive.

Understanding and forgiveness create gravity. As you explore these and freely grant them, you will draw others to the peaceful soul within you. You will become a beacon of light in a sometimes dark and unforgiving world. Breathe in love—exhale understanding and forgiveness.

You may certainly allow and assist God in transforming your world and the world of those whose lives you touch. Your *Nourished Soul* can contribute greatly to the healing of broken hearts everywhere. We all need love.

Jesus loves you as you are. He accepts you as you are. He understands why you are the way you are and longs to heal you of all your unease. You, too, may accept and love yourself and others just as you and they are.

You will love yourself and others better when you accept all God's children for who they are and understand that you, as well as everyone else, are in the same challenging situation.

Pause when agitated with yourself or any other broken human, and ask God to heal your thinking. We all make mistakes. We mess things up. We hurt one another. There are people you have harmed, and there are people that have harmed you. These situations can be healed.

Throw away the keys to the hurt locker where you have stored the pain of yours and other's mistakes. Let it go. Forgiveness heals the world. Why destroy your joy by continuing to strain your vitality with the weighty load of past misery? Drop the rock. Give yourself and others a break.

No matter what you or anyone else has done, forgiveness is the path out of the pain. Don't burden your soul with resentment, condemning, criticizing, and complaining. Allow God to set your heart free.

God has forgiven you, and you should follow His example. Release yourself. Release others. It is in pardoning that you are pardoned. Be restored to love. Allow God to swaddle your broken heart in a contented cocoon of compassion, kindness, humility, gentleness, patience, and love.

Allow the soul-enriching love and care of God to untangle your mind to understand and forgive.

The book of Colossians encourages you:

> *Therefore, as God's chosen people, holy and dearly loved, clothe yourselves with compassion, kindness, humility, gentleness and patience. Bear with each other and forgive whatever grievances you may have against one another. Forgive as the Lord forgave you. And over all these virtues put on love, which binds them all together in perfect unity.* Colossians 3:12-14 NIV

Love binds these virtues. You are chosen and dearly loved by God. Clothe yourself rightly and stretch these virtues over your heart. Forgive yourself and others as the Lord forgives you.

God loves you so much. Be like Him. Be victorious. Die to self-centeredness. Be restored, forgiven, gracious, and saved. Demonstrate His love. Walk free and untangled. Utilize pain to progress. Use each trial to propel you forward. Find the silver linings.

The challenges you face can be your greatest assets and adventures. Use them as the blessings they are. Rely on God to show you how to sacrifice your resentments, fears, pains, and hurts on the altar of forgiveness.

Understand that everyone is broken. Forgive yourself and others. What have you got to lose?

It's important to note that to understand and forgive does not mean that you must subject yourself to someone who harms you. In some situations, you may need to seek safety and help.

But once you are safe, don't burden yourself with resentment, bitterness, pain, and anger. Don't chain yourself to the darkness. Be free. Allow God to heal your soul. Forgive grievances and hurts.

Most of us find great joy in relationships where we experience acceptance, understanding, and forgiveness. Seek to grant this joy to yourself and others.

Train your mind to focus on the beauty in your life and on the hope of the coming life that is yours—thanks to the gift of Jesus, your Friend, Savior, and King. Even though someone may have caused you harm, set them free in healthy, safe, and forgiving ways.

God Frees My Heart to Love and Encourage

"As you free love—love will free you." James Bars

Thinking, believing, and speaking critically about yourself and others is a heavy burden to bear. God will empower you to lift yourself and others above the dreary tasks and negative weight of criticism. Please remember and understand that all humans, including yourself, are broken. Strive to refrain from being critical; instead, focus on everyone's positive features. A lighter and much more rewarding path is found on the trail of love and encouragement. Your love and encouragement are revealed to yourself and others through your actions and words.

Body language is often the dominant form of communication used to reveal one's attitude; it will convey your emotions, whether critical or uplifting. The majority of your emotional communication is most likely non-verbal When your love and encouragement are true, your entire being reveals it.

The fruit of criticism is picked at your own peril. Being critical and condemning of yourself and others is a weapon of the dark side. God has called you to love. In the process of being restored to your original design and intent, your compassion and love for yourself and others will thrive. Consider these well-known Bible verses.

For God so loved the world that he gave his one and only Son, that whoever believes in him shall not perish but have eternal life. For God did not send his Son into the world to condemn the world, but to save the world through him. John 3:16-17 NIV

God did not give and send Himself in the form of His Son—Jesus into the world to condemn us. He gave and sent Himself in the form of His Son—Jesus into the world to save us. Jesus was not given and sent to condemn or criticize, but to lift up, to restore—to cause health, happiness, hope, new life, and beautiful emotions to spring from the hearts of all. He came to make known the Father. He came to reveal the foundation of God's kingdom—self-sacrificing love. He came to redeem, to restore, and to encourage. He came to inspire with hope, grit, and confidence. He came to demonstrate God's boundless grace. Then He said, *"follow me."* This, He will empower you to do. Through His Spirit's indwelling power—self will fall away, and you will treat others like Jesus treated others.

You reap what you sow. As you love, encourage, and inspire others, you will be loved, encouraged, and inspired.

You will discover that silence in the face of the desire to criticize yourself or others will become a pathway to peace and may keep you out of negative situations. *"Watch your words and hold your tongue; you'll save yourself a lot of grief."* Proverbs 21:23 MSG

Noticing and speaking of the faults of others will recoil on your soul and diminish your movement into the light of God's love. *"Whoever derides their neighbor has no sense, but the one who has understanding holds their tongue."* Proverbs 11:12 NIV

Voicing and attempting to correct the faults of others may be a way to distract you from dealing with your own difficulties. You may find that you have developed a habit of discrediting others for their faults. You may very well suffer from the same faults. You know what they say, *"If you spot it—you got it."* The function of this process is often discovered to be nothing more than an attempt to lift yourself up by putting others down. This creates a fruitless circle of negativity and frustration in your heart. It will suck the love, joy, peace, and patience from your soul.

You are already worthy. So are they. You needn't put anyone down—God, yourself, or others.

Love, joy, peace, and patience unfold and mature more readily in your soul when you allow God to restructure your perspectives and attitudes toward Him, yourself, and others. As you continue to germinate, sprout, grow, and harvest positive patterns that focus on loving others and encouraging their assets, your *Nourished Soul* will rise from the pit. You will soar above the sinking quagmire of belittling the beautiful creations of God.

Loving and encouraging others will bring the same back to you. Let compassion and gentleness reign in your heart. Look for the good in yourself, and others and you will find it. Find good words to speak to all and about all. Replanting the garden of your mind with the soul-enriching roots and fruits of love and encouragement will often cut across the grain of negativity and habitual patterns.

Your mind's garden may have been seeded by the invasive weeds of darkness. However, the benefits derived from shifting your thought and action patterns away from the dark side into the light of God's loving ways are eternal. Consider the outgrowth of these hope-filled words of love and encouragement: *"Do not judge others, and you will not be judged. For you will be treated as you treat others. The standard you use in judging is the standard by which you will be judged."* Matthew 7:1-2 NLT

Strive to learn from each soul you encounter with an eye toward their benefit. Don't criticize. Allow the Holy Spirit to convict your soul and the souls of others. Remember—convicting and changing hearts is His job—not yours. Don't preach change—be the change you wish to see. People are often more inspired by seeing a sermon than by listening to one.

> *A great teacher never strives to explain his vision—he simply invites you to stand beside him and see for yourself.* —The Rev. R. Inman

This is what God did in the form of His Son, Jesus. As He lifts you above the negative patterns of your old life, you will become a more valuable witness to His power and ability to restore the human soul. You will be free to love and encourage.

Make yourself available to others in the ways God inspires, equips, and motivates you. Follow your own sacred pathways to the throne of God and the ancient ways of love and care. There is only one you. Be you. Only *you* can love like *you* do. *Love in your heart isn't put there to stay. Love isn't love till you give it away.*

A critical attitude will rob you of your joy, but a positive attitude of gratitude coupled with honest actions of love and encouragement will bring joy to you and others.

Most seem to respond well to positive reinforcement. Love and encouragement are generously granted to you through God's Spirit. He can create a positive and uplifting environment within you. A refreshing river of living water can flow through you. Jesus reveals this truth: *"The one who believes in Me, as the Scripture said, from his innermost being will flow rivers of living water."* John 7:38 NASB

Demonstrating love and encouragement through your attitudes, actions, words, and body language are positive ways to refresh yourself and others with living waters.

Understandably, each person senses love and encouragement in different ways. Learning how those whose lives you touch experience love can be a rewarding tool for all.

Dr. Gary Chapman has written an enlightening book that is helpful in discovering how you and others experience love. You may wish to obtain his book, *The 5 Love Languages: The Secret to Love that Lasts.* [KK]

As you remember to love God first, your love for others will flow more freely. It is in experiencing God's love that you become equipped to love and encourage yourself and others more effectively. Paul tells us:

> *If you have any encouragement from being united with Christ, if any comfort from his love ... then make my joy complete by being like-minded, having the same love, being one in spirit and purpose. Do nothing out of selfish ambition or vain conceit, but in humility consider others better than yourselves. Each of you should look not only to your own interests, but also to the interests of others.* Philippians 2:1-4 NIV

You freely receive love and encouragement from God; you will profit from offering the same to yourself and your fellow man. Paul often wrote on the importance of love and encouragement:

My goal is that they may be encouraged in heart and united in love, so that they may have the full riches of complete understanding. Colossians 2:2 NIV

Your love has given me great joy and encouragement, because you, brother, have refreshed the hearts of the Lord's people. Philemon 1:7 NIV

Finally, brothers and sisters, rejoice! Strive for full restoration, encourage one another, be of one mind, live in peace. And the God of love and peace will be with you. 2 Corinthians 13:11 NIV

As you practice focusing your efforts on loving and encouraging yourself and others, you will find understanding, purpose, and peace. Remember—you are to love others as yourself.

Do you love yourself? Many people are harder on themselves than anyone else would dare to be. Strive to monitor your self-talk and seek to love yourself humbly and appropriately as God's child.

You will love others better when you love and care for yourself properly. One of the best things you can do for your own health and happiness is to love and encourage yourself and others. *"A cheerful disposition is good for your health; gloom and doom leave you bone-tired."* Proverbs 17:22 MSG

Love and encouragement can accomplish what criticism never will. They will break down the walls that separate. As God's child, you are dearly loved and richly encouraged. You are enabled to put to death vain conceit and selfish ambition and set free to cheerfully love and encourage yourself and others. What a beautiful day it is when you lay your head on the pillow at night and realize you didn't criticize anyone or anything that day. Oh—sweet freedom!

God Liberates My Soul to Help and Heal

The most efficient and effective way to participate in the divine nature (self-sacrificing love) and escape the corruption in the world caused by evil desires is to allow your Papa God to rewire your *MADFATs.*

As you progressively possess the characteristics of a peace-filled, heaven-bound soul, your being will advance in the light of love. You will be all the more eager to make your calling and election sure. You will walk in ever-expanding, heart-warming contentment. The number of regretful moments in your life will continue to decrease.

It is common to cause harm when under the influence of self-centered anger. This is a fear-based emotion. As your *MADFATs* are rewired by God, your emotions will become more consistently love-based. You may still experience anger, but the motives behind your anger will change. You will dissolve fear-based, self-centered anger. Your anger will become like God's love-based, righteous anger.

The person suffering from the ravages of rebellion may not even understand why they are the way they are. Why get angry with them for being born broken? They didn't ask for it.

When you find that you are becoming frustrated with yourself or others, seek to comprehend the underlying entanglements and employ your energies to bring healing to each conflicted experience. *"Anyone can become angry—that is easy, but to be angry with the right person at the right time, and for the right purpose and in the right way—that is not within everyone's power, and that is not easy."* Aristotle CCC

Have you ever harmed another while feeling peaceful, loving, calm, and relaxed? Probably not. I guess that your harming of others has to do with moments of intense flash-anger or the development of long-term resentment building and revenge planning.

Has resentment, revenge, hatred, or animosity ever delivered positive, satisfying, free-flowing rivers of peace to your soul? Not likely. These experiences will generally deliver more of the same. Especially if bad words are spoken against you or action is taken against you, either for seemingly uncalled-for reasons or in retaliation for your bad words or actions.

Is all anger wrong? No. Anger at injustice—perceived or real—is the human heart's following the divine Creator's response within. You are made in God's image and likeness. God gets angry.

He gets angry for your good. You get angry when injustice occurs—just like God. His divine image in you generates your response to injustice, unfairness, and unrighteousness.

Righteous anger can be evidence that God dwells in you. To become angry at the wrongness of this dark world may display your nobility. This is righteous anger. Righteous anger is your physical, emotional, and spiritual response to wrongs. However, as a human functioning outside the full ability to cooperate with God's laws of love and liberty, you are at a disadvantage. Selfishness, self-centeredness, and fear are often the basis of your anger. This is not righteous anger.

Turning again to Scripture, you will discover revealed within its pages that love casts out fear. You may abide in love. In so doing, you are delivered from self-centeredness and unrighteous anger.

> *We have come to know and have believed the love which God has for us. God is love, and the one who abides in love abides in God, and God abides in him. By this, love is perfected with us, so that we may have confidence in the day of judgment; because as He is, so also are we in this world.*
>
> *There is no fear in love; but perfect love casts out fear, because fear involves punishment, and the one who fears is not perfected in love.* [1 John 4:16-18 NASB]

Perfect love casts out fear. Does God walk in fear? No. God is love!

But He does know sorrow and righteous anger. Does His anger flow from love? Yes—always. God's anger is always righteous anger.

I believe God is not angry with us because we were born broken. I believe He gets angry when we reject the light He freely offers us at our own peril. I believe He is angry at the injustice we must endure under the lash of rebellion, self-centeredness, and fear.

Even so, as broken as we may be, we can still behave as God does concerning anger—*because as He is, so also are we in this world.* We, too, may experience righteous anger.

If your two-year-old child is running toward a cliff and you shout at him in an angry, forceful voice in an attempt to save him and get him to stop—are you angry at the child? No. Your apparent anger is motivated by love and concern for your child. I believe God is doing the same for you. Should you fear God? It depends on which definition of the word "fear" you use.

Scripture states that you are to fear God, *"You must fear the LORD your God and worship him and cling to him. Your oaths must be in his name alone."* [Deuteronomy 10:20 NLT]

Consider this revelation from the psalmist: *"Lord, if you kept a record of our sins, who, O Lord, could ever survive? But you offer forgiveness, that we might learn to fear you."* [Psalm 130:3-4 NLT]

I believe when Scripture tells you to fear God, it is not telling you to be afraid of Him but to hold Him in awe and reverence. And when Scripture talks about God's anger, I believe that it is talking about His righteous, love-based anger.

During my travels through the Scriptures, I have come across many situations where God seemed cruel. It was difficult to see Him as love in most of those confusing actions. Until my Counselor—the Holy Spirit, began to enlighten me. It was revealed to me that God always tries to warn souls before any catastrophe falls. And He does so repeatedly with compassionate concern.

He warned of the great flood for a hundred and twenty years before it came. It is when we ignore Him and choose to push Him and His warnings aside to follow our own twisted desires that devastation comes. He is a perfect Father. His motive is always soul-enriching love and care. When I looked behind the destruction caused by God's mysterious acts, I always found a parent's warning. A loud cry to stop before we careen off the cliff.

The entire Bible is a warning for us—today. He must purge His universe of evil for the eternal safety of His children. A cleansing fire is coming. He has provided a fire escape—a Way out. His Daddy's heart breaks for His precious children who choose to reject Him. I believe He will suffer forever over each child who said no to His freely granted offer of an eternal life luscious with adventure. God is love. I believe His anger is the result of sorrow over losing any of His children forever. His anger source is always love. Your anger source is not. Not yet. Your anger source is often self-centeredness or fear. These unrighteous anger sources may cause you to lash out and harm yourself or others. The source of your anger will often determine if you need to make amends.

If you harm someone out of self-centeredness or fear and the anger that arises from them, then you are most likely in the wrong and need to make amends. Sincere amends—no falsies.

But if your anger is righteous anger and your words and actions come from a place of love, you are probably okay. However, those involved must believe in the truth of your motives. This is usually apparent, especially if you have a history of this type of love-based, righteous anger.

How can God rewire you so that self-centered, fear-based anger-related harm stops causing you and those around you pain and suffering? This is a part of gaining new *MADFATs.*

As you walk in God's inspiring power to transform you by renewing your motives, affections, desires, feelings, actions, and thoughts—fear-based, self-centered anger will fade.

New neural pathways will be wired into your brain, and your actions and reactions will become regulated by love-based patterns. This will take time and practice. Some useful tools to help in this ongoing process are:

The Nine Steps to Resolve Conflict and Manage Anger

1.) **The Pause**. *When anger is rising—pause and pray for the right thoughts and actions. Detach from the negative emotions as soon as possible. Take a few deep breaths.*

2.) The Closed Mouth. *"Fools vent their anger, but the wise quietly hold it back."* Proverbs 29:11 NLT *Never miss an appropriate opportunity to keep your mouth shut—especially when angry. "A gentle answer turns away wrath, but a harsh word stirs up anger."* Proverbs 15:1 NIV

3.) The Escape. *It can help diffuse the situation if you politely withdraw. Say that you would like to take time to consider the other person's point of view and you wish to be alone to pray.*

4.) The Return. *While you are away, actually pray and see the other person's side. Ask yourself this question: "What part of this am I responsible for?" Go back and admit it. Go in an attitude of love.*

5.) **The Replay.** *If, at first, you don't succeed—take another break. Some people need more time to cool.*

6.) **The Apology.** *Make sincere amends. Strive not to do it again. Laugh at the situation as soon as it seems right to do so.*

7.) **The Forgiven**. *Everyone wants to be forgiven for their errors. So do it. Forgive, and let it go. Don't haunt yourself or others with past mistakes.*

8.) **The Lesson.** *Debrief yourself after each anger experience. What worked? What made things worse? What can you do next time to make the situation better or dissolve it completely?*

9.) The Happiness Garden. *A good offense is the best defense. Consistently plant peace, love, joy, patience, acceptance, understanding, wisdom, goodness, and all other beautiful spiritual flowers in the garden of your mind. Their abundance will cause the weeds of distress and anger to be uprooted.*

Take charge of your brains' neuroplasticity. If you don't purposely plant seeds in your brain that produce the desired fruit—other forces will plant weeds to choke off your bounty of joy.

Nourish your mind. Plant good seeds in its fertile soil and expose its sprouts to the Son-light. Seek and follow your own sacred pathway back to the Garden-of-Eden *Nourished Soul* you are meant to be. Enlist the Spirit of God's guidance and light, and you will produce a vast harvest of beautiful, abundant, love-expanding deliciousness. Plant, germinate, sprout, and nourish sweet, succulent crops for the eternal universe to enjoy. Fertilize your soul with nutritious spiritual goodness. Eat freely and often of the Bread of Life. Drink deeply of the satisfying Water that flows from the Rock. Jesus is the Bread of Life. He is the Water and the Rock. He is the Fire Escape. Obtain life-saving vital nourishment from God's Word. Jesus is the Word.

> *In the beginning was the Word, and the Word was with God, and the Word was God. He was with God in the beginning.*
> *Through Him all things were made; without Him nothing was made that has been made. In Him was life, and that life was the light of men.* John 1:1-5 NIV

This book is designed to help facilitate the healthy, happy, fruitful gardening of your heart, mind, and soul by exposing you to relevant concepts of science, as well as the inspiring light found in the Word of God. But please know this—the written word of God has special messages for you, and you must find them for yourself by reading, studying, and absorbing its power directly.

You can utilize the guides outlined in this book as you invite God to rewire your *MADFATs.* Be that as it may, you will find the greatest benefit by going directly to His word. Doing so will enable you to richly access His Spirit's transforming power personally from the Source.

As He restores your neural pathways back to His original design, before the fall in the Garden, you will be refreshed and remade. Love will take the place of unrighteous anger. Your heart will receive the divine similitude. You will find that you will not need to make amends as often.

But don't avoid this vital process. Making amends is the fruit of a mature soul.

The humility gained and the healing produced by admitting your wrongs and making amends enriches the souls of all involved. All will enjoy the fruits of love. *"Love does no harm to a neighbor. Therefore love is the fulfillment of the law."* Romans 13:10 NIV

Mending your relationships with others will fill your soul with ever-increasing peace and provide all whose lives you touch with a much less drama-driven life. You should always seek to live at peace with those around you. Paul advises: *"If it is possible, as far as it depends on you, live at peace with everyone."* Romans 12:18 NIV

Jesus believed it was so important that you mend your relationships with others that in the Sermon on the Mount He said: *"Therefore, if you are offering your gift at the altar and there remember that your brother has something against you, leave your gift there in front of the altar. First go and be reconciled to your brother; then come and offer your gift."* Matthew 5:23-24 NIV

You may not have control over the wrong others do to you, but you can take responsibility for your role in any conflict you experience. You do have control when it comes to making amends for the harm you cause others.

As you walk closely with the Spirit of the Lord, He will convict you of the restitution you owe, and in obedience, you should strive to make amends quickly. Taking responsibility, confessing your failure, and changing your ways are strong steps toward peaceful, loving, open relationships. You will be able to look the world in the eye.

Don't dwell on the harm another may have caused you in any situation, but promptly forgive and make amends for your part. Don't allow pride to keep you from living in peace with yourself and others. Seek ways to benefit everyone and not harm them.

You must be tender, careful, and considerate when making amends. If you have caused someone harm they don't know about, and it would harm them even more to discover what you have done, it may not be best to tell them. Pray about what you should do. God will direct you. You may wish to find an alternative means of making amends other than apologizing directly for the wrong you have done. However, if a person does know what you have done, you should make amends directly. Strive to benefit others always and avoid harming anyone.

If you are exhibiting a certain behavior that harms others, your amends will have little effect if you continue to participate in that behavior. True amends will include discontinuing harmful choices and actively seeking ways to help and heal yourself and others.

If you suffer under the ravages of overwhelming confusion, depression, addiction, compulsion, or obsession, the information in this book can help. In addition, there are great benefits enjoyed by those who actively participate in support groups. There is also an army of clergy, counselors, mentors, and other professionals available. You may need some help with skin on it. And, you may very well discover that you will heal and grow more solidly by being helpful to others. As you give—you receive.

Each day, as you focus on that day's *Nourished Soul Gardening Guide*, you will be nurturing and growing the new neural habits God's Holy Spirit is implanting in you. You will move forward through His wisdom, guidance, and power. You will truthfully say:

God untangles my mind to understand and forgive.
God frees my heart to love and encourage.
God liberates my soul to help and heal.

Mr. Paul's Insights, Inspirations, and Experiences Chapter Eight

As each Chapter neared completion, Mr. Paul would review it. Then, we would discuss it. I recorded our post review discussions. What follows are poignant and interesting excerpts from his recorded comments.

* This chapter talks about forgiveness. This reminded me that when I first moved to our place here, there was a group of Viet Nam Veterans that met in Port Townsend every week. The government had hired a state counselor to come and deal with us. But it was so pathetic. This guy just had the group continue to repeat their war stories over and over again. These guys were all divorced, none of them had a job, they were living out in the woods, and they were still talking the same jargon they did in Viet Nam twenty years ago. I said, "You guys, this is no way to live. You've got to move on. And forgiveness is the only way to get free. Continually repeating all this stuff and holding resentments will keep you there. You'll never be free." I said, "Forgiveness is a gift. It sets you free. The government couldn't care less about you. But if you choose to forgive, then you get the load off of you; and you'll be free." It was so pathetic how this counselor handled the group. They would never be free, but his job was secure. It seemed like he didn't care. It just amazes me how people don't grasp the benefits of forgiveness. It is such a gift. It fully delivers you from whatever bondages or afflictions were put upon you. I just love that for us as believers; we can forgive because we have been forgiven. We've seen forgiveness, so we can give it. You can't give what you don't have. It's such an awesome thing how God has forgiven us, and because of that, we can forgive and be set free.

* When the chapter mentioned, *"The fear of the Lord"* and how fearing Him means to hold Him in reverence and awe. It reminded me of a verse that I love. Psalm 147:11. *"The LORD taketh pleasure in them that fear him, in those that hope in his mercy."* I love that! *"God takes pleasure when we fear Him and hope in His mercy."* That, I think, is just so cool.

* The problem with us is separation from God. It happened in the Garden. It's the work of the enemy, and he continues to do his best to separate us from God. We were created to know God. To fellowship with Him. It's by design. He is our Father. Abba means Father God.

Chapter Notes and Discussion Topics

Notes ______________________________

How did this chapter affect you? And why? ______________________________

Did you gain any new perspectives or perceptions? ______________________________

What changed in you after reading this chapter? ______________________________

How can you use this knowledge to help improve your relationships with God, yourself, and others?

Chapter Nine

The Nourished Soul Gardening Guide for:

Happy You, in God's Temple of Light

Or do you not know that your body is the temple of the Holy Spirit who is in you, whom you have from God, and you are not your own? For you were bought at a price; therefore glorify God in your body and in your spirit, which are God's [1 Corinthians 6:19-20 NKJV]

God's Spirit Illuminates His Temple of Light

God made you in His image and likeness. He gave you a body wherein you experience a spiritual, mental, and physical existence that is unique to you. Your complete being (spirit, mind, and body) is designed to be a temple for Him—a home where His Spirit may dwell, illuminate your soul, and enrich your journey here and hereafter. Honor God by caring for the temple He has given you. This should be done in ways that are uniquely effective in helping Him achieve His will for your life. There has never been, and never will be, another you. You are a rare and priceless gem. Care for yourself.

God often uses symbolism when attempting to enlighten His children. Christ regularly drew upon the power of parables, symbolism, and object lessons to open the minds of His listeners.

God's temple is to be His dwelling place. It is a sacred place.

The actual and symbolic temple built in ancient Jerusalem by King Solomon was constructed of the very finest stone, wood, bronze, precious jewels, silver, and gold. A very costly temple, but not nearly as costly as you.

> *For you know that God paid a ransom to save you from the empty life you inherited from your ancestors. And it was not paid with mere gold or silver, which lose their value. It was the precious blood of Christ, the sinless, spotless Lamb of God.* [1 Peter 1:18-19 NLT]

At the heart of the temple was the Most Holy Place where God's Presence dwelt above the Mercy Seat. The Mercy Seat was over the Ark of the Covenant. Above the Ark were two golden angels. Inside the Ark of the Covenant was Aaron's rod that had sprouted, a jar of manna, and the law of God written in stone by His own hand (see Exodus Chapter 26).

In the courtyard, outside of the temple, the animal sacrifices that pointed to Christ's sacrifice on our behalf occurred. These were symbolic of His bearing the sins of all humanity and providing the means by which we are sanctified and saved. Thank you—our wonder-filled Friend, Savior, and King—Jesus.

Through the symbolism contained in the temple and the courtyard practices, God is conveying to you life's most valuable object lessons.

I believe that occupying a temple of stone, wood, and metal is not His desire. I believe He desires to live in and through you and every other human being.

You are the most valuable and precious dwelling place on earth. Your being is to be His temple—His temple of light (goodness and truth). Since this is true, how can you apply to your own being the object lessons illustrated in the ancient temple and its symbols?

Let us focus on the Most Holy Place, which I believe is symbolic of your brain—the central location of your heart, mind, and soul. In the Most Holy Place was kept one very important and symbolic item. It was the Ark of the Covenant, which I believe symbolizes the truly desired vessel wherein God will dwell—you. You are the ark.

Covering the Ark of the Covenant was God's Mercy Seat, which is symbolic of the Messiah—Jesus Christ, mercifully covering you.

Since Scripture declares that you are to be God's temple, it just makes sense that the Most Holy Place in your temple would be your brain, where the essence of you—your heart, mind, and soul reside.

Your heart, mind, and soul are where the symbolic items kept in the Ark are to infuse you with His promises—His covenant. It is within your heart and mind that God's Holy Spirit illuminates your soul, gives you new life, restores you, and brings to fruition the truths behind the symbols placed inside the Ark of the Covenant.

Inside the Ark, three symbolic objects were safely preserved—a jar of manna, Aaron's lifeless yet blossoming staff, and God's laws of love, written in stone by His own hand.

1.) The jar of manna is symbolic of the Bread of Life that comes down from heaven to feed the hungry travelers in the desert of hardship. *"Then Jesus said to them, "Most assuredly, I say to you, Moses did not give you the bread from heaven, but My Father gives you the true bread from heaven. For the bread of God is He who comes down from heaven and gives life to the world."*

Then they said to Him, "Lord, give us this bread always."

And Jesus said to them, "I am the bread of life. He who comes to Me shall never hunger, and he who believes in Me shall never thirst." [John 6:32-35 NKJV]

2.) Aaron's lifeless yet blossoming staff is symbolic of God giving new life to a dead branch. This is symbolic of all who have placed their faith in the Messiah. *"But God, who is rich in mercy, because of His great love with which He loved us, even when we were dead in trespasses, made us alive together with Christ ... "* Ephesians 2:4 NKJV

3.) The Ten Commandments—written by the hand of God in stone is symbolic of His laws of love, written by Him, in your mind, and on your heart of stone. *"But this is the covenant that I will make with the house of Israel after those days, says the Lord: I will put My law in their minds, and write it on their hearts; and I will be their God, and they shall be My people."* Jeremiah 31:33 NKJV

"Moreover, I will give you a new heart and put a new spirit within you; and I will remove the heart of stone from your flesh and give you a heart of flesh." Ezekiel 36:26 NASB

You are to be His temple. The items placed in the Ark of the Covenant are symbols of the promises that are to bear fruit in you. You are to be the dead branch brought to new life. You are to be the consumer of the manna, the Bread of life that came down from heaven—Jesus. And through God's new covenant, He will put His laws in your mind and write them on your heart. He will be your God, and you shall be one of His people—a soul temple illuminated by His Holy Spirit.

God's promises to Israel are good for all time. Not just for the biological descendants of Abraham or the physical nation of Israel that existed at the time the promises were delivered. *"If you belong to Christ, then you are Abraham's seed, and heirs according to the promise.."* Galatians 3:29 NIV

You, like most of us, were grafted into the vine that is spiritual Israel. You have an inheritance among the other tribal members. You are spiritual Israel because of your belief in your Messiah—Jesus Christ. You are granted access to His Holy Spirit's illuminating presence. You are His temple of light (goodness and truth)!

Your experience will be this—the Bread of heaven will nourish and strengthen your soul as you affirm His laws of love in your new life. All the while, guardian angels will surround you, and God's Mercy Seat, representing the atoning sacrifice of Jesus, mercifully covers you. Beautiful!

Outside the actual yet symbolic Temple in ancient Jerusalem was the altar upon which the daily sacrifices occurred. You are not only to be the temple of God; you are to sacrifice self on the altar. You are to be a living sacrifice. The center of this experience is the surrendering of your will, your life, and your *MADFATs* to God and allowing Him to transform you by the renewing of your mind.

Therefore, I urge you, brothers and sisters, in view of God's mercy, to offer your bodies as a living sacrifice, holy and pleasing to God—this is your true and proper worship. Do not conform to the pattern of this world, but be transformed by the renewing of your mind. Romans 12:1-2 NIV

Since you are honored to be God's temple and His Spirit is illuminating you, don't you want to maintain His temple in the best condition—inside and out? Sure you do. As you care for the temple of God, you will be cared for. As you destroy the temple of God, you will suffer.

> *Do you not know that you are a temple of God and that the Spirit of God dwells in you? If any man destroys the temple of God, God will destroy him, for the temple of God is holy, and that is what you are.* 1 Corinthians 3:16-17 NIV

God grants free will. It is the only way His kingdom of love can function. Your choices will obviously dictate the quality of your life. If you choose to ignore and violate the laws of love, the laws of health, and the laws of nature, your temple will suffer. Poor choices can be catastrophic and result in the destruction of the temple God has entrusted to you.

It is true that you will encounter a life-ending event that will destroy your earthly temple. But you might not be accountable for it.

You might not be accountable for the calamities that encroach upon your life, but there are issues you will stand accountable for. You are the only being who can allow God's Holy Spirit to illuminate your soul and repair your broken heart and mind. You are the only being who can claim faith in Jesus Christ—for you. You are the only being who can consistently allow His Spirit to rewire, restore and renew your *MADFATs.* You are the only being who can surrender yourself to God. You are the only being who can do the part you need to do because; you are the only being who can daily open your heart and mind to allow His Spirit to continually beautify and illuminate your *Nourished Soul's* temple. And, you are the only being who can offer yourself as a slave of righteousness—a slave of God.

> *Just as you used to offer yourselves as slaves to impurity and to ever-increasing wickedness, so now offer yourselves as slaves to righteousness leading to holiness.*
>
> *When you were slaves to sin, you were free from the control of righteousness. What benefit did you reap at that time from the things you are now ashamed of? Those things result in death!*
>
> *But now that you have been set free from sin and have become slaves of God, the benefit you reap leads to holiness, and the result is eternal life.*
>
> *For the wages of sin is death, but the gift of God is eternal life in Christ Jesus our Lord.*
> Romans 6:19-23 NIV

You, now, are set free from violating God's laws of love—His covenant. The benefit you reap leads to holiness, and the result is eternal life in Jesus Christ! Exciting!

Even though the wages of sin is death—the gift of God is eternal life in Christ Jesus. Oh, sweet hope! Since you are now set free from the lifestyle choices that destroy you and bring you shame—rejoice! Your soul is free of the dark side. *"So if the Son makes you free, you will be free indeed."* John 8:36 NASB

You are now a slave of God. He is a wonderful Master. He sets you free from slavery to the dark side and calls you His coheir. You will find complete joy in serving a King like Him. Choose to serve Him daily. Strive to experience the very best spiritual, mental, and physical health possible.

The enemy desires to steal, kill, and destroy you—forever. He desires to rob God of your sweet, eternal friendship. But God desires to redeem and restore you—spirit, mind, and body.

Keeping your spirit, mind, and body in the best health possible will help greatly in strengthening your ability to maintain mental alertness and a spiritually astute state of being.

Performing the tasks necessary to care for God's temple, such as seeking to be pure in heart and developing and maintaining a sound mind and body, may prove to be the most essential and enriching missions you participate in here on this temporary home called earth.

King Solomon, the man charged with building the temple of God in Jerusalem, neglected these tasks and lost sight of the importance of manifesting the character of God in his life by proper care of his own personal temple. He may very well have been the wisest, wealthiest man to have ever walked beneath the sun. *"King Solomon was greater in riches and wisdom than all the other kings of the earth. The whole world sought audience with Solomon to hear the wisdom God had put in his heart.* 1 Kings 10:23-24 NIV

Although Solomon was honored by God and chosen to build His symbolic temple on earth, he gave himself over to the worship of other gods. God granted him wisdom and wealth. However, he became self-indulgent and lost sight of the need to keep his own temple holy. He rejected the Spirit of God's illuminating light and became self-indulgent rather than generous with his blessings.

In his old age, Solomon wrote of his understanding of life under the sun. His thoughts are found in the book of Ecclesiastes. He came to see that life here was temporal and that selfishly seeking the things of this world is like chasing after the wind. He claimed that nearly all of his earthly achievements were meaningless. He wrote:

I said to myself, "Look, I have increased in wisdom more than anyone who has ruled over Jerusalem before me; I have experienced much of wisdom and knowledge."

Then I applied myself to the understanding of wisdom, and also of madness and folly, but I learned that this, too, is a chasing after the wind.

For with much wisdom comes much sorrow; the more knowledge, the more grief.

I said to myself, "Come now, I will test you with pleasure to find out what is good." But that also proved to be meaningless. "Laughter," I said, "is madness. And what does pleasure accomplish?" I tried cheering myself with wine, and embracing folly—my mind still guiding me with wisdom. I wanted to see what was good for people to do under the heavens during the few days of their lives.

I undertook great projects: I built houses for myself and planted vineyards. I made gardens and parks and planted all kinds of fruit trees in them. I made reservoirs to water groves of flourishing trees. I bought male and female slaves and had other slaves who were born in my house. I also owned more herds and flocks than anyone in Jerusalem before me. I amassed silver and gold for myself, and the treasure of kings and provinces.

I acquired male and female singers, and a harem as well—the delights of a man's heart. I became greater by far than anyone in Jerusalem before me. In all this my wisdom stayed with me. I denied myself nothing my eyes desired; I refused my heart no pleasure.

My heart took delight in all my labor, and this was the reward for all my toil.

Yet when I surveyed all that my hands had done and what I had toiled to achieve, everything was meaningless, a chasing after the wind; nothing was gained under the sun. Ecclesiastes 1:16-2:11 NIV

It's not likely that you will have the opportunity to plumb the depths of self-indulgence like Solomon. But he could not find satisfaction. This world and the things in it will never satisfy the deepest hungers of the human heart. All of your chasing after the wind, whether through wisdom, pleasures, work, sex, riches, feasting, or whatever else you chase, are manifestations of an unfulfilled God-hunger. Only by being connected with God and accepting the lot He assigns you here will you come to satisfy your soul. Solomon realized that this world and the temple he built, as well as the personal one he occupied, were temporary.

As his life was ebbing away, he realized the futility of all he had toiled for here. It would not last. Solomon, like you, understood that this life and all that is in it will only last for a time. Then it will end.

He also discovered the futility of attempting to satisfy his unfulfilled God-hunger with the distractions of this world. He did recognize that happiness was achievable here, and one could find satisfaction in their labors under the sun. In the same book of Ecclesiastes, he wrote:

This is what I have observed to be good: that it is appropriate for a person to eat, to drink and to find satisfaction in their toilsome labor under the sun during the few days of life God has

given them—for this is their lot.

Moreover, when God gives someone wealth and possessions, and the ability to enjoy them, to accept their lot and be happy in their toil—this is a gift of God. They seldom reflect on the days of their life, because God keeps them occupied with gladness of heart. Ecclesiastes 5:18-20 NIV

Solomon obviously saw happy people enjoying their lives. Unlike him, they seldom reflected on their days, for God kept them occupied with gladness of heart. They were eating and drinking and finding satisfaction in their labors under the sun, just like some people are today.

Whether you have wealth and possessions or not, you can accept your lot and be happy. It is a gift from God.

I have met some of the world's wealthiest and most powerful people personally. US Presidents, Congressmen, Senators, and Billionaires. I have also met what I believed were some of the happiest people in the world. Yet, it's interesting that they were rarely the same people. Where did we get the idea that power, wealth, and possessions lead to happiness? It didn't work for Solomon. He was wiser, richer, and more powerful than anyone else, but he was not satisfied. Despite all of his wisdom, he allowed his many wives to turn his heart from God. His soul-temple became impure as he lost his single-hearted devotion to the One who gave him all. He sought other gods. He lost focus. He lost the ability to enjoy the gifts of God. He was not occupied with gladness of heart.

Solomon did come to understand the perils of turning from God and seeking fulfillment in other gods and the things of this world. He discovered the emptiness of self-indulgence and the sorrow of occupying an unclean temple. In turning from the Lord to other gods, Solomon lost his kingdom and began the downfall of Israel.

The Lord became angry with Solomon because his heart had turned away from the Lord, the God of Israel, who had appeared to him twice. Although he had forbidden Solomon to follow other gods, Solomon did not keep the Lord's command. So the Lord said to Solomon, "Since this is your attitude and you have not kept my covenant and my decrees, which I commanded you, I will most certainly tear the kingdom away from you and give it to one of your subordinates. 1 Kings 11:9-11 NIV

It appears that Solomon had allowed his temple to become polluted with the worship of other gods, and he neglected to keep his Most Holy Place illuminated by God's Spirit. He stopped being the temple of God wherein His Holy Spirit wishes to dwell. He stopped feasting on the Bread of life. The laws of love were no longer emblazoned upon his heart and mind. The power of God that had brought new life to bloom in him was turned away as lust devoured love. His branch lost connection with the Vine, and he experienced the painful shallowness of life without his Lord. He came to a deeper understanding of God's love through God's discipline: *"...because the Lord disciplines those he loves, as a father the son he delights in."* Proverbs 3:12 NIV

Toward the end, his heart sought to warn you:

Remember your Creator in the days of your youth, before the days of trouble come and the years approach when you will say, "I find no pleasure in them"

... Remember him—before the silver cord is severed, and the golden bowl is broken; before the pitcher is shattered at the spring, and the wheel broken at the well, and the dust returns to the ground it came from, and the spirit returns to God who gave it.

"Meaningless! Meaningless!" says the Teacher. "Everything is meaningless!" ... Now all has been heard; here is the conclusion of the matter: Fear God and keep his commandments, for this is the duty of all mankind. For God will bring every deed into judgment, including every hidden thing, whether it is good or evil. Ecclesiastes 12:1-14 NIV

Remember your Creator in the days of your youth, before the days of trouble come, and the years approach when you will say, *"I find no pleasure in them."*

The core message of Solomon's sad tale is this—love God, and you will keep His commandments. His commands are to love. Don't chase after the wind. Care for, don't defile God's temple. Eat of the Bread of life. Connect to the Vine, and allow new life to bloom through you. Let Him write His laws of love on your heart and mind. Be a healthy and happy you in God's temple of light—forever!

Remember, God has your name written on the palm of His hand. He rejoices over you with singing and takes great pleasure in your presence. You are worthy of being taken care of. Within your temple dwells the greatest treasure in the universe—the Spirit of God. His Spirit of power, love, and self-control will illuminate you. Your renewed heart and mind will be inspired to focus on making healthy, joy-rich, productive life choices.

It's true that life on earth is often a struggle. It is within struggles that the strength of your connection with and trust in God are often enhanced. Trials and struggles provide super opportunities for growth and victory. Use them to your benefit rather than allowing them to bruise your soul.

Enemies of goodness and truth do exist on earth—the dark one and his cohorts are thieves and liars. They want you to lose. They misguide, misdirect, and mislead souls away from the Gateway to heaven. The dark one and his followers wish to steal, kill, and destroy you. However, Jesus desires to give you life to the full. He said:

Very truly I tell you, I am the gate for the sheep. All who have come before me are thieves and robbers, but the sheep have not listened to them. I am the gate; whoever enters through me will be saved. They will come in and go out, and find pasture. The thief comes only to steal and kill and destroy; I have come that they may have life, and have it to the full. John 10:7-10 NIV

Life to the full is what Jesus wishes to grant you. He is able to free you from all destructive lifestyle choices—if you allow Him. Remember, however; *you* are to participate in the healing.

There are measures you can take to help keep God's temple in the best condition possible. All aspects of your being are united into the whole you. Your spirit, mind, and body make up your temple. They all function together.

The majority of this book has been directed at enhancing health and happiness in the spiritual and mental aspects of your being. However, the most effective transformations are not complete without addressing the issues of attitude and physical health.

Let's first discuss attitude. What I am talking about is your ability to experience *all* of life with an attitude of gratitude. And to believe that God and you together can elevate and dominate your days with free-flowing positivity and rejoicing—regardless of any situation.

It is written: *"Rejoice always, pray continually, give thanks in all circumstances; for this is God's will for you in Christ Jesus."* 1 Thessalonians 5:16-18 NIV

God can eliminate all negativity and replace all remains of a complaining attitude from your being. As you focus on Him and the many endowments He wishes to reveal and bestow upon you; you will no longer find it necessary to dwell on negativity or reserve the capacity to complain.

Instead, you will spend the precious moments of your life in praise, rejoicing, and giving thanks in all of life's circumstances. No matter what is thrown at you, it is God's will, in Christ Jesus, that you have an attitude of gratitude, even amidst the hard trials. Your new, default attitude toward life's challenges will be to find value in each and every situation, especially the difficult and painful ones.

God Urges Gratitude Amidst the Struggles of Life

"Gratitude is the attitude that enables the aptitude
to enjoy the certitude that all of life is a blessed gift." James Bars

Scripture advises you to: *"Rejoice always, pray continually, give thanks in all circumstances; for this is God's will for you in Christ Jesus."* 1 Thessalonians 5:16-18 NIV

Tragedy, loss, suffering, pain—have these been part of your life? Most likely. Were they seen as opportunities? Did you rejoice and give thanks? Are they still a part of your essence today? Does their memory haunt you? Are they sucking the sweetness from your soul? What would it take for you to see them as some of your greatest gifts? Which could be a greater danger to your soul—prosperity and wealth or persecution and pain? Many people have discovered their greatest growth and most satisfying blessings during their most difficult trials. Let's review some interesting perspectives on and attitudes toward these matters.

Benjamin Franklin stated in his ageless, creative work entitled, *The Way to Wealth (Little Books of Wisdom), "There are no gains without pains."* MM

Scripture declares:

> *And we boast in the hope of the glory of God. Not only so, but we also glory in our sufferings, because we know that suffering produces perseverance; perseverance, character; and character, hope. And hope does not put us to shame, because God's love has been poured out into our hearts through the Holy Spirit, who has been given to us.* Romans 5:2-5 NIV

> *Consider it pure joy, my brothers and sisters, whenever you face trials of many kinds, because you know that the testing of your faith produces perseverance. Let perseverance finish its work so that you may be mature and complete, not lacking anything.* James 1:2-4 NIV

> *That is why, for Christ's sake, I delight in weaknesses, in insults, in hardships, in persecutions, in difficulties. For when I am weak, then I am strong.* 2 Corinthians 12:10 NIV

> *Though the fig tree does not bud and there are no grapes on the vines, though the olive crop fails and the fields produce no food, though there are no sheep in the pen and no cattle in the stalls, yet I will rejoice in the LORD, I will be joyful in God my Savior. The Sovereign LORD is my strength; he makes my feet like the feet of a deer, he enables me to tread on the heights.* Habakkuk 3:17-19 NIV

Your perspective on and attitude toward life's difficulties is your choice. The wise souls among us quickly grasp the truth concerning the struggles of life. They come to an early understanding that—difficulties often prove to be a soul's greatest assets. Gratitude prepares the enjoyment of the moment you're in right now. Train your brain to settle on the good in each moment and to relish it.

The wisdom to pray continually, give thanks in every circumstance, rejoice in every challenge, and experience gratitude amidst every struggle, reveals the deepest faith and trust in God's benevolence—despite hardships.

Wisdom processes pain in healthy ways. Wisdom does not deny emotions. Wisdom cries. Wisdom weeps. Wisdom laughs. Wisdom loves. Wisdom dispenses compassion like rain. Wisdom shines its light—dispelling the darkness. Wisdom cleanses the soul and uses opposing forces to propel the heart onward; into the light. Be wise—rejoice always.

Rebellious self-centeredness and fear occupy the core of all complaining. Fear breeds insecurity. Insecurity breeds negativity. Negativity breeds complaint.

If you are not certain about your place in the universe and don't recognize your true worth as a child of the King of creation, this low self-image may produce within you the need to complain about people, places, and things in an effort to raise yourself up in status and vision. A large share of all complaining has this deficiency at its core.

Complaining is a pervasive noise penetrating the essence of your existence and annihilating the joy-filled and undeniably abundant list of reasons you have to celebrate. This black tool is skillfully used by the dark one to steal your ability and desire to flourish in the atmosphere of praise and rejoicing. How often have you found yourself in an attitude of rejoicing and complaining at the same time? Never. Gratitude, praising, and rejoicing are the antidotes for complaining, self-centeredness, and fear. Inject yourself with these life-enhancing medications.

You can struggle in the dark with a complaining attitude, or you can step into the light and enjoy an attitude of gratitude and a heart full of praise and rejoicing. The choice is yours. Regardless of what life brings to you—you decide how to respond. Look beyond the clouds—see refreshing amidst the rain. Has complaining about God, yourself, others, or life's challenges ever brought you a moment's peace? No.

Why not seek the silver lining in all of life's challenges? Why not find ways to praise God, and lift yourself and others up instead of sitting in a bucket of sour grapes? Why not rejoice in all circumstances and recognize that God can use any situation to bring about His good, pleasing and perfect will?

Open the eyes of your heart. Look for the lesson. Seek the Teacher's wisdom. *"If any of you lacks wisdom, you should ask God, who gives generously to all without finding fault, and it will be given to you."* James 1:5 NIV

To complain is defined as expressing grief, pain, or discontentment. If the dominant outflow of your thoughts and words come in the form of grief, pain, or discontentment, you will find little joy in life.

An attitude of gratitude is vital to your spiritual, emotional, and physical health. Self-centered anger, fear, and frustration are toxic thinking patterns that actually disrupt the positive attributes of your very DNA. [B]

Refrain from complaining; instead, be grateful for the growth opportunities found in the heartaches, pains, hardships, difficulties, struggles, weaknesses, insults, and persecutions that God has allowed and will continue to allow you the opportunity to experience. Now that's a paradigm shift that will free your soul to revel in all aspects of life and allow your spirit, mind, and body to enjoy vibrant health.

Rather than condemn, criticize, or complain, choose to focus on the good in life; with purpose. Fold your soul into goodness by savoring the multitude of good experiences that envelope your days. It only takes a few seconds of soothing reflection on a consistent basis to rewire your brain away from a negativity bias.

Nearly all humans are infected with a bias toward negativity. The prevalence of this distortion among this world's inhabitants is well documented and easily observable. This challenge is a direct result of being born and raised in a fear-based, self-centered society. To counter this wilting constraint, all one needs to do is purposely look for and absorb good experiences. Goodness exists in every moment of life. Strive to take a few seconds each hour and observe or remember a good experience. Make it a priority to gain from goodness by noticing it, memorizing it, relishing it, and allowing it to fill your entire being. Take a few seconds each hour to reflect on the good all around, and you will soon create a positivity bias within the depths of your happy heart.

To accompany this growing tone, you may wish to design and adopt some personalized affirmations. Each morning I often declare: *"This is the day the Lord has made; I will rejoice and be glad in it."* Psalm 118:24 NASB

It's easy, effective, rewarding, and as I practice it, others around me seem to be happier. Weird, right?

By gratefully focusing on and absorbing the good, you will rebuild the architecture of your brain's neural pathways and elevate your emotions into ever-expanding horizons of health and happiness. Bad days are ripe with opportunities to reframe them into good ones.

Consider the attitude of Christ as He endured the worst experience any human ever has or ever will endure and focused on the good that would come from it and not the pain of enduring it:

> *Therefore, since we are surrounded by such a huge crowd of witnesses to the life of faith, let us strip off every weight that slows us down, especially the sin that so easily trips us up. And let us run with endurance the race God has set before us. We do this by keeping our eyes on Jesus, the champion who initiates and perfects our faith.*
>
> *Because of the joy awaiting him, he endured the cross, disregarding its shame. Now he is seated in the place of honor beside God's throne. Think of all the hostility he endured from sinful people; then you won't become weary and give up.* Hebrews 12:1-3 NLT

Be free to endure, to persevere, to see the joy that awaits and the goodness that exists.

Mental and emotional well-being are invaluable assets. They aid in moving toward achieving and maintaining your soul's health and happiness. Have an attitude of gratitude. Watch your attitude and your words. Stay positive. Solomon may have had many problems, he was human, but he had great wisdom as well. Let's take advantage of his wise revelations. He wrote:

> *A joyful heart is good medicine, but a crushed spirit dries up the bones.* Proverbs 17:22 ESV

> *Be not wise in your own eyes; fear the LORD, and turn away from evil. It will be healing to your flesh and refreshment to your bones.* Proverbs 3:7-8 ESV

> *Gracious words are like a honeycomb, sweetness to the soul and health to the body.* Proverbs 16:24 ESV
>
> *The light of the eyes rejoices the heart, and good news refreshes the bones.* Proverbs 15:30 ESV

Want healthy DNA and a happy, hope-filled life? Rejoice always and absorb goodness and truth consistently!

Many disregard the cause of our troubles—the enemy of souls—and directly throw the blame for any pain on God. Remember—God is not your enemy. He is your Friend, your Savior, and your King. He is your hope. He is your creator. He is your strength. He is your Redeemer. He is your future.

Absorb and realize the following truth—God is love. Always!

Love cannot exist without free will. Free will made it possible for beings of light to choose the darkness. This darkness, we now live in.

Please realize that the pain you experience in this life is the result of sin—the result of rebellion against God's laws of love and liberty. It is not your fault. However, it is your good fortune as a child of God to be His witness. This is your chance. How will the cause of God gain from your pain? What message will your life send? Will your testimony have a positive impact? *This* life, *this* day, *this* experience—*this* is your opportunity to allow God to shine through you before all creation.

Will you surrender your victory to the dark one? Will you join his team of complainers and allow him to steal your right to experience joy during life's difficulties? Or will you transcend your struggles? Will the strength of Jesus be exposed through you? Will your testimony reveal the God who holds you tenderly in His arms and carries you securely up the cliffs and over the hurdles of life?

Since the fall of man in the Garden of Eden, all humans have suffered the consequences of our original parents' rebellion. Through the millennia, our souls have become increasingly corrupted, defiled, broken, beaten down, and alienated from the throne of God.

Do not fear, for God offers you restoration, salvation, and hope through His Son, Jesus Christ. At the end of this age, sin will be destroyed forever. But for now, the evil rebellion is being allowed to complete its course on this quarantined planet.

What is happening in this world is not being conducted in secret. All eyes are upon the great controversy between goodness and truth (God) and evil and lies (satan).

When the end comes, and throughout all eternity, every existing and newly created being will be able to completely know and understand the devastating consequences of ignoring God's laws of love. The benefits of this knowledge far outweigh any temporary struggles you may experience here.

Every created being will understand the falseness of the evil one's lies. They will all know that God's laws of love are not meant to dominate and inhibit but to protect and enhance. Each intelligent soul will fully comprehend that God is love and that living within His design is ultimately and completely superior to jumping off the cliff of rebellion.

You, my dear friend, are being allowed to share your testimony at the great trial of God. Eternal eyes are upon you. Seize this once-in-forever opportunity to testify on the Father's behalf. When you accept Jesus Christ as your soul's Savior, you become a citizen of heaven with all attendant rights and privileges. Be a witness for His kingdom.

Continually acknowledge the weakness of your human side and invite the Holy Spirit into your heart as your personal power Source. Don't complain about your struggles, troubles, pains, or anything else here. *"Be joyful in hope, patient in affliction, faithful in prayer."* Romans 12:12 NIV

Jesus made clear what your attitude toward trouble should be. *"Here on earth you will have many trials and sorrows. But take heart, because I have overcome the world."* John 16:33 NLT

Seize the day! Seize your chance to make your mark on the side of your Friend, Creator, and Savior. Allow God to rewire your *MADFATs* into heaven-inspired ones.

Be heavenly. Don't complain about life's struggles. Praise and rejoice in the trust that has been placed in you. Do not fear, worry, or complain. A greater purpose is at work. Good is already victorious over evil. Open the eyes of your heart. Lay your self-centeredness and fear on the altar of self-sacrifice, and your complaints will fade away.

Everyone knows that life on earth is a combination of painful struggles and joyful experiences. It's easy to focus on the negative. Our human culture is programmed for that. Be different. Stretch beyond the temporary. See the eternal.

Therefore we do not lose heart. Though outwardly we are wasting away, yet inwardly we are being renewed day by day.

For our light and momentary troubles are achieving for us an eternal glory that far outweighs them all. So we fix our eyes not on what is seen, but on what is unseen, since what is seen is temporary, but what is unseen is eternal. 2 Corinthians 4:16-18 NIV

Don't drift with the crowd into the river of doubt and despair. Stand up and praise God that you are counted worthy of the great trust. Even if you should be allowed to suffer in the cause of God, don't complain—rejoice and praise Him. As you rise to this level on your spiritual journey, you will know that you can endure every moment and experience in your life.

The Apostle Paul was well acquainted with the spiritual war you currently find yourself in. He was familiar with persecution and violence. They were often perpetrated against him as a witness in the great trial. Yet, he was driven to preach the Gospel. He saw the big picture—the unseen.

When you find yourself wanting to complain about yourself, others, or life's circumstances, try to remember when Paul and Silas were put in prison:

The crowd joined in the attack against Paul and Silas, and the magistrates ordered them to be stripped and beaten. After they had been severely flogged, they were thrown into prison, and the jailer was commanded to guard them carefully. Upon receiving such orders, he put them in the inner cell and fastened their feet in the stocks.

About midnight Paul and Silas were praying and singing hymns to God, and the other prisoners were listening to them. Acts 16:22-25 NIV

After being severely flogged, beaten, and thrown into prison, they were praising God! They were put in prison for their faith—for doing the Lord's work—for preaching the Good News. They weren't focused on the short-term pain and discomfort. Their attitude was revealed through their actions. They did not complain but praised God for the troubles they faced and rejoiced in the fact that they were counted worthy to suffer for the cause of Christ.

They persevered, and God miraculously released them. This God will do for you also. Through the power of His Holy Spirit, you can face the troubles in this life with perseverance—without complaining—so that God can complete His work in you.

Don't live in denial of life's painful struggles, but don't spend your energies focusing on them. Acknowledge the realities of human trials and joys and relate to them in healthy ways. Use them to propel you forward. Trust God. *"And we know that in all things God works for the good of those who love him, who have been called according to his purpose."* Romans 8:28 NIV

Have faith in God's will, even when you don't understand the trial. Seek the lesson. Grow strong amidst the weeds. Expose your soul to the light of the Son. Strive for gratitude amidst the struggles of life. Flourish in the hardships. See the silver linings. Enjoy an experience of complete joy here on earth, and live with the hope of eternal life in heaven. Seek Him with all your heart. Know that God's plans for you are great. It is written:

For I know the plans I have for you, declares the Lord, plans to prosper you and not to harm you, plans to give you hope and a future. Then you will call upon me and come and pray to me, and I will listen to you.

You will seek me and find me when you seek me with all your heart. I will be found by you, declares the Lord, and I will bring you back from captivity. Jeremiah 29:11-14 NIV

Whether your struggles are small or great, whether you are a little upset with yourself or someone else, or you are in the midst of your deepest loss—trust God. His love for you and His promise of life beyond this troubled world will comfort you and give you hope. Walk in His joy as you make time to give thanks for His gifts of a prosperous, free and victorious life here and eternally hereafter. Focus your heart's desires and thoughts on Him. God will nourish your soul and fill you with His Spirit of power, love, and self-control. Praise Him during the troubling storms. He will calm the rough seas within you and those around you. Know His peace.

Jesus promised, *"Peace I leave with you, My peace I give to you; not as the world gives do I give to you. Let not your heart be troubled, neither let it be afraid."* John 14:27 NKJV

There is beauty and goodness all around you—in every moment of life—in every person you meet—in every struggle. There is no joy in complaining. Nothing good comes from condemning or criticizing. Let it go! Be free and be joyful. Plant seeds of faith and trust in the garden of your mind. Germinate the soul-enhancing crops of understanding and forgiving, loving and encouraging, helping and healing, and praising and rejoicing. Encourage your *Nourished Soul* to sprout and grow in the Son-light of God's gracious and lavish love.

> *Rejoice in the Lord always. I will say it again: Rejoice! Let your gentleness be evident to all. The Lord is near. Do not be anxious about anything, but in every situation, by prayer and petition, with thanksgiving, present your requests to God. And the peace of God, which transcends all understanding, will guard your hearts and your minds in Christ Jesus.*
> Philippians 4:4-7 NIV

God Revives With Daily Delights

Now let's discuss physical health and fitness. Your temple *is* the dwelling place for God's Holy Spirit. If your temple is in a state of disrepair due to poor lifestyle choices, you may not enjoy the full life Jesus came to grant you. He is the Great Physician. He can heal all manner of disease and brokenness. Does He always heal a person's physical body? No.

Paul, one of His Apostles, didn't get the healing he wished for, yet he didn't give up. Through his hardship and weakness, you are exposed to a very vital message. May his attitude toward his hardship and weakness transform your perspectives and attitudes concerning your own.

> *Therefore, in order to keep me from becoming conceited, I was given a thorn in my flesh, a messenger of Satan, to torment me. Three times I pleaded with the Lord to take it away from me. But he said to me, "My grace is sufficient for you, for my power is made perfect in weakness."*
>
> *Therefore I will boast all the more gladly about my weaknesses, so that Christ's power may rest on me. That is why, for Christ's sake, I delight in weaknesses, in insults, in hardships, in persecutions, in difficulties. For when I am weak, then I am strong.* 2 Corinthians 12:7-10 NIV

Jesus Himself, in the garden of Gethsemane, prayed for a different path—one without pain.

Before He was dragged away to be tortured and crucified as the unblemished sacrificial Lamb of God, He prayed that He would not need to endure the physical, psychological, and spiritual pain He was facing. His human side staggered at the immensity of the task before Him, but He submitted to God. He trusted the Father. In the Garden of Gethsemane, before He was seized, He prayed:

"Father, if you are willing, please take this cup of suffering away from me. Yet I want your will to be done, not mine." Then an angel from heaven appeared and strengthened him. He prayed more fervently, and he was in such agony of spirit that his sweat fell to the ground like great drops of blood. Luke 22:42 -44 NLT

Jesus never denied the painful, troubling experiences of life on earth. He didn't spend His time and energy focusing on them either. He acknowledged that life was difficult. He also instructed us to be at peace and take courage, for He had overcome the world. *"These things I have spoken to you, so that in Me you may have peace. In the world you have tribulation, but take courage; I have overcome the world."* John 16:33 NASB

You may never, in this life, know why you are not always relieved and healed upon request. More answers will be revealed in the next life. Walk in faith. Be patient. God knows what is best for you.

Should you continue to believe for and seek His healing? Yes. Should you take advantage of every available resource to secure a pure, holy, and healthy temple? Yes!

The spirit, mind, and body God built for you possess tremendous healing power. There are habits you can develop that will help to create a healthy environment within you so that faith in the healing power God can grant and has placed in your body can work effectively. It is often about proper care.

Immediately after creating Adam and Eve, God directed their attention to the sources of nourishment and healthy care of their physical bodies.

Then God said, "I give you every seed-bearing plant on the face of the whole earth and every tree that has fruit with seed in it. They will be yours for food. And to all the beasts of the earth and all the birds in the sky and all the creatures that move along the ground—everything that has the breath of life in it—I give every green plant for food." And it was so.

God saw all that he had made, and it was very good. And there was evening, and there was morning—the sixth day. Genesis 1:29-31 NIV

After creating Adam, and even before He created Eve, God established a healthy, plant-based diet and invigorating, body-moving work for man in nature. He provided Adam with succulent, mouth-watering foods and enjoyable, fulfilling employment that kept him outside in the exhilarating sunlight, clean air, and in direct contact with the Creator's exquisite, enlivening touch. *"The Lord God took the man and put him in the garden of Eden to work it and keep it."* Genesis 2:15 NIV

Then God said, "I give you every seed-bearing plant on the face of the whole earth and every tree that has fruit with seed in it. They will be yours for food." Genesis 1:29 NIV

God, in His loving care, gave man life, an abundance of life-sustaining, plant-based, healthy foods, and productive, happy employment that allowed him to physically move about in the presence of His awe-inspiring creation. I believe that God desires the best for you. This includes healthy fuel for your body and activities involving moving about in His creation.

Nearly all health and nutrition experts tout the vital importance of pure water, sunshine, fresh air, exercise, and eating well to provide your body with the essentials for repair, healing, and health.

I encourage everyone who really desires health and happiness to watch the *Back To Eden Gardening Documentary Film - How to Grow a Vegetable Garden,* with Mr. Paul Gautchi, the co-author of this book. Wow!

The first designs for man, revealed by God, were the need for healthy food and movement in His life-enhancing creation. He started with a focus on healthy food. If you struggle with food issues, you are not alone. Eating disorders are among the deadliest mental illnesses, second only to opioid overdose. [GGG]

Life-threatening food is the first item satan focused on in turning Adam and Eve from obedience to God. Food is the first item satan focused on in trying to tempt Jesus in the wilderness.

Look around—is food still an issue for many today? There is either too much, not enough, and often not the healthiest options or portion sizes.

God designed your body and provided the best fuel for it. He knows what will give you optimal health. In caring for your temple's physical well-being, do as He suggests; include nutrient-dense foods in your diet and move about in His creation.

Consider the story of Daniel and his friends Hananiah, Mishael, and Azariah. They were exiled to Babylon and forced into King Nebuchadnezzar's service. Since they displayed an aptitude for every kind of learning, they were elevated in the King's service and required to eat the food from the King's table, which was likely to be thought of as the best available. However, they refused to put unhealthy, unclean food in their bodies and said to the chief official over them, *"Please test your servants for ten days, and let them give us vegetables to eat and water to drink. Then let our appearance be examined before you, and the appearance of the young men who eat the portion of the king's delicacies; and as you see fit, so deal with your servants."* Daniel 1:12-13 NKJV

"Now at the end of the days, when the king had said that they should be brought in, the chief of the eunuchs brought them in before Nebuchadnezzar. Then the king interviewed them, and among them all none was found like Daniel, Hananiah, Mishael, and Azariah; therefore they served before the king. And in all matters of wisdom and understanding about which the king examined them, he found them ten times better than all the magicians and astrologers who were in all his realm." Daniel 1:18-20 NKJV

After suffering from several health issues, I began eating a plant-based diet about two years ago. I'm now nearly 70 years old and experiencing the best health I've known for many decades. I am able to do pullups once again and can hike up and down high mountains better than I've been able to for a long time. Among the many benefits I am enjoying on a God-designed, organic, plant-based diet are the facts that I seldom feel as hungry as I used to, and I rarely worry about how much I eat. I've gone gluten-free but still lost twenty pounds of fat even though I eat a large amount of carbs each day. Also, my tastes have changed. I actually crave my daily cruciferous-rich bowl of nutrient-dense delights with my homemade, organic Catalina dressing. I'm salivating just thinking about it.

More and more people are discovering the truths that they are not only destroying their health by consuming animal products but are seriously damaging our delicate planet as well. Think about how strong elephants and gorillas are. They eat nothing but plants. In 2021 the World's Strongest Man competition partnered with Burger Patch, a vegan fast-food chain, to power the competitors. Bodybuilders around the world are riding the beneficial wave of plant-based diets.

Watch the film titled: *The Game Changers.* You will be astonished at the gains people are enjoying by simply altering their eating habits.

There are thousands of exercise programs available as well. Look for the one that works for you and may also get you out in God's creation. Garden, if you are able. Seek good counsel concerning the food you are using to energize God's temple. Watch *Paul Gautschi's Back-to-Eden* garden tours on Youtube. Hippocrates, the father of western medicine, made this often-quoted statement, *"Let food be thy medicine and medicine be thy food."*

Many enlightening books and videos have been produced on health and nutrition. The best ones seem to focus often on using food for health and healing, such as *What the Health, The Game Changers,* and *Food Matters.* Read Andreas Moritz's book *The Amazing Liver and Gallbladder Flush.* Many of today's illnesses are caused by living in a polluted world that may have clogged your liver.

As part of my recovery from the many health issues I've been suffering from for decades, I am currently doing the Amazing Liver and Gallbladder Flush. It's been amazing.

There is a nearly unlimited amount of information available to help you find the eating plan and exercise program that will work best for you. The important thing is to be consistent and to seek God's guidance. He will help you build neural pathways in your brain that will enable you to develop healthy exercise and eating habits. You should check with a knowledgeable medical professional before starting any diet or exercise program.

There are many positive benefits and rewards associated with the proper care of God's temple. Here are a few: You are likely to; Live longer, thrive—not just survive, have more energy, avoid disease, and illness, keep medical costs down, enjoy life with your children and grandchildren, feel more empowered and confident, look and feel better, enjoy better sex and better mental health.

In addition to these enjoyable benefits, you will remain in a more constant state of homeostasis and peace because of the neural pleasure cascade God built into you.

Recall what was mentioned earlier: Your brain distributes happy drugs, such as dopamine and serotonin. These drugs serve as natural antidepressants. They are often released through exercising positive mental states, life-enhancing nutrition, being outdoors, physical movement, and other positive lifestyle choices.

Serotonin and dopamine levels are reduced as a result of stress, sleep loss, lack of exposure to sunlight, poor nutrition, and lack of exercise. Low levels of serotonin and dopamine can be the source of issues such as restlessness, tiredness, irritability, obsessive compulsions, weight gain, anxiety, chronic body pains, depression, and aggressiveness.

Lifestyle choices do affect your life. God designed you for optimal functioning when you properly maintain your systems as a whole and observe His laws of health.

In searching for advice on achieving and maintaining physical health and wholeness, we discovered a concise and holistic formula. It was developed by Linda Clayville. Linda is a Certified Nutritionist who has spent decades helping others balance all areas of their lives.

Linda's guide, entitled: *How I Spell Health and Fitness,* uses the word *WHOLENESS* as an acronym. We have included a brief message from Linda as well as her *WHOLENESS* formula for health.

> *"Healthy living has been a passion for most of my adult life. True health and fitness depend on treating the body, mind, and soul as a whole unit. The acronym "WHOLENESS" outlines the basic principles that I have learned in my formal studies in nutrition and have observed in truly healthy people. Thinking about wholeness can help keep us on track when enthusiasm for taking care of our bodies wanes."* [QQ]

W = Water

Drink water like a camel! Since the human body is more than 70% water, not drinking enough of it can dehydrate every body system. But 6-8 glasses of pure water a day can protect your joints, heart, pancreas, and skin, help to control false hunger pangs, aid in elimination, and stave off premature aging. Drink about one half your body weight in ounces every day.

H = Healthy Habits

Establish a regular, healthy circadian rhythm. The body is programmed to work optimally on a

24-hour circadian cycle. Eating, sleeping and exercising at regular times each day supports health and fitness and can actually prolong life! Many people who live to be 100+ say that they followed regular routines in their lives.

O= Outside Air

Go outdoors and breathe deeply every day. Diseases, including the dreaded cancers, thrive when there is a lack of oxygen. So does brain fog. Getting outside for a breath of fresh air can clear the mental cobwebs. Filling your lungs and life with fresh outside air will help to keep you physically fit and mentally sharp.

L= Love

Cultivate a love of God, love of others and a lifestyle of forgiveness. Don't hesitate to actively seek help in coming to terms with present pain or with old issues. Nine out of ten illnesses originate in the mind. Worry, bitterness, and unresolved anger can wreak havoc on every system in the body. On the other hand, love, trust, and forgiveness are life giving and health preserving.

E= Exercise & Elimination

Get moving and make sure to keep your colon moving, as well. Walk, swim, or rebound, etc. 30+ minutes daily and rotate resistance exercises every other day for bone health. S-T-R-E-T-C-H like a cat upon arising and right before you exercise. Exercise is good for mood, circulation, digestion, respiration and elimination. Just like exercise, regular elimination is a key to wholeness. Nutrition and natural aids can help regularity, if you struggle in that area.

N= Nutrition

Eat a fibrous, unprocessed "rainbow." The fiber in grains, beans, nuts and seeds helps keep your colon swept out. Five to seven servings of dark, bright colored fruits and vegetables every day provide your body with very powerful antioxidants and enzymes it needs for both function and repair. To preserve valuable nutrients, look for food grown without much processing.

E= Endorphins

Tickle your funny bone and avoid "stinking thinking." Laughter and a positive attitude release endorphins. Endorphins are the feel-good hormones that help keep your body healthy. Laughter is good medicine and a happy heart can actually strengthen the bones! So make a point to laugh every day and go out of your way to interact with people who support positive thinking.

S= Sunshine

Soak up sunshine for 15 minutes every day. Exposing just your face to sunlight for that short amount of time, whatever the season, causes the body to produce Vitamin D. (Vitamin D helps strengthen bones, improve mood, and prevent cancer.) Sunlight also can lift the mood and help to prevent seasonal affective disorder. Take precautions against sunburn, but don't fear the sun.

S= Sleep

Don't burn the midnight oil. Go to bed early and get six to eight hours of sleep every night. Because the body is programmed to heal and repair itself during sleep, going to bed too late and/ or not getting enough rest can short circuit physical and emotional health. Conversely, regular, adequate rest can support health and lead to a longer life.

Linda's suggestions are thoughtful and beneficial to overall health and happiness. I strive to incorporate them into my habitual daily cycles. I've paraphrased her advice in the *Nourished Soul Eden Treats Sheets* that follow. I also added a couple of items—worship and work. I believe that a healthy lifestyle includes a balance between worship, work, rest, and play. The rewards of worship and work cannot be underestimated in their value to the human spirit, mind, and body. It's exciting to continue to discover new and healthful ways to enjoy these life experiences. It's also important to prayerfully consider and ensure that your daily activities are worthy and pleasing to God. Seek His direction, guidance, and counsel in all your pursuits. He declares: *"I am the Lord your God, who teaches you what is best for you, who directs you in the way you should go."* Isaiah 48:17 NIV

One pursuit I have found powerfully beneficial is prayer with fasting. There are huge spiritual and health benefits found in fasting with humble prayer. Jesus used this during His defeat of satan in the desert. Some of my most powerful and memorable times with God occurred during times of fasting and prayer. There are many different ways to fast. Talk with your enlightened medical professional to choose a fasting style that will work for you.

As you follow the suggestions outlined in this book, God and you together will plant key spiritual concepts and patterns in your mind. In practicing them, you will be increasingly transformed and restored to the Garden-of-Eden *Nourished Soul* you were meant to be. You will flourish as you enjoy the heavenly art of mind renewal and rewired *MADFATs*. You will know what David declared:

> *The Lord is my shepherd, I will not be in need. He lets me lie down in green pastures; He leads me beside quiet waters. He restores my soul; He guides me in the paths of righteousness for the sake of His name. Even though I walk through the valley of the shadow of death, I fear no evil, for You are with me; your rod and Your staff, they comfort me. You prepare a table before me in the presence of my enemies; You have anointed my head with oil; My cup overflows.*
>
> *Certainly goodness and faithfulness will follow me all the days of my life, And my dwelling will be in the house of the Lord forever.* Psalm 23 NASB

Mr. Paul's Insights, Inspirations, and Experiences
Chapter Nine

As each Chapter neared completion, Mr. Paul would review it. Then, we would discuss it. I recorded our post review discussions. What follows are poignant and interesting excerpts from his recorded comments.

* Early in this chapter, you quoted 1 Corinthians 3:16-17 *"Do you not know that you are a temple of God and that the Spirit of God dwells in you? If any man destroys the temple of God, God will destroy him, for the temple of God is holy, and that is what you are."* 1 Corinthians 3:16-17 NIV

What I think is very significant about this Scripture is, this is the New Testament, under the New Covenant. Are you hearing me? The New Testament, under the New Covenant. God's saying, *"I'll destroy you."* I think that's making a statement—big time! It's huge! It's a big deal to God how we care for our bodies. And people take it so lightly. This is His temple! This is where He dwells! You should respect that. It's a big deal. I love that Scripture, *"Be not deceived, God will not be mocked. Whatever you sow, you'll reap."* Our tendency is to think we are going to get away with it. That's human nature. I love how God prefaces that statement, *"Don't be deceived."* You're not going to mock God. You will reap what you sow. It's a given.

God is so, so righteous. It's all about righteousness. It's just so right to do right.

We take for granted this amazing, incredible body He has given to us. And we abuse it. It's a gift! It's a total gift of God, and we're responsible for how we care for it. Give account. We are going to give account.

* I was really blessed. My parents and my grandmother always had gardens, and we always had really good food. As kids growing up, my parents never let us drink sodas or eat any junk food. We always had really good live food. I went through high school with three years of perfect attendance because I never got sick. Again, you reap what you sow. It's a given.

When you're a kid growing up, you're hungry. Whenever we were hungry, we could walk outside and access the most amazing fruits and vegetables all year long. In California, you could grow all year. I remember if I ever did get a little cold or something, I'd go to my mom's kumquat tree. A kumquat is like a small orange, but the skin is the sweet part, and the interior is tart. I'd eat the whole thing. And because I'd eat the skin, which is the most nutritious part. I'm telling you, in twenty minutes, no matter what I had, I was well. It was phenomenal how quickly that thing worked! It was huge! It's like, whoa! That thing is like—instant healing. You know, maximum vitamin C. They were bitesize. You could put the whole thing in your mouth. I'd chew those things and just go for it. I would just eat those things and eat those things, and I'd get totally well.

* When people ask me what's my favorite kind of apple, I tell them, "The last one I ate." When people tour my place, they're shocked at how all of my apples are so different. They each have a completely different flavor. It's like a whole new reality. When you buy apples from the store, they all taste so bland and the same—nothing. Again it comes back to the character of God. God is awesome! He's unique. He didn't make things boring. Everything has a unique awesome flavor.

The thing I'm observing after gardening here for forty-two years I've seen the incredible change that the covering of wood chips has made to the soil. It's been such an education for me. To me, it shows the character of God and how redeeming He is, and how He'll transform, and change, and bless under His rules. Under His ways of doing things.

Again, I so see the significance of Him putting us in the Garden of Eden because the garden reveals the character of God. It makes Him so visible and tangible. Again, after being here for forty-two years, I've seen the effects, and it keeps getting better.

* In this chapter, you also quoted 1 Thessalonians 5:16-18. *"Rejoice always, pray continually, give thanks in all circumstances; for this is God's will for you in Christ Jesus."* 1 Thessalonians 5:16-18 NIV

This Scripture totally changed my life. It says to give thanks in everything. You see, when I would head out to work, I would plan my day. I would always plan more than I could get done. I always did that. I don't know why. I just did. And I would go to bed at night whining, "I didn't get this done. I didn't get that done." I'd be just miserable. Then when the Holy Spirit really spoke this Scripture to me, "In everything give thanks." Now I go to bed and say, "Father, we had a great day today! We got a lot done, and tomorrow is a new day." It changes everything! It changes your whole perspective. When you sit there whining and complaining. It doesn't get anything done. All you are is miserable. And I think, "God, Your owner's manual teaches us how to live in an effective, awesome way! In everything, give thanks. It's so powerful!

* The Scripture is so clear. It says, *"As a man thinks in his heart, so is he."* Your thoughts create your reality. When you're whining and complaining, it's gonna create that kind of reality. It's like, come on, wake up!

My wife found a video where a brain surgeon was somehow photographing the brains of people he was working on. He could see that the people who had gratitude, their brains were significantly healthier. It was visible on the screen. It was huge! It was totally huge to look at anatomy as proof of His Word, *"As a man thinks in his heart, so is he."* God is so good. The owner's manual is amazing. It really teaches you how to live. And, if you pay attention to it, it's such an advantage. He's being very real. *"Be not deceived; God will not be mocked. You reap what you sow."* There are consequences to your actions. He's just being very, very real.

* This is a really significant and awesome chapter and a perfect one to tie the entire book together. It's hard to watch how believers are so negligent in caring for their health and eating right. It's scary man. It's almost like they're brain dead. They act like they don't know any better. You gotta be kidding me. It's so sad. S A D: Standard American Diet. The standard American diet is sad. It's really pathetic.

Again, the Word is so clear. We think we are going to get away with it, but we are not. I love how God warns us. *"Be not deceived. God will not be mocked. You will reap what you sow."* That's a reality, and you're not going to change it. The human mind keeps thinking, "I can do this and get away with it." I just love God's wording; He's really upfront. *"Don't be deceived; I will not be mocked. You're gonna reap what you sow."* It's a given.

* It's very interesting when you look at Scripture. David is the only individual in Scripture who got the title, *"A man after God's own heart."* No one else in Scripture got that. Look at the life of Daniel. Seventy years with no record of any sin. And the Bible doesn't hide things. It's very upfront. It tells you everything. That man lived a totally righteous life. No record of sin. But he was not given the title: *"A man after God's own heart."* I believe the reason is because David was so real. He was so totally transparent. He was completely in the light. All the time. The Word says, *"If we walk in the light as He is in the light, we have fellowship with one another, and the blood of Jesus Christ His Son cleanses us from all sin."* It's all about being in the light. And that's what David was. He was totally in the light. He was totally transparent. That's why I believe God said, *"That's a man after my own heart."*

I love Psalm 51. What an incredible statement of repentance. When Nathan confronted him, he didn't make excuses; he totally acknowledged his sinfulness. That's such a powerful, powerful statement there in Psalm 51. That is the part that got God's heart because David was so real. Completely transparent. Nothing hidden. God honored him because of that.

Chapter Notes and Discussion Topics

Notes

How did this chapter affect you? And why?

Did you gain any new perspectives or perceptions?

What changed in you after reading this chapter?

How can you use this knowledge to help improve your relationships with God, yourself, and others?

Chapter Ten

The Nourished Soul Eden Treats Sheets

—Intro

Gardening your *Nourished Soul:* As you write about, meditate on, visualize, practice, and embody God's Spirit's light and power, He will re-wire your mind and re-focus your patterns of life on Him; He will recreate you and the character traits you will certainly enjoy.

On your *Nourished Soul Eden Treats Sheets*, you and God together will continually elevate your inspired *Nourished Soul*. This is where many positive, healthy, and inspiring neural pathways will grow solidly in the garden of your mind. Your new *MADFATs* will be strengthened through the process of writing them down, meditating on them, practicing them, and visualizing them as you embody them in your life's reality.

As you begin your journey, please remember the immense value in seeing God as He truly is—Love. I believe He loves you and wants nothing but the very best for your life.

It is imperative that you see God clearly. You were created in His image and likeness. Your insight into His love-based character and movements is fundamental to who you will become.

On your *Nourished Soul Eden Treats Sheets,* you will realize and embody the wonderful benefits of living life under the influence and direction of your loving Papa God's Holy Spirit. He is the one who has instilled in you the desire to seek godly motives, affections, desires, feelings, actions, and thoughts. It is by consistently exposing yourself to God's love and light that you become enlightened, and your heart, mind, and soul are healed. The importance of documenting your journey cannot be overemphasized.

Your *Nourished Soul Eden Treats Sheets* will become the joyous home of your ever-expanding renewal. The work, you and God's Spirit, do together on these pages will greatly assist in the growth of your *Nourished Soul*. It is important to record your transformation process in each section.

You will find the *Prayer and Learning Journal* section very beneficial in opening doors for new light to enter.

Remember, this is a process—allow God to work. You never know what He will use to draw your heart into His kingdom of light. Don't become discouraged should you seem to fail and fall back into acting out dark deeds. Treat yourself with tenderness as a child of the King of heaven. It is easy and common to judge, criticize, dislike, and complain about yourself. Instead, rejoice in the lessons and place your challenges amidst your blessings as learning experiences.

When disharmony clouds your day, grasp the opportunity to study it. Record what you learn from your experiences in the *Prayer and Learning Journal* section of your *Nourished Soul Eden Treats Sheets*. Aristotle wrote: *"Excellence is an art won by training and habituation. We do not act rightly because we have virtue and excellence. But we rather have those because we have acted rightly. We are what we repeatedly do. Excellence, then, is not an act but a habit."*

As you are inspired, take a moment and record what works for you, what doesn't work for you, and what your strategy will be the next time the evil one tries to steal you away. Don't simply focus on the failure experiences—record inspiring insights. Primarily focus on victories and how God and you together will achieve ever-increasing advantage in your character building and love-based life. Keep in mind that godly deeds lead to true pleasure, peace, and joy. Dark deeds always end in pain. Understand the pain and use it to propel you into ever-advancing growth.

The pain you experience as a result of dark life choices is a beneficial learning tool. The pain they produce can chase you away from them and bring about the realization of the goodness of God's will in your life. Many won't willingly run to the light but rather find themselves backing away from the darkness—because of the pain. Your *Prayer and Learning Journal* is a great place to reinforce the lessons learned in victory and defeat. Record personal challenges, memorable experiences, and attentive prayers as you envision communicating directly with God in writing.

The act of visualizing and recording events in writing holds particular interest. It seems that visualizing and writing affects the brain's ability to retain information in powerfully unique ways.[T]

This is why your *Nourished Soul Eden Treats Sheets* are so vital to your regeneration process. As you visualize and record an event in writing, your brain has the propensity to interpret what you write as reality. Here you will daily record, meditate on, visualize, practice, realize, and embody God's transformation of your being. His Spirit will win sway over your soul. Your spirit will tune to His and will assert influence over your entire being, thus, moving your spirit, mind, and body toward vibrant happiness and health. The garden of your mind will increasingly produce the fruits of heaven.

Don't forget, all of life is a lesson. Some experiences will require that you trust God even if you don't understand why—yet.

Scripture declares: *"Trust in the Lord with all your heart and do not lean on your own understanding. In all your ways acknowledge Him, and He will make your paths straight. Do not be wise in your own eyes; Fear the Lord and turn away from evil. It will be healing to your body and refreshment to your bones. Honor the Lord from your wealth, and from the first of all your produce;*

Then your barns will be filled with plenty, and your vats will overflow with new wine. My son, do not reject the discipline of the Lord or loathe His rebuke, for whom the Lord loves He disciplines, just as a father disciplines the son in whom he delights." Proverbs 3:5-12 NASB

On your *Nourished Soul Eden Treats Sheets,* record desired, divine patterns. You may copy our words or paraphrase each day's sentiments into your own Spirit-led version. Be creative. Bare yourself before God. Know His love. Listen. Learn. Transcribe inspirations. Be honest. Be gritty. Cry. Laugh. Allow light to dispel the darkness. Be patient. Repetition and practice are key to your unending renewal and growth. Feed your *Nourished Soul.*

Read a page or two each day of the text portion of this book, as well as a chapter each day in the Bible. When you reach the end, begin again. When you run out of blank *Nourished Soul Eden Treats Sheets,* get a fresh copy of the book and continue your journey. The deeper you plant your *Eden Treats*, the richer your harvest will be. Don't throw away completed books. It is exciting to review your growth as the years pass and see clearly the evidence of answered prayers and a mind that has been transformed through the renewing powers of God and your improving desires to follow His lead back to the Garden.

I am sorry to say that if you are reading this in an E-book format, you don't have the *Nourished Soul Eden Treats Sheets*. You may wish to own a printed copy of this book. I believe that owning and utilizing the printed book is the best option because of the enhanced learning that writing allows.

However you decide to move forward, I pray that God's Holy Spirit will continually ignite deep truths about His character within you. May you enjoy the endless benefits of knowing and following Jesus—the Way, the Truth, and the Life.

May you flourish richly as your precious Father God plants His laws of love and liberty in the garden of your mind.

We hope to meet you here on earth and in the kingdom of heaven. Until then, our prayer for you and yours will be: *The Lord bless you and keep you; the Lord make his face shine on you and be gracious to you; the Lord turn his face toward you and give you peace.* Numbers 6:24-26 NIV

If you feel moved to, please bless this book with your much appreciated review on Amazon.com.

Thank you.

Paul Gautschi and James Bars

Disclaimer: *The authors and publishers in this book strongly recommend that you consult with your physician before beginning any diet or exercise program. You should be in good physical condition and be able to participate in the mentioned recommendations and exercises. The authors and publishers in this book are not licensed medical care providers and represent that they have no expertise in diagnosing, examining, or treating medical conditions of any kind, or in determining the effect of any specific diet or exercise on a medical condition. You should understand that when participating in any diet or exercise program, there is the possibility of physical injury. If you engage in any portion of these recommendations or exercises, you agree that you do so at your own risk, are voluntarily participating in these activities, assume all risk of sickness or injury to yourself, and agree to release and discharge the authors and publishers in this book from any and all claims or causes of action, known or unknown, arising out of their negligence.*

The Laws of Love and Liberty

I am the Lord your God, who rescued you from the land of Egypt, the place of your slavery.

You must not have any other god but me.

You must not make for yourself an idol of any kind or an image of anything in the heavens or on the earth or in the sea. You must not bow down to them or worship them, for I, the Lord your God, am a jealous God who will not tolerate your affection for any other gods. I lay the sins of the parents upon their children; the entire family is affected—even children in the third and fourth generations of those who reject me. But I lavish unfailing love for a thousand generations on those who love me and obey my commands.

You must not misuse the name of the Lord your God. The Lord will not let you go unpunished if you misuse his name.

Remember to observe the Sabbath day by keeping it holy. You have six days each week for your ordinary work, but the seventh day is a Sabbath day of rest dedicated to the Lord your God. On that day no one in your household may do any work. This includes you, your sons and daughters, your male and female servants, your livestock, and any foreigners living among you. For in six days the Lord made the heavens, the earth, the sea, and everything in them; but on the seventh day he rested. That is why the Lord blessed the Sabbath day and set it apart as holy.

Honor your father and mother. Then you will live a long, full life in the land the Lord your God is giving you.

You must not murder.

You must not commit adultery.

You must not steal.

You must not testify falsely against your neighbor.

You must not covet your neighbor's house. You must not covet your neighbor's wife, male or female servant, ox or donkey, or anything else that belongs to your neighbor. Exodus 20:2-17 NLT

Keep this Book of the Law always on your lips; meditate on it day and night, so that you may be careful to do everything written in it. Then you will be prosperous and successful. Joshua 1:8 NIV

You may copy our words or paraphrase each day's treat sheet into your own Spirit-led expressions. Be creative. Connect with and write to God directly. Know His love. Listen. Transcribe inspirations. Be honest. Be gritty. Cry. Laugh. Use pain and temptation to trigger God's light. Be patient. Repetition and practice are key to your unending renewal and growth.

Sunday: Planting My New MADFATs — God Loves Me Day

God's soul-enriching love and care breathe His ways into all my motives.

God's loving-kindness warms my affections for Him, myself, and others.

God's enduring faithfulness energizes my desires to know, obey, and honor Him.

God's soothing fruit of love, joy, peace, and patience seasons all my feelings.

God's life-supporting laws of love mother my improving actions.

God's tender love shepherds my thoughts with captivating wisdom.

Monday: The Good Soil Promise — Spirit Day

The Holy Spirit's soil of power, love, and self-control nourishes the roots and fruits of my soul.

Tuesday: Amazing Grace and the Touchstones — Grace Day

God's amazing grace corrects all my mistakes.

Touchstone #1: *God's willing meekness inspires my humility.*

Touchstone #2: *God loves me tenderly.*
Touchstone #3: *God strives to recreate, redeem, and enrich me.*

Wednesday: The Covering and the Way Up — Jesus Day

Christ's Robe of Right Covers My Life.

Jesus is my Friend, my Savior, and my King.

Jesus loves well and shows me how.
Jesus cares well and shows me how.

Thursday: Untangling the Night — Freedom Day

I *escape the darkness by remaining in God's light.*

Through pain and God's light my MADFATs are made right.

Papa's Love PATERNs of light dissolve my night.

____

Friday: IOU Love — Love Day

God untangles my mind to understand and forgive.______________

God frees my heart to love and encourage. ______________

God liberates my soul to help and heal.______________

Saturday: Happy You, in God's Temple of Light — Joy and Rest Day

God's Spirit illuminates His temple of light.______________

God urges gratitude amidst the struggles of life.______________

God revives with daily delights—water, nature, love, motion, food, worship, work, rest, and play.____

Prayer and Learning Journal: ______________

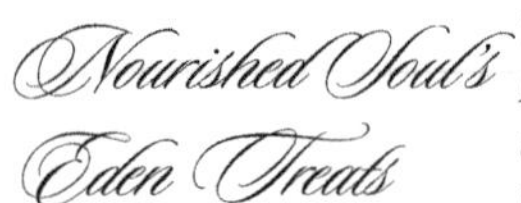

You may copy our words or paraphrase each day's treat sheet into your own Spirit-led expressions. Be creative. Connect with and write to God directly. Know His love. Listen. Transcribe inspirations. Be honest. Be gritty. Cry. Laugh. Use pain and temptation to trigger God's light. Be patient. Repetition and practice are key to your unending renewal and growth.

Sunday: Planting My New MADFATs — God Loves Me Day

God's soul-enriching love and care breathe His ways into all my motives.

God's loving-kindness warms my affections for Him, myself, and others.

God's enduring faithfulness energizes my desires to know, obey, and honor Him.

God's soothing fruit of love, joy, peace, and patience seasons all my feelings.

God's life-supporting laws of love mother my improving actions.

God's tender love shepherds my thoughts with captivating wisdom.

Monday: The Good Soil Promise — Spirit Day

The Holy Spirit's soil of power, love, and self-control nourishes the roots and fruits of my soul.

Tuesday: Amazing Grace and the Touchstones — Grace Day

God's amazing grace corrects all my mistakes.

Touchstone #1: *God's willing meekness inspires my humility.*

Touchstone #2: *God loves me tenderly.*
Touchstone #3: *God strives to recreate, redeem, and enrich me.*

Wednesday: The Covering and the Way Up — Jesus Day

Christ's Robe of Right Covers My Life.

Jesus is my Friend, my Savior, and my King.

Jesus loves well and shows me how.
Jesus cares well and shows me how.

Thursday: Untangling the Night — Freedom Day

I *escape the darkness by remaining in God's light.*

Through pain and God's light my MADFATs are made right.

Papa's Love PATERNs of light dissolve my night.

"It gave me great joy to have some brothers come and tell about your faithfulness to the truth and how you continue to walk in the truth." 3 John 1:3 NIV

Friday: IOU Love — Love Day

God untangles my mind to understand and forgive.

God frees my heart to love and encourage.

God liberates my soul to help and heal.

Saturday: Happy You, in God's Temple of Light — Joy and Rest Day

God's Spirit illuminates His temple of light.

God urges gratitude amidst the struggles of life.

God revives with daily delights—water, nature, love, motion, food, worship, work, rest, and play.

Prayer and Learning Journal:

You may copy our words or paraphrase each day's treat sheet into your own Spirit-led expressions. Be creative. Connect with and write to God directly. Know His love. Listen. Transcribe inspirations. Be honest. Be gritty. Cry. Laugh. Use pain and temptation to trigger God's light. Be patient. Repetition and practice are key to your unending renewal and growth.

Sunday: Planting My New MADFATs — God Loves Me Day

God's soul-enriching love and care breathe His ways into all my motives.

God's loving-kindness warms my affections for Him, myself, and others.

God's enduring faithfulness energizes my desires to know, obey, and honor Him.

God's soothing fruit of love, joy, peace, and patience seasons all my feelings.

God's life-supporting laws of love mother my improving actions.

God's tender love shepherds my thoughts with captivating wisdom.

Monday: The Good Soil Promise — Spirit Day

The Holy Spirit's soil of power, love, and self-control nourishes the roots and fruits of my soul.

Tuesday: Amazing Grace and the Touchstones — Grace Day

God's amazing grace corrects all my mistakes.

Touchstone #1: *God's willing meekness inspires my humility.*

Touchstone #2: *God loves me tenderly.*
Touchstone #3: *God strives to recreate, redeem, and enrich me.*

Wednesday: The Covering and the Way Up — Jesus Day

Christ's Robe of Right Covers My Life.

Jesus is my Friend, my Savior, and my King.

Jesus loves well and shows me how.
Jesus cares well and shows me how.

Thursday: Untangling the Night — Freedom Day

I *escape the darkness by remaining in God's light.*

Through pain and God's light my MADFATs are made right.

Papa's Love PATERNs of light dissolve my night.

"We write this to make our joy complete. This is the message we have heard from him and declare to you: God is light; in him there is no darkness at all." 1 John 1:4-5 NIV

Friday: IOU Love — Love Day

God untangles my mind to understand and forgive. ______________________

God frees my heart to love and encourage. ______________________

God liberates my soul to help and heal. ______________________

Saturday: Happy You, in God's Temple of Light — Joy and Rest Day

God's Spirit illuminates His temple of light. ______________________

God urges gratitude amidst the struggles of life. ______________________

God revives with daily delights—water, nature, love, motion, food, worship, work, rest, and play. ______

Prayer and Learning Journal: ______________________

You may copy our words or paraphrase each day's treat sheet into your own Spirit-led expressions. Be creative. Connect with and write to God directly. Know His love. Listen. Transcribe inspirations. Be honest. Be gritty. Cry. Laugh. Use pain and temptation to trigger God's light. Be patient. Repetition and practice are key to your unending renewal and growth.

Sunday: Planting My New MADFATs — God Loves Me Day

*God's soul-enriching love and care breathe His ways into all my motives.*____________________

*God's loving-kindness warms my affections for Him, myself, and others.*____________________

*God's enduring faithfulness energizes my desires to know, obey, and honor Him.*____________________

*God's soothing fruit of love, joy, peace, and patience seasons all my feelings.*____________________

*God's life-supporting laws of love mother my improving actions.*____________________

God's tender love shepherds my thoughts with captivating wisdom. ____________________

Monday: The Good Soil Promise — Spirit Day

*The Holy Spirit's soil of power, love, and self-control nourishes the roots and fruits of my soul.*______

Tuesday: Amazing Grace and the Touchstones — Grace Day

God's amazing grace corrects all my mistakes. ____________________

Touchstone #1: God's willing meekness inspires my humility.____________________

Touchstone #2: God loves me tenderly. ____________________

Touchstone #3: God strives to recreate, redeem, and enrich me.____________________

Wednesday: The Covering and the Way Up — Jesus Day

*Christ's Robe of Right Covers My Life.*____________________

*Jesus is my Friend, my Savior, and my King.*____________________

Jesus loves well and shows me how. ____________________

Jesus cares well and shows me how. ____________________

Thursday: Untangling the Night — Freedom Day

I *escape the darkness by remaining in God's light.* ____________________

Through pain and God's light my MADFATs are made right. ____________________

Papa's Love PATERNs of light dissolve my night. ____________________

Even Thanks for the week of: ____________________

"Though you have not seen him, you love him; and even though you do not see him now, you believe in him and are filled with an inexpressible and glorious joy, for you are receiving the goal of your faith, the salvation of your souls." 1 Peter 1:8-9 NIV

<u>Friday: IOU Love — Love Day</u>

*God untangles my mind to understand and forgive.*____

____

God frees my heart to love and encourage. ____

____

*God liberates my soul to help and heal.*____

____

<u>Saturday: Happy You, in God's Temple of Light — Joy and Rest Day</u>

*God's Spirit illuminates His temple of light.*____

____

*God urges gratitude amidst the struggles of life.*____

____

*God revives with daily delights—water, nature, love, motion, food, worship, work, rest, and play.*____

____

____

Prayer and Learning Journal: ____

____

____

____

____

____

____

____

____

____

____

____

____

____

____

____

____

____

____

____

____

____

____

____

____

____

____

____

____

You may copy our words or paraphrase each day's treat sheet into your own Spirit-led expressions. Be creative. Connect with and write to God directly. Know His love. Listen. Transcribe inspirations. Be honest. Be gritty. Cry. Laugh. Use pain and temptation to trigger God's light. Be patient. Repetition and practice are key to your unending renewal and growth.

Sunday: Planting My New MADFATs — God Loves Me Day

*God's soul-enriching love and care breathe His ways into all my motives.*____________

*God's loving-kindness warms my affections for Him, myself, and others.*____________

*God's enduring faithfulness energizes my desires to know, obey, and honor Him.*____________

*God's soothing fruit of love, joy, peace, and patience seasons all my feelings.*____________

*God's life-supporting laws of love mother my improving actions.*____________

God's tender love shepherds my thoughts with captivating wisdom. ____________

Monday: The Good Soil Promise — Spirit Day

*The Holy Spirit's soil of power, love, and self-control nourishes the roots and fruits of my soul.*______

Tuesday: Amazing Grace and the Touchstones — Grace Day

God's amazing grace corrects all my mistakes. ____________

Touchstone #1: *God's willing meekness inspires my humility.*____________

Touchstone #2: *God loves me tenderly.* ____________

Touchstone #3: *God strives to recreate, redeem, and enrich me.*____________

Wednesday: The Covering and the Way Up — Jesus Day

*Christ's Robe of Right Covers My Life.*____________

*Jesus is my Friend, my Savior, and my King.*____________

Jesus loves well and shows me how. ____________

Jesus cares well and shows me how. ____________

Thursday: Untangling the Night — Freedom Day

I *escape the darkness by remaining in God's light.* ____________

Through pain and God's light my MADFATs are made right. ____________

Papa's Love PATERNs of light dissolve my night. ____________

Friday: IOU Love — Love Day

God untangles my mind to understand and forgive.

God frees my heart to love and encourage.

God liberates my soul to help and heal.

Saturday: Happy You, in God's Temple of Light — Joy and Rest Day

God's Spirit illuminates His temple of light.

God urges gratitude amidst the struggles of life.

God revives with daily delights—water, nature, love, motion, food, worship, work, rest, and play.

Prayer and Learning Journal:

You may copy our words or paraphrase each day's treat sheet into your own Spirit-led expressions. Be creative. Connect with and write to God directly. Know His love. Listen. Transcribe inspirations. Be honest. Be gritty. Cry. Laugh. Use pain and temptation to trigger God's light. Be patient. Repetition and practice are key to your unending renewal and growth.

Sunday: Planting My New MADFATs — God Loves Me Day

God's soul-enriching love and care breathe His ways into all my motives.

God's loving-kindness warms my affections for Him, myself, and others.

God's enduring faithfulness energizes my desires to know, obey, and honor Him.

God's soothing fruit of love, joy, peace, and patience seasons all my feelings.

God's life-supporting laws of love mother my improving actions.

God's tender love shepherds my thoughts with captivating wisdom.

Monday: The Good Soil Promise — Spirit Day

The Holy Spirit's soil of power, love, and self-control nourishes the roots and fruits of my soul.

Tuesday: Amazing Grace and the Touchstones — Grace Day

God's amazing grace corrects all my mistakes.

Touchstone #1: God's willing meekness inspires my humility.

Touchstone #2: God loves me tenderly.
Touchstone #3: God strives to recreate, redeem, and enrich me.

Wednesday: The Covering and the Way Up — Jesus Day

Christ's Robe of Right Covers My Life.

Jesus is my Friend, my Savior, and my King.

Jesus loves well and shows me how.
Jesus cares well and shows me how.

Thursday: Untangling the Night — Freedom Day

I escape the darkness by remaining in God's light.

Through pain and God's light my MADFATs are made right.

Papa's Love PATERNs of light dissolve my night.

"Obey your leaders and submit to their authority. They keep watch over you as men who must give an account. Obey them so that their work will be a joy, not a burden, for that would be of no advantage to you." Hebrews 13:17 NIV

Friday: IOU Love — Love Day

*God untangles my mind to understand and forgive.*____________________

____

God frees my heart to love and encourage. ____________________

____

*God liberates my soul to help and heal.*____________________

____

Saturday: Happy You, in God's Temple of Light — Joy and Rest Day

*God's Spirit illuminates His temple of light.*____________________

____

*God urges gratitude amidst the struggles of life.*____________________

____

*God revives with daily delights—water, nature, love, motion, food, worship, work, rest, and play.*____

____

____

Prayer and Learning Journal: ____________________

You may copy our words or paraphrase each day's treat sheet into your own Spirit-led expressions. Be creative. Connect with and write to God directly. Know His love. Listen. Transcribe inspirations. Be honest. Be gritty. Cry. Laugh. Use pain and temptation to trigger God's light. Be patient. Repetition and practice are key to your unending renewal and growth.

Sunday: Planting My New MADFATs — God Loves Me Day

God's soul-enriching love and care breathe His ways into all my motives.

God's loving-kindness warms my affections for Him, myself, and others.

God's enduring faithfulness energizes my desires to know, obey, and honor Him.

God's soothing fruit of love, joy, peace, and patience seasons all my feelings.

God's life-supporting laws of love mother my improving actions.

God's tender love shepherds my thoughts with captivating wisdom.

Monday: The Good Soil Promise — Spirit Day

The Holy Spirit's soil of power, love, and self-control nourishes the roots and fruits of my soul.

Tuesday: Amazing Grace and the Touchstones — Grace Day

God's amazing grace corrects all my mistakes.

***Touchstone #1:** God's willing meekness inspires my humility.*

***Touchstone #2:** God loves me tenderly.*

***Touchstone #3:** God strives to recreate, redeem, and enrich me.*

Wednesday: The Covering and the Way Up — Jesus Day

Christ's Robe of Right Covers My Life.

Jesus is my Friend, my Savior, and my King.

Jesus loves well and shows me how.

Jesus cares well and shows me how.

Thursday: Untangling the Night — Freedom Day

***I** escape the darkness by remaining in God's light.*

Through pain and God's light my MADFATs are made right.

Papa's Love PATERNs of light dissolve my night.

Extra Thanks for the week of:

"Let us fix our eyes on Jesus, the author and perfecter of our faith, who for the joy set before him endured the cross, scorning its shame, and sat down at the right hand of the throne of God." Hebrews 12:2 NIV

Friday: IOU Love — Love Day

God untangles my mind to understand and forgive.

God frees my heart to love and encourage.

God liberates my soul to help and heal.

Saturday: Happy You, in God's Temple of Light — Joy and Rest Day

God's Spirit illuminates His temple of light.

God urges gratitude amidst the struggles of life.

God revives with daily delights—water, nature, love, motion, food, worship, work, rest, and play.

Prayer and Learning Journal:

You may copy our words or paraphrase each day's treat sheet into your own Spirit-led expressions. Be creative. Connect with and write to God directly. Know His love. Listen. Transcribe inspirations. Be honest. Be gritty. Cry. Laugh. Use pain and temptation to trigger God's light. Be patient. Repetition and practice are key to your unending renewal and growth.

Sunday: Planting My New MADFATs — God Loves Me Day

God's soul-enriching love and care breathe His ways into all my motives.

God's loving-kindness warms my affections for Him, myself, and others.

God's enduring faithfulness energizes my desires to know, obey, and honor Him.

God's soothing fruit of love, joy, peace, and patience seasons all my feelings.

God's life-supporting laws of love mother my improving actions.

God's tender love shepherds my thoughts with captivating wisdom.

Monday: The Good Soil Promise — Spirit Day

The Holy Spirit's soil of power, love, and self-control nourishes the roots and fruits of my soul.

Tuesday: Amazing Grace and the Touchstones — Grace Day

God's amazing grace corrects all my mistakes.

Touchstone #1: *God's willing meekness inspires my humility.*

Touchstone #2: *God loves me tenderly.*
Touchstone #3: *God strives to recreate, redeem, and enrich me.*

Wednesday: The Covering and the Way Up — Jesus Day

Christ's Robe of Right Covers My Life.

Jesus is my Friend, my Savior, and my King.

Jesus loves well and shows me how.
Jesus cares well and shows me how.

Thursday: Untangling the Night — Freedom Day

I *escape the darkness by remaining in God's light.*

Through pain and God's light my MADFATs are made right.

Papa's Love PATERNs of light dissolve my night.

Eden Treats for the week of:

____

"Your love has given me great joy and encouragement, because you, brother, have refreshed the hearts of the saints." PHILEMON 1:7 NIV

Friday: IOU Love — Love Day

God untangles my mind to understand and forgive.

God frees my heart to love and encourage.

God liberates my soul to help and heal.

Saturday: Happy You, in God's Temple of Light — Joy and Rest Day

God's Spirit illuminates His temple of light.

God urges gratitude amidst the struggles of life.

God revives with daily delights—water, nature, love, motion, food, worship, work, rest, and play.

Prayer and Learning Journal:

You may copy our words or paraphrase each day's treat sheet into your own Spirit-led expressions. Be creative. Connect with and write to God directly. Know His love. Listen. Transcribe inspirations. Be honest. Be gritty. Cry. Laugh. Use pain and temptation to trigger God's light. Be patient. Repetition and practice are key to your unending renewal and growth.

Sunday: Planting My New MADFATs — God Loves Me Day

God's soul-enriching love and care breathe His ways into all my motives.

God's loving-kindness warms my affections for Him, myself, and others.

God's enduring faithfulness energizes my desires to know, obey, and honor Him.

God's soothing fruit of love, joy, peace, and patience seasons all my feelings.

God's life-supporting laws of love mother my improving actions.

God's tender love shepherds my thoughts with captivating wisdom.

Monday: The Good Soil Promise — Spirit Day

The Holy Spirit's soil of power, love, and self-control nourishes the roots and fruits of my soul.

Tuesday: Amazing Grace and the Touchstones — Grace Day

God's amazing grace corrects all my mistakes.

Touchstone #1: *God's willing meekness inspires my humility.*

Touchstone #2: *God loves me tenderly.*
Touchstone #3: *God strives to recreate, redeem, and enrich me.*

Wednesday: The Covering and the Way Up — Jesus Day

Christ's Robe of Right Covers My Life.

Jesus is my Friend, my Savior, and my King.

Jesus loves well and shows me how.
Jesus cares well and shows me how.

Thursday: Untangling the Night — Freedom Day

I *escape the darkness by remaining in God's light.*

Through pain and God's light my MADFATs are made right.

Papa's Love PATERNs of light dissolve my night.

<u>*Friday: IOU Love — Love Day*</u>

God untangles my mind to understand and forgive.

God frees my heart to love and encourage.

God liberates my soul to help and heal.

<u>*Saturday: Happy You, in God's Temple of Light — Joy and Rest Day*</u>

God's Spirit illuminates His temple of light.

God urges gratitude amidst the struggles of life.

God revives with daily delights—water, nature, love, motion, food, worship, work, rest, and play.

Prayer and Learning Journal:

You may copy our words or paraphrase each day's treat sheet into your own Spirit-led expressions. Be creative. Connect with and write to God directly. Know His love. Listen. Transcribe inspirations. Be honest. Be gritty. Cry. Laugh. Use pain and temptation to trigger God's light. Be patient. Repetition and practice are key to your unending renewal and growth.

Sunday: Planting My New MADFATs — God Loves Me Day

*God's soul-enriching love and care breathe His ways into all my motives.*____________________

*God's loving-kindness warms my affections for Him, myself, and others.*____________________

*God's enduring faithfulness energizes my desires to know, obey, and honor Him.*________________

*God's soothing fruit of love, joy, peace, and patience seasons all my feelings.*________________

*God's life-supporting laws of love mother my improving actions.*____________________

God's tender love shepherds my thoughts with captivating wisdom. ____________________

Monday: The Good Soil Promise — Spirit Day

*The Holy Spirit's soil of power, love, and self-control nourishes the roots and fruits of my soul.*______

Tuesday: Amazing Grace and the Touchstones — Grace Day

God's amazing grace corrects all my mistakes. ____________________

Touchstone #1: *God's willing meekness inspires my humility.*____________________

Touchstone #2: *God loves me tenderly.* ____________________

Touchstone #3: *God strives to recreate, redeem, and enrich me.*____________________

Wednesday: The Covering and the Way Up — Jesus Day

*Christ's Robe of Right Covers My Life.*____________________

*Jesus is my Friend, my Savior, and my King.*____________________

Jesus loves well and shows me how. ____________________

Jesus cares well and shows me how. ____________________

Thursday: Untangling the Night — Freedom Day

I *escape the darkness by remaining in God's light.* ____________________

Through pain and God's light my MADFATs are made right. ____________________

Papa's Love PATERNs of light dissolve my night. ____________________

Eden Treats for the week of: _______________

"If you have any encouragement from being united with Christ, if any comfort from his love, if any fellowship with the Spirit, if any tenderness and compassion, then make my joy complete by being like-minded, having the same love, being one in spirit and purpose." PHILIPPIANS 2:1-2 NIV

Friday: IOU Love — Love Day

God untangles my mind to understand and forgive.

God frees my heart to love and encourage.

God liberates my soul to help and heal.

Saturday: Happy You, in God's Temple of Light — Joy and Rest Day

God's Spirit illuminates His temple of light.

God urges gratitude amidst the struggles of life.

God revives with daily delights—water, nature, love, motion, food, worship, work, rest, and play.

Prayer and Learning Journal:

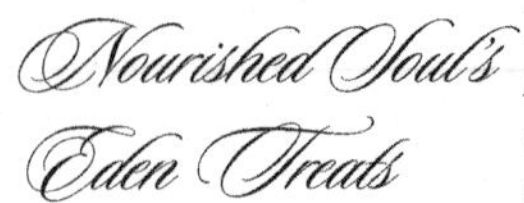

You may copy our words or paraphrase each day's treat sheet into your own Spirit-led expressions. Be creative. Connect with and write to God directly. Know His love. Listen. Transcribe inspirations. Be honest. Be gritty. Cry. Laugh. Use pain and temptation to trigger God's light. Be patient. Repetition and practice are key to your unending renewal and growth.

Sunday: Planting My New MADFATs — God Loves Me Day

God's soul-enriching love and care breathe His ways into all my motives.

God's loving-kindness warms my affections for Him, myself, and others.

God's enduring faithfulness energizes my desires to know, obey, and honor Him.

God's soothing fruit of love, joy, peace, and patience seasons all my feelings.

God's life-supporting laws of love mother my improving actions.

God's tender love shepherds my thoughts with captivating wisdom.

Monday: The Good Soil Promise — Spirit Day

The Holy Spirit's soil of power, love, and self-control nourishes the roots and fruits of my soul.

Tuesday: Amazing Grace and the Touchstones — Grace Day

God's amazing grace corrects all my mistakes.

Touchstone #1: *God's willing meekness inspires my humility.*

Touchstone #2: *God loves me tenderly.*
Touchstone #3: *God strives to recreate, redeem, and enrich me.*

Wednesday: The Covering and the Way Up — Jesus Day

Christ's Robe of Right Covers My Life.

Jesus is my Friend, my Savior, and my King.

Jesus loves well and shows me how.
Jesus cares well and shows me how.

Thursday: Untangling the Night — Freedom Day

I *escape the darkness by remaining in God's light.*

Through pain and God's light my MADFATs are made right.

Papa's Love PATERNs of light dissolve my night.

"In all my prayers for all of you, I always pray with joy because of your partnership in the gospel from the first day until now, being confident of this, that he who began a good work in you will carry it on to completion until the day of Christ Jesus." Philippians 1:4-6 NIV

Friday: IOU Love — Love Day

*God untangles my mind to understand and forgive.*______________________________

____

God frees my heart to love and encourage. ______________________________

____

*God liberates my soul to help and heal.*______________________________

____

Saturday: Happy You, in God's Temple of Light — Joy and Rest Day

*God's Spirit illuminates His temple of light.*______________________________

____

*God urges gratitude amidst the struggles of life.*______________________________

____

*God revives with daily delights—water, nature, love, motion, food, worship, work, rest, and play.*____

____

____

Prayer and Learning Journal: ______________________________

You may copy our words or paraphrase each day's treat sheet into your own Spirit-led expressions. Be creative. Connect with and write to God directly. Know His love. Listen. Transcribe inspirations. Be honest. Be gritty. Cry. Laugh. Use pain and temptation to trigger God's light. Be patient. Repetition and practice are key to your unending renewal and growth.

Sunday: Planting My New MADFATs — God Loves Me Day

God's soul-enriching love and care breathe His ways into all my motives.

God's loving-kindness warms my affections for Him, myself, and others.

God's enduring faithfulness energizes my desires to know, obey, and honor Him.

God's soothing fruit of love, joy, peace, and patience seasons all my feelings.

God's life-supporting laws of love mother my improving actions.

God's tender love shepherds my thoughts with captivating wisdom.

Monday: The Good Soil Promise — Spirit Day

The Holy Spirit's soil of power, love, and self-control nourishes the roots and fruits of my soul.

Tuesday: Amazing Grace and the Touchstones — Grace Day

God's amazing grace corrects all my mistakes.

Touchstone #1: God's willing meekness inspires my humility.

Touchstone #2: God loves me tenderly.
Touchstone #3: God strives to recreate, redeem, and enrich me.

Wednesday: The Covering and the Way Up — Jesus Day

Christ's Robe of Right Covers My Life.

Jesus is my Friend, my Savior, and my King.

Jesus loves well and shows me how.
Jesus cares well and shows me how.

Thursday: Untangling the Night — Freedom Day

***I** escape the darkness by remaining in God's light.*

Through pain and God's light my MADFATs are made right.

Papa's Love PATERNs of light dissolve my night.

Friday: IOU Love — Love Day

God untangles my mind to understand and forgive. _______________

God frees my heart to love and encourage. _______________

God liberates my soul to help and heal. _______________

Saturday: Happy You, in God's Temple of Light — Joy and Rest Day

God's Spirit illuminates His temple of light. _______________

God urges gratitude amidst the struggles of life. _______________

God revives with daily delights—water, nature, love, motion, food, worship, work, rest, and play. _______________

Prayer and Learning Journal: _______________

You may copy our words or paraphrase each day's treat sheet into your own Spirit-led expressions. Be creative. Connect with and write to God directly. Know His love. Listen. Transcribe inspirations. Be honest. Be gritty. Cry. Laugh. Use pain and temptation to trigger God's light. Be patient. Repetition and practice are key to your unending renewal and growth.

Sunday: Planting My New MADFATs — God Loves Me Day

God's soul-enriching love and care breathe His ways into all my motives.

God's loving-kindness warms my affections for Him, myself, and others.

God's enduring faithfulness energizes my desires to know, obey, and honor Him.

God's soothing fruit of love, joy, peace, and patience seasons all my feelings.

God's life-supporting laws of love mother my improving actions.

God's tender love shepherds my thoughts with captivating wisdom.

Monday: The Good Soil Promise — Spirit Day

The Holy Spirit's soil of power, love, and self-control nourishes the roots and fruits of my soul.

Tuesday: Amazing Grace and the Touchstones — Grace Day

God's amazing grace corrects all my mistakes.

***Touchstone #1:** God's willing meekness inspires my humility.*

***Touchstone #2:** God loves me tenderly.*
***Touchstone #3:** God strives to recreate, redeem, and enrich me.*

Wednesday: The Covering and the Way Up — Jesus Day

Christ's Robe of Right Covers My Life.

Jesus is my Friend, my Savior, and my King.

Jesus loves well and shows me how.
Jesus cares well and shows me how.

Thursday: Untangling the Night — Freedom Day

***I** escape the darkness by remaining in God's light.*

Through pain and God's light my MADFATs are made right.

Papa's Love PATERNs of light dissolve my night.

"I have great confidence in you; I take great pride in you. I am greatly encouraged; in all our troubles my joy knows no bounds." 2 Corinthians 7:4 NIV

Friday: IOU Love — Love Day

God untangles my mind to understand and forgive.

God frees my heart to love and encourage.

God liberates my soul to help and heal.

Saturday: Happy You, in God's Temple of Light — Joy and Rest Day

God's Spirit illuminates His temple of light.

God urges gratitude amidst the struggles of life.

God revives with daily delights—water, nature, love, motion, food, worship, work, rest, and play.

Prayer and Learning Journal:

You may copy our words or paraphrase each day's treat sheet into your own Spirit-led expressions. Be creative. Connect with and write to God directly. Know His love. Listen. Transcribe inspirations. Be honest. Be gritty. Cry. Laugh. Use pain and temptation to trigger God's light. Be patient. Repetition and practice are key to your unending renewal and growth.

Sunday: Planting My New MADFATs — God Loves Me Day

*God's soul-enriching love and care breathe His ways into all my motives.*____________________

*God's loving-kindness warms my affections for Him, myself, and others.*____________________

*God's enduring faithfulness energizes my desires to know, obey, and honor Him.*________________

*God's soothing fruit of love, joy, peace, and patience seasons all my feelings.*__________________

*God's life-supporting laws of love mother my improving actions.*__________________________

God's tender love shepherds my thoughts with captivating wisdom. ________________________

Monday: The Good Soil Promise — Spirit Day

*The Holy Spirit's soil of power, love, and self-control nourishes the roots and fruits of my soul.*______

Tuesday: Amazing Grace and the Touchstones — Grace Day

God's amazing grace corrects all my mistakes. ___________________________________

Touchstone #1: *God's willing meekness inspires my humility.*____________________________

Touchstone #2: *God loves me tenderly.* ____

Touchstone #3: *God strives to recreate, redeem, and enrich me.*___________________________

Wednesday: The Covering and the Way Up — Jesus Day

*Christ's Robe of Right Covers My Life.*____

*Jesus is my Friend, my Savior, and my King.*_______________________________________

Jesus loves well and shows me how. ____

Jesus cares well and shows me how. ____

Thursday: Untangling the Night — Freedom Day

I *escape the darkness by remaining in God's light.* __________________________________

Through pain and God's light my MADFATs are made right. ____________________________

Papa's Love PATERNs of light dissolve my night. ___________________________________

<u>*Friday: IOU Love — Love Day*</u>

*God untangles my mind to understand and forgive.*______________________________

____

God frees my heart to love and encourage. ______________________________

____

*God liberates my soul to help and heal.*______________________________

____

<u>*Saturday: Happy You, in God's Temple of Light — Joy and Rest Day*</u>

*God's Spirit illuminates His temple of light.*______________________________

____

*God urges gratitude amidst the struggles of life.*______________________________

____

*God revives with daily delights—water, nature, love, motion, food, worship, work, rest, and play.*____

____

____

Prayer and Learning Journal: ______________________________

You may copy our words or paraphrase each day's treat sheet into your own Spirit-led expressions. Be creative. Connect with and write to God directly. Know His love. Listen. Transcribe inspirations. Be honest. Be gritty. Cry. Laugh. Use pain and temptation to trigger God's light. Be patient. Repetition and practice are key to your unending renewal and growth.

Sunday: Planting My New MADFATs — God Loves Me Day

God's soul-enriching love and care breathe His ways into all my motives.

God's loving-kindness warms my affections for Him, myself, and others.

God's enduring faithfulness energizes my desires to know, obey, and honor Him.

God's soothing fruit of love, joy, peace, and patience seasons all my feelings.

God's life-supporting laws of love mother my improving actions.

God's tender love shepherds my thoughts with captivating wisdom.

Monday: The Good Soil Promise — Spirit Day

The Holy Spirit's soil of power, love, and self-control nourishes the roots and fruits of my soul.

Tuesday: Amazing Grace and the Touchstones — Grace Day

God's amazing grace corrects all my mistakes.

Touchstone #1: *God's willing meekness inspires my humility.*

Touchstone #2: *God loves me tenderly.*

Touchstone #3: *God strives to recreate, redeem, and enrich me.*

Wednesday: The Covering and the Way Up — Jesus Day

Christ's Robe of Right Covers My Life.

Jesus is my Friend, my Savior, and my King.

Jesus loves well and shows me how.

Jesus cares well and shows me how.

Thursday: Untangling the Night — Freedom Day

I *escape the darkness by remaining in God's light.*

Through pain and God's light my MADFATs are made right.

Papa's Love PATERNs of light dissolve my night.

Seven Truths for the week of: ______________

"May the God of hope fill you with all joy and peace as you trust in him, so that you may overflow with hope by the power of the Holy Spirit." Romans 15:13 NIV

Friday: IOU Love — Love Day

*God untangles my mind to understand and forgive.*______________________________

____

God frees my heart to love and encourage. ______________________________

____

*God liberates my soul to help and heal.*______________________________

____

Saturday: Happy You, in God's Temple of Light — Joy and Rest Day

*God's Spirit illuminates His temple of light.*______________________________

____

*God urges gratitude amidst the struggles of life.*______________________________

____

*God revives with daily delights—water, nature, love, motion, food, worship, work, rest, and play.*____

____

____

Prayer and Learning Journal: ______________________________

You may copy our words or paraphrase each day's treat sheet into your own Spirit-led expressions. Be creative. Connect with and write to God directly. Know His love. Listen. Transcribe inspirations. Be honest. Be gritty. Cry. Laugh. Use pain and temptation to trigger God's light. Be patient. Repetition and practice are key to your unending renewal and growth.

Sunday: Planting My New MADFATs — God Loves Me Day

God's soul-enriching love and care breathe His ways into all my motives.

God's loving-kindness warms my affections for Him, myself, and others.

God's enduring faithfulness energizes my desires to know, obey, and honor Him.

God's soothing fruit of love, joy, peace, and patience seasons all my feelings.

God's life-supporting laws of love mother my improving actions.

God's tender love shepherds my thoughts with captivating wisdom.

Monday: The Good Soil Promise — Spirit Day

The Holy Spirit's soil of power, love, and self-control nourishes the roots and fruits of my soul.

Tuesday: Amazing Grace and the Touchstones — Grace Day

God's amazing grace corrects all my mistakes.

Touchstone #1: *God's willing meekness inspires my humility.*

Touchstone #2: *God loves me tenderly.*
Touchstone #3: *God strives to recreate, redeem, and enrich me.*

Wednesday: The Covering and the Way Up — Jesus Day

Christ's Robe of Right Covers My Life.

Jesus is my Friend, my Savior, and my King.

Jesus loves well and shows me how.
Jesus cares well and shows me how.

Thursday: Untangling the Night — Freedom Day

I *escape the darkness by remaining in God's light.*

Through pain and God's light my MADFATs are made right.

Papa's Love PATERNs of light dissolve my night.

Eden Treats for the week of:

"For the kingdom of God is not a matter of eating and drinking, but of righteousness, peace and joy in the Holy Spirit, because anyone who serves Christ in this way is pleasing to God and approved by men." Romans 14:17-18 NIV

Friday: IOU Love — Love Day

God untangles my mind to understand and forgive.

God frees my heart to love and encourage.

God liberates my soul to help and heal.

Saturday: Happy You, in God's Temple of Light — Joy and Rest Day

God's Spirit illuminates His temple of light.

God urges gratitude amidst the struggles of life.

God revives with daily delights—water, nature, love, motion, food, worship, work, rest, and play.

Prayer and Learning Journal:

You may copy our words or paraphrase each day's treat sheet into your own Spirit-led expressions. Be creative. Connect with and write to God directly. Know His love. Listen. Transcribe inspirations. Be honest. Be gritty. Cry. Laugh. Use pain and temptation to trigger God's light. Be patient. Repetition and practice are key to your unending renewal and growth.

Sunday: Planting My New MADFATs — God Loves Me Day

*God's soul-enriching love and care breathe His ways into all my motives.*____________________

*God's loving-kindness warms my affections for Him, myself, and others.*____________________

*God's enduring faithfulness energizes my desires to know, obey, and honor Him.*________________

*God's soothing fruit of love, joy, peace, and patience seasons all my feelings.*________________

*God's life-supporting laws of love mother my improving actions.*____________________

God's tender love shepherds my thoughts with captivating wisdom. ____________________

Monday: The Good Soil Promise — Spirit Day

*The Holy Spirit's soil of power, love, and self-control nourishes the roots and fruits of my soul.*______

Tuesday: Amazing Grace and the Touchstones — Grace Day

God's amazing grace corrects all my mistakes. ____________________

Touchstone #1: *God's willing meekness inspires my humility.*____________________

Touchstone #2: *God loves me tenderly.* ____________________

Touchstone #3: *God strives to recreate, redeem, and enrich me.*____________________

Wednesday: The Covering and the Way Up — Jesus Day

*Christ's Robe of Right Covers My Life.*____________________

*Jesus is my Friend, my Savior, and my King.*____________________

Jesus loves well and shows me how. ____________________

Jesus cares well and shows me how. ____________________

Thursday: Untangling the Night — Freedom Day

I *escape the darkness by remaining in God's light.* ____________________

Through pain and God's light my MADFATs are made right. ____________________

Papa's Love PATERNs of light dissolve my night. ____________________

"When the crowds heard Philip and saw the miraculous signs he did, they all paid close attention to what he said. With shrieks, evil spirits came out of many, and many paralytics and cripples were healed. So there was great joy in that city." Acts 8:6-8 NIV

Friday: IOU Love — Love Day

God untangles my mind to understand and forgive.

God frees my heart to love and encourage.

God liberates my soul to help and heal.

Saturday: Happy You, in God's Temple of Light — Joy and Rest Day

God's Spirit illuminates His temple of light.

God urges gratitude amidst the struggles of life.

God revives with daily delights—water, nature, love, motion, food, worship, work, rest, and play.

Prayer and Learning Journal:

You may copy our words or paraphrase each day's treat sheet into your own Spirit-led expressions. Be creative. Connect with and write to God directly. Know His love. Listen. Transcribe inspirations. Be honest. Be gritty. Cry. Laugh. Use pain and temptation to trigger God's light. Be patient. Repetition and practice are key to your unending renewal and growth.

Sunday: Planting My New MADFATs — God Loves Me Day

*God's soul-enriching love and care breathe His ways into all my motives.*___________________

____

____

*God's loving-kindness warms my affections for Him, myself, and others.*___________________

____

____

*God's enduring faithfulness energizes my desires to know, obey, and honor Him.*___________

____

____

*God's soothing fruit of love, joy, peace, and patience seasons all my feelings.*____________

____

____

*God's life-supporting laws of love mother my improving actions.*______________________

____

God's tender love shepherds my thoughts with captivating wisdom. ____________________

____

____

Monday: The Good Soil Promise — Spirit Day

*The Holy Spirit's soil of power, love, and self-control nourishes the roots and fruits of my soul.*______

____

____

Tuesday: Amazing Grace and the Touchstones — Grace Day

God's amazing grace corrects all my mistakes. _____________________________

____

Touchstone #1: *God's willing meekness inspires my humility.*____________________

____

Touchstone #2: *God loves me tenderly.* _______________________________

Touchstone #3: *God strives to recreate, redeem, and enrich me.*________________

____

Wednesday: The Covering and the Way Up — Jesus Day

*Christ's Robe of Right Covers My Life.*_____________________________________

____

*Jesus is my Friend, my Savior, and my King.*________________________________

____

Jesus loves well and shows me how. _______________________________

Jesus cares well and shows me how. _______________________________

Thursday: Untangling the Night — Freedom Day

I *escape the darkness by remaining in God's light.* ___________________________

____

Through pain and God's light my MADFATs are made right. ____________________

____

Papa's Love PATERNs of light dissolve my night. ___________________________

____

> "Until now you have not asked for anything in my name. Ask and you will receive, and your joy will be complete." John 16:24 NIV

Friday: IOU Love — Love Day

God untangles my mind to understand and forgive.

God frees my heart to love and encourage.

God liberates my soul to help and heal.

Saturday: Happy You, in God's Temple of Light — Joy and Rest Day

God's Spirit illuminates His temple of light.

God urges gratitude amidst the struggles of life.

God revives with daily delights—water, nature, love, motion, food, worship, work, rest, and play.

Prayer and Learning Journal:

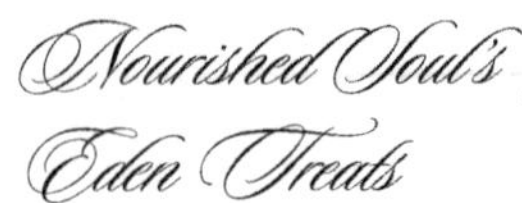

You may copy our words or paraphrase each day's treat sheet into your own Spirit-led expressions. Be creative. Connect with and write to God directly. Know His love. Listen. Transcribe inspirations. Be honest. Be gritty. Cry. Laugh. Use pain and temptation to trigger God's light. Be patient. Repetition and practice are key to your unending renewal and growth.

Sunday: Planting My New MADFATs — God Loves Me Day

God's soul-enriching love and care breathe His ways into all my motives.

God's loving-kindness warms my affections for Him, myself, and others.

God's enduring faithfulness energizes my desires to know, obey, and honor Him.

God's soothing fruit of love, joy, peace, and patience seasons all my feelings.

God's life-supporting laws of love mother my improving actions.

God's tender love shepherds my thoughts with captivating wisdom.

Monday: The Good Soil Promise — Spirit Day

The Holy Spirit's soil of power, love, and self-control nourishes the roots and fruits of my soul.

Tuesday: Amazing Grace and the Touchstones — Grace Day

God's amazing grace corrects all my mistakes.

Touchstone #1: *God's willing meekness inspires my humility.*

Touchstone #2: *God loves me tenderly.*

Touchstone #3: *God strives to recreate, redeem, and enrich me.*

Wednesday: The Covering and the Way Up — Jesus Day

Christ's Robe of Right Covers My Life.

Jesus is my Friend, my Savior, and my King.

Jesus loves well and shows me how.

Jesus cares well and shows me how.

Thursday: Untangling the Night — Freedom Day

I *escape the darkness by remaining in God's light.*

Through pain and God's light my MADFATs are made right.

Papa's Love PATERNs of light dissolve my night.

Eden Treats for the week of: ____________

"If you obey my commands, you will remain in my love, just as I have obeyed my Father's commands and remain in his love. I have told you this so that my joy may be in you and that your joy may be complete." John 15:10-11 NIV

Friday: IOU Love — Love Day

God untangles my mind to understand and forgive.

God frees my heart to love and encourage.

God liberates my soul to help and heal.

Saturday: Happy You, in God's Temple of Light — Joy and Rest Day

God's Spirit illuminates His temple of light.

God urges gratitude amidst the struggles of life.

God revives with daily delights—water, nature, love, motion, food, worship, work, rest, and play.

Prayer and Learning Journal:

You may copy our words or paraphrase each day's treat sheet into your own Spirit-led expressions. Be creative. Connect with and write to God directly. Know His love. Listen. Transcribe inspirations. Be honest. Be gritty. Cry. Laugh. Use pain and temptation to trigger God's light. Be patient. Repetition and practice are key to your unending renewal and growth.

Sunday: Planting My New MADFATs — God Loves Me Day

God's soul-enriching love and care breathe His ways into all my motives.

God's loving-kindness warms my affections for Him, myself, and others.

God's enduring faithfulness energizes my desires to know, obey, and honor Him.

God's soothing fruit of love, joy, peace, and patience seasons all my feelings.

God's life-supporting laws of love mother my improving actions.

God's tender love shepherds my thoughts with captivating wisdom.

Monday: The Good Soil Promise — Spirit Day

The Holy Spirit's soil of power, love, and self-control nourishes the roots and fruits of my soul.

Tuesday: Amazing Grace and the Touchstones — Grace Day

God's amazing grace corrects all my mistakes.

***Touchstone #1:** God's willing meekness inspires my humility.*

***Touchstone #2:** God loves me tenderly.*
***Touchstone #3:** God strives to recreate, redeem, and enrich me.*

Wednesday: The Covering and the Way Up — Jesus Day

Christ's Robe of Right Covers My Life.

Jesus is my Friend, my Savior, and my King.

Jesus loves well and shows me how.
Jesus cares well and shows me how.

Thursday: Untangling the Night — Freedom Day

***I** escape the darkness by remaining in God's light.*

Through pain and God's light my MADFATs are made right.

Papa's Love PATERNs of light dissolve my night.

"Then Jesus led them to Bethany, and lifting his hands to heaven, he blessed them. While he was blessing them, he left them and was taken up to heaven. So they worshiped him and then returned to Jerusalem filled with great joy." Luke 24:50-52 NLT

Friday: IOU Love — Love Day

God untangles my mind to understand and forgive.

God frees my heart to love and encourage.

God liberates my soul to help and heal.

Saturday: Happy You, in God's Temple of Light — Joy and Rest Day

God's Spirit illuminates His temple of light.

God urges gratitude amidst the struggles of life.

God revives with daily delights—water, nature, love, motion, food, worship, work, rest, and play.

Prayer and Learning Journal:

You may copy our words or paraphrase each day's treat sheet into your own Spirit-led expressions. Be creative. Connect with and write to God directly. Know His love. Listen. Transcribe inspirations. Be honest. Be gritty. Cry. Laugh. Use pain and temptation to trigger God's light. Be patient. Repetition and practice are key to your unending renewal and growth.

Sunday: Planting My New MADFATs — God Loves Me Day

*God's soul-enriching love and care breathe His ways into all my motives.*________________

*God's loving-kindness warms my affections for Him, myself, and others.*________________

*God's enduring faithfulness energizes my desires to know, obey, and honor Him.*____________

*God's soothing fruit of love, joy, peace, and patience seasons all my feelings.*____________

*God's life-supporting laws of love mother my improving actions.*________________

God's tender love shepherds my thoughts with captivating wisdom. ________________

Monday: The Good Soil Promise — Spirit Day

*The Holy Spirit's soil of power, love, and self-control nourishes the roots and fruits of my soul.*______

Tuesday: Amazing Grace and the Touchstones — Grace Day

God's amazing grace corrects all my mistakes. ________________

Touchstone #1: *God's willing meekness inspires my humility.*________________

Touchstone #2: *God loves me tenderly.* ________________
Touchstone #3: *God strives to recreate, redeem, and enrich me.*________________

Wednesday: The Covering and the Way Up — Jesus Day

*Christ's Robe of Right Covers My Life.*________________

*Jesus is my Friend, my Savior, and my King.*________________

Jesus loves well and shows me how. ________________
Jesus cares well and shows me how. ________________

Thursday: Untangling the Night — Freedom Day

I *escape the darkness by remaining in God's light.* ________________

Through pain and God's light my MADFATs are made right. ________________

Papa's Love PATERNs of light dissolve my night. ________________

"At that time Jesus, full of joy through the Holy Spirit, said, "I praise you, Father, Lord of heaven and earth, because you have hidden these things from the wise and learned, and revealed them to little children. Yes, Father, for this was your good pleasure." Luke 10:21 NIV

Friday: IOU Love — Love Day

God untangles my mind to understand and forgive.

God frees my heart to love and encourage.

God liberates my soul to help and heal.

Saturday: Happy You, in God's Temple of Light — Joy and Rest Day

God's Spirit illuminates His temple of light.

God urges gratitude amidst the struggles of life.

God revives with daily delights—water, nature, love, motion, food, worship, work, rest, and play.

Prayer and Learning Journal:

You may copy our words or paraphrase each day's treat sheet into your own Spirit-led expressions. Be creative. Connect with and write to God directly. Know His love. Listen. Transcribe inspirations. Be honest. Be gritty. Cry. Laugh. Use pain and temptation to trigger God's light. Be patient. Repetition and practice are key to your unending renewal and growth.

Sunday: Planting My New MADFATs — God Loves Me Day

God's soul-enriching love and care breathe His ways into all my motives.

God's loving-kindness warms my affections for Him, myself, and others.

God's enduring faithfulness energizes my desires to know, obey, and honor Him.

God's soothing fruit of love, joy, peace, and patience seasons all my feelings.

God's life-supporting laws of love mother my improving actions.

God's tender love shepherds my thoughts with captivating wisdom.

Monday: The Good Soil Promise — Spirit Day

The Holy Spirit's soil of power, love, and self-control nourishes the roots and fruits of my soul.

Tuesday: Amazing Grace and the Touchstones — Grace Day

God's amazing grace corrects all my mistakes.

***Touchstone #1:** God's willing meekness inspires my humility.*

***Touchstone #2:** God loves me tenderly.*

***Touchstone #3:** God strives to recreate, redeem, and enrich me.*

Wednesday: The Covering and the Way Up — Jesus Day

Christ's Robe of Right Covers My Life.

Jesus is my Friend, my Savior, and my King.

Jesus loves well and shows me how.

Jesus cares well and shows me how.

Thursday: Untangling the Night — Freedom Day

***I** escape the darkness by remaining in God's light.*

Through pain and God's light my MADFATs are made right.

Papa's Love PATERNs of light dissolve my night.

Eden Treats for the week of:

____

"Blessed are you when men hate you, when they exclude you and insult you and reject your name as evil, because of the Son of Man. Rejoice in that day and leap for joy, because great is your reward in heaven. For that is how their fathers treated the prophets." Luke 6:22-23 NIV

Friday: IOU Love — Love Day

*God untangles my mind to understand and forgive.*_______________

God frees my heart to love and encourage. _______________

*God liberates my soul to help and heal.*_______________

Saturday: Happy You, in God's Temple of Light — Joy and Rest Day

*God's Spirit illuminates His temple of light.*_______________

*God urges gratitude amidst the struggles of life.*_______________

*God revives with daily delights—water, nature, love, motion, food, worship, work, rest, and play.*____

Prayer and Learning Journal: _______________

You may copy our words or paraphrase each day's treat sheet into your own Spirit-led expressions. Be creative. Connect with and write to God directly. Know His love. Listen. Transcribe inspirations. Be honest. Be gritty. Cry. Laugh. Use pain and temptation to trigger God's light. Be patient. Repetition and practice are key to your unending renewal and growth.

Sunday: Planting My New MADFATs — God Loves Me Day

God's soul-enriching love and care breathe His ways into all my motives.

God's loving-kindness warms my affections for Him, myself, and others.

God's enduring faithfulness energizes my desires to know, obey, and honor Him.

God's soothing fruit of love, joy, peace, and patience seasons all my feelings.

God's life-supporting laws of love mother my improving actions.

God's tender love shepherds my thoughts with captivating wisdom.

Monday: The Good Soil Promise — Spirit Day

The Holy Spirit's soil of power, love, and self-control nourishes the roots and fruits of my soul.

Tuesday: Amazing Grace and the Touchstones — Grace Day

God's amazing grace corrects all my mistakes.

Touchstone #1: *God's willing meekness inspires my humility.*

Touchstone #2: *God loves me tenderly.*
Touchstone #3: *God strives to recreate, redeem, and enrich me.*

Wednesday: The Covering and the Way Up — Jesus Day

Christ's Robe of Right Covers My Life.

Jesus is my Friend, my Savior, and my King.

Jesus loves well and shows me how.
Jesus cares well and shows me how.

Thursday: Untangling the Night — Freedom Day

I *escape the darkness by remaining in God's light.*

Through pain and God's light my MADFATs are made right.

Papa's Love PATERNs of light dissolve my night.

Extra Thanks for the week of: ____________

"But the angel said to them, "Do not be afraid. I bring you good news of great joy that will be for all the people. Today in the town of David a Savior has been born to you; he is Christ the Lord." Luke 2:10–11 NIV

Friday: IOU Love — Love Day

God untangles my mind to understand and forgive. ____________

God frees my heart to love and encourage. ____________

God liberates my soul to help and heal. ____________

Saturday: Happy You, in God's Temple of Light — Joy and Rest Day

God's Spirit illuminates His temple of light. ____________

God urges gratitude amidst the struggles of life. ____________

God revives with daily delights—water, nature, love, motion, food, worship, work, rest, and play. ____________

Prayer and Learning Journal: ____________

You may copy our words or paraphrase each day's treat sheet into your own Spirit-led expressions. Be creative. Connect with and write to God directly. Know His love. Listen. Transcribe inspirations. Be honest. Be gritty. Cry. Laugh. Use pain and temptation to trigger God's light. Be patient. Repetition and practice are key to your unending renewal and growth.

Sunday: Planting My New MADFATs — God Loves Me Day

*God's soul-enriching love and care breathe His ways into all my motives.*____________________

*God's loving-kindness warms my affections for Him, myself, and others.*____________________

*God's enduring faithfulness energizes my desires to know, obey, and honor Him.*____________________

*God's soothing fruit of love, joy, peace, and patience seasons all my feelings.*____________________

*God's life-supporting laws of love mother my improving actions.*____________________

God's tender love shepherds my thoughts with captivating wisdom. ____________________

Monday: The Good Soil Promise — Spirit Day

*The Holy Spirit's soil of power, love, and self-control nourishes the roots and fruits of my soul.*______

Tuesday: Amazing Grace and the Touchstones — Grace Day

God's amazing grace corrects all my mistakes. ____________________

Touchstone #1: *God's willing meekness inspires my humility.*____________________

Touchstone #2: *God loves me tenderly.* ____________________

Touchstone #3: *God strives to recreate, redeem, and enrich me.*____________________

Wednesday: The Covering and the Way Up — Jesus Day

*Christ's Robe of Right Covers My Life.*____________________

*Jesus is my Friend, my Savior, and my King.*____________________

Jesus loves well and shows me how. ____________________

Jesus cares well and shows me how. ____________________

Thursday: Untangling the Night — Freedom Day

I *escape the darkness by remaining in God's light.* ____________________

Through pain and God's light my MADFATs are made right. ____________________

Papa's Love PATERNs of light dissolve my night. ____________________

"... 'He has risen from the dead and is going ahead of you into Galilee. There you will see him.' Now I have told you." So the women hurried away from the tomb, afraid yet filled with joy, and ran to tell his disciples." Matthew 28:7-8 NIV

Friday: IOU Love — Love Day

God untangles my mind to understand and forgive.

God frees my heart to love and encourage.

God liberates my soul to help and heal.

Saturday: Happy You, in God's Temple of Light — Joy and Rest Day

God's Spirit illuminates His temple of light.

God urges gratitude amidst the struggles of life.

God revives with daily delights—water, nature, love, motion, food, worship, work, rest, and play.

Prayer and Learning Journal:

You may copy our words or paraphrase each day's treat sheet into your own Spirit-led expressions. Be creative. Connect with and write to God directly. Know His love. Listen. Transcribe inspirations. Be honest. Be gritty. Cry. Laugh. Use pain and temptation to trigger God's light. Be patient. Repetition and practice are key to your unending renewal and growth.

Sunday: Planting My New MADFATs — God Loves Me Day

God's soul-enriching love and care breathe His ways into all my motives.

God's loving-kindness warms my affections for Him, myself, and others.

God's enduring faithfulness energizes my desires to know, obey, and honor Him.

God's soothing fruit of love, joy, peace, and patience seasons all my feelings.

God's life-supporting laws of love mother my improving actions.

God's tender love shepherds my thoughts with captivating wisdom.

Monday: The Good Soil Promise — Spirit Day

The Holy Spirit's soil of power, love, and self-control nourishes the roots and fruits of my soul.

Tuesday: Amazing Grace and the Touchstones — Grace Day

God's amazing grace corrects all my mistakes.

Touchstone #1: *God's willing meekness inspires my humility.*

Touchstone #2: *God loves me tenderly.*
Touchstone #3: *God strives to recreate, redeem, and enrich me.*

Wednesday: The Covering and the Way Up — Jesus Day

Christ's Robe of Right Covers My Life.

Jesus is my Friend, my Savior, and my King.

Jesus loves well and shows me how.
Jesus cares well and shows me how.

Thursday: Untangling the Night — Freedom Day

I *escape the darkness by remaining in God's light.*

Through pain and God's light my MADFATs are made right.

Papa's Love PATERNs of light dissolve my night.

"The kingdom of heaven is like treasure hidden in a field. When a man found it, he hid it again, and then in his joy went and sold all he had and bought that field." Matthew 13:44 NIV

Friday: IOU Love — Love Day

God untangles my mind to understand and forgive.

God frees my heart to love and encourage.

God liberates my soul to help and heal.

Saturday: Happy You, in God's Temple of Light — Joy and Rest Day

God's Spirit illuminates His temple of light.

God urges gratitude amidst the struggles of life.

God revives with daily delights—water, nature, love, motion, food, worship, work, rest, and play.

Prayer and Learning Journal:

You may copy our words or paraphrase each day's treat sheet into your own Spirit-led expressions. Be creative. Connect with and write to God directly. Know His love. Listen. Transcribe inspirations. Be honest. Be gritty. Cry. Laugh. Use pain and temptation to trigger God's light. Be patient. Repetition and practice are key to your unending renewal and growth.

Sunday: Planting My New MADFATs — God Loves Me Day

God's soul-enriching love and care breathe His ways into all my motives.

God's loving-kindness warms my affections for Him, myself, and others.

God's enduring faithfulness energizes my desires to know, obey, and honor Him.

God's soothing fruit of love, joy, peace, and patience seasons all my feelings.

God's life-supporting laws of love mother my improving actions.

God's tender love shepherds my thoughts with captivating wisdom.

Monday: The Good Soil Promise — Spirit Day

The Holy Spirit's soil of power, love, and self-control nourishes the roots and fruits of my soul.

Tuesday: Amazing Grace and the Touchstones — Grace Day

God's amazing grace corrects all my mistakes.

***Touchstone #1:** God's willing meekness inspires my humility.*

***Touchstone #2:** God loves me tenderly.*

***Touchstone #3:** God strives to recreate, redeem, and enrich me.*

Wednesday: The Covering and the Way Up — Jesus Day

Christ's Robe of Right Covers My Life.

Jesus is my Friend, my Savior, and my King.

Jesus loves well and shows me how.

Jesus cares well and shows me how.

Thursday: Untangling the Night — Freedom Day

***I** escape the darkness by remaining in God's light.*

Through pain and God's light my MADFATs are made right.

Papa's Love PATERNs of light dissolve my night.

"When I discovered your words, I devoured them. They are my joy and my heart's delight, for I bear your name, O LORD God of Heaven's Armies." Jeremiah 15:16 NLT

Friday: IOU Love — Love Day

God untangles my mind to understand and forgive.

God frees my heart to love and encourage.

God liberates my soul to help and heal.

Saturday: Happy You, in God's Temple of Light — Joy and Rest Day

God's Spirit illuminates His temple of light.

God urges gratitude amidst the struggles of life.

God revives with daily delights—water, nature, love, motion, food, worship, work, rest, and play.

Prayer and Learning Journal:

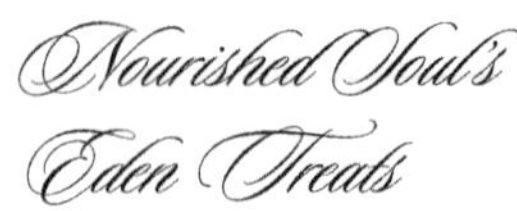

You may copy our words or paraphrase each day's treat sheet into your own Spirit-led expressions. Be creative. Connect with and write to God directly. Know His love. Listen. Transcribe inspirations. Be honest. Be gritty. Cry. Laugh. Use pain and temptation to trigger God's light. Be patient. Repetition and practice are key to your unending renewal and growth.

Sunday: Planting My New MADFATs — God Loves Me Day

God's soul-enriching love and care breathe His ways into all my motives.

God's loving-kindness warms my affections for Him, myself, and others.

God's enduring faithfulness energizes my desires to know, obey, and honor Him.

God's soothing fruit of love, joy, peace, and patience seasons all my feelings.

God's life-supporting laws of love mother my improving actions.

God's tender love shepherds my thoughts with captivating wisdom.

Monday: The Good Soil Promise — Spirit Day

The Holy Spirit's soil of power, love, and self-control nourishes the roots and fruits of my soul.

Tuesday: Amazing Grace and the Touchstones — Grace Day

God's amazing grace corrects all my mistakes.

Touchstone #1: *God's willing meekness inspires my humility.*

Touchstone #2: *God loves me tenderly.*

Touchstone #3: *God strives to recreate, redeem, and enrich me.*

Wednesday: The Covering and the Way Up — Jesus Day

Christ's Robe of Right Covers My Life.

Jesus is my Friend, my Savior, and my King.

Jesus loves well and shows me how.

Jesus cares well and shows me how.

Thursday: Untangling the Night — Freedom Day

I *escape the darkness by remaining in God's light.*

Through pain and God's light my MADFATs are made right.

Papa's Love PATERNs of light dissolve my night.

Eden Treats for the week of: ____________________

"Instead of their shame my people will receive a double portion, and instead of disgrace they will rejoice in their inheritance; and so they will inherit a double portion in their land, and everlasting joy will be theirs." Isaiah 61:7 NIV

Friday: IOU Love — Love Day

God untangles my mind to understand and forgive.

God frees my heart to love and encourage.

God liberates my soul to help and heal.

Saturday: Happy You, in God's Temple of Light — Joy and Rest Day

God's Spirit illuminates His temple of light.

God urges gratitude amidst the struggles of life.

God revives with daily delights—water, nature, love, motion, food, worship, work, rest, and play.

Prayer and Learning Journal:

You may copy our words or paraphrase each day's treat sheet into your own Spirit-led expressions. Be creative. Connect with and write to God directly. Know His love. Listen. Transcribe inspirations. Be honest. Be gritty. Cry. Laugh. Use pain and temptation to trigger God's light. Be patient. Repetition and practice are key to your unending renewal and growth.

Sunday: Planting My New MADFATs — God Loves Me Day

God's soul-enriching love and care breathe His ways into all my motives.

God's loving-kindness warms my affections for Him, myself, and others.

God's enduring faithfulness energizes my desires to know, obey, and honor Him.

God's soothing fruit of love, joy, peace, and patience seasons all my feelings.

God's life-supporting laws of love mother my improving actions.

God's tender love shepherds my thoughts with captivating wisdom.

Monday: The Good Soil Promise — Spirit Day

The Holy Spirit's soil of power, love, and self-control nourishes the roots and fruits of my soul.

Tuesday: Amazing Grace and the Touchstones — Grace Day

God's amazing grace corrects all my mistakes.

Touchstone #1: *God's willing meekness inspires my humility.*

Touchstone #2: *God loves me tenderly.*
Touchstone #3: *God strives to recreate, redeem, and enrich me.*

Wednesday: The Covering and the Way Up — Jesus Day

Christ's Robe of Right Covers My Life.

Jesus is my Friend, my Savior, and my King.

Jesus loves well and shows me how.
Jesus cares well and shows me how.

Thursday: Untangling the Night — Freedom Day

I *escape the darkness by remaining in God's light.*

Through pain and God's light my MADFATs are made right.

Papa's Love PATERNs of light dissolve my night.

"Shout for joy, O heavens; rejoice, O earth; burst into song, O mountains! For the LORD comforts his people and will have compassion on his afflicted ones." Isaiah 49:13 NIV

Friday: IOU Love — Love Day

God untangles my mind to understand and forgive.

God frees my heart to love and encourage.

God liberates my soul to help and heal.

Saturday: Happy You, in God's Temple of Light — Joy and Rest Day

God's Spirit illuminates His temple of light.

God urges gratitude amidst the struggles of life.

God revives with daily delights—water, nature, love, motion, food, worship, work, rest, and play.

Prayer and Learning Journal:

You may copy our words or paraphrase each day's treat sheet into your own Spirit-led expressions. Be creative. Connect with and write to God directly. Know His love. Listen. Transcribe inspirations. Be honest. Be gritty. Cry. Laugh. Use pain and temptation to trigger God's light. Be patient. Repetition and practice are key to your unending renewal and growth.

Sunday: Planting My New MADFATs — God Loves Me Day

*God's soul-enriching love and care breathe His ways into all my motives.*____________________

*God's loving-kindness warms my affections for Him, myself, and others.*____________________

*God's enduring faithfulness energizes my desires to know, obey, and honor Him.*____________________

*God's soothing fruit of love, joy, peace, and patience seasons all my feelings.*____________________

*God's life-supporting laws of love mother my improving actions.*____________________

God's tender love shepherds my thoughts with captivating wisdom. ____________________

Monday: The Good Soil Promise — Spirit Day

*The Holy Spirit's soil of power, love, and self-control nourishes the roots and fruits of my soul.*______

Tuesday: Amazing Grace and the Touchstones — Grace Day

God's amazing grace corrects all my mistakes. ____________________

Touchstone #1: *God's willing meekness inspires my humility.*____________________

Touchstone #2: *God loves me tenderly.* ____________________

Touchstone #3: *God strives to recreate, redeem, and enrich me.*____________________

Wednesday: The Covering and the Way Up — Jesus Day

*Christ's Robe of Right Covers My Life.*____________________

*Jesus is my Friend, my Savior, and my King.*____________________

Jesus loves well and shows me how. ____________________

Jesus cares well and shows me how. ____________________

Thursday: Untangling the Night — Freedom Day

I *escape the darkness by remaining in God's light.* ____________________

Through pain and God's light my MADFATs are made right. ____________________

Papa's Love PATERNs of light dissolve my night. ____________________

"But your dead will live; their bodies will rise. You who dwell in the dust, wake up and shout for joy. Your dew is like the dew of the morning; the earth will give birth to her dead." Isaiah 26:19 NIV

Friday: IOU Love — Love Day

God untangles my mind to understand and forgive. ____________________

God frees my heart to love and encourage. ____________________

God liberates my soul to help and heal. ____________________

Saturday: Happy You, in God's Temple of Light — Joy and Rest Day

God's Spirit illuminates His temple of light. ____________________

God urges gratitude amidst the struggles of life. ____________________

God revives with daily delights—water, nature, love, motion, food, worship, work, rest, and play. ____

Prayer and Learning Journal: ____________________

You may copy our words or paraphrase each day's treat sheet into your own Spirit-led expressions. Be creative. Connect with and write to God directly. Know His love. Listen. Transcribe inspirations. Be honest. Be gritty. Cry. Laugh. Use pain and temptation to trigger God's light. Be patient. Repetition and practice are key to your unending renewal and growth.

Sunday: Planting My New MADFATs — God Loves Me Day

*God's soul-enriching love and care breathe His ways into all my motives.*____________________

*God's loving-kindness warms my affections for Him, myself, and others.*____________________

*God's enduring faithfulness energizes my desires to know, obey, and honor Him.*____________________

*God's soothing fruit of love, joy, peace, and patience seasons all my feelings.*____________________

*God's life-supporting laws of love mother my improving actions.*____________________

God's tender love shepherds my thoughts with captivating wisdom. ____________________

Monday: The Good Soil Promise — Spirit Day

*The Holy Spirit's soil of power, love, and self-control nourishes the roots and fruits of my soul.*______

Tuesday: Amazing Grace and the Touchstones — Grace Day

God's amazing grace corrects all my mistakes. ____________________

Touchstone #1: *God's willing meekness inspires my humility.*____________________

Touchstone #2: *God loves me tenderly.* ____________________
Touchstone #3: *God strives to recreate, redeem, and enrich me.*____________________

Wednesday: The Covering and the Way Up — Jesus Day

*Christ's Robe of Right Covers My Life.*____________________

*Jesus is my Friend, my Savior, and my King.*____________________

Jesus loves well and shows me how. ____________________
Jesus cares well and shows me how. ____________________

Thursday: Untangling the Night — Freedom Day

I *escape the darkness by remaining in God's light.* ____________________

Through pain and God's light my MADFATs are made right. ____________________

Papa's Love PATERNs of light dissolve my night. ____________________

"So I commend the enjoyment of life, because nothing is better for a man under the sun than to eat and drink and be glad. Then joy will accompany him in his work all the days of the life God has given him under the sun." Ecclesiastes 8:15 NIV

Friday: IOU Love — Love Day

God untangles my mind to understand and forgive.

God frees my heart to love and encourage.

God liberates my soul to help and heal.

Saturday: Happy You, in God's Temple of Light — Joy and Rest Day

God's Spirit illuminates His temple of light.

God urges gratitude amidst the struggles of life.

God revives with daily delights—water, nature, love, motion, food, worship, work, rest, and play.

Prayer and Learning Journal:

You may copy our words or paraphrase each day's treat sheet into your own Spirit-led expressions. Be creative. Connect with and write to God directly. Know His love. Listen. Transcribe inspirations. Be honest. Be gritty. Cry. Laugh. Use pain and temptation to trigger God's light. Be patient. Repetition and practice are key to your unending renewal and growth.

Sunday: Planting My New MADFATs — God Loves Me Day

*God's soul-enriching love and care breathe His ways into all my motives.*________________

*God's loving-kindness warms my affections for Him, myself, and others.*________________

*God's enduring faithfulness energizes my desires to know, obey, and honor Him.*________________

*God's soothing fruit of love, joy, peace, and patience seasons all my feelings.*________________

*God's life-supporting laws of love mother my improving actions.*________________

God's tender love shepherds my thoughts with captivating wisdom. ________________

Monday: The Good Soil Promise — Spirit Day

*The Holy Spirit's soil of power, love, and self-control nourishes the roots and fruits of my soul.*______

Tuesday: Amazing Grace and the Touchstones — Grace Day

God's amazing grace corrects all my mistakes. ________________

Touchstone #1: *God's willing meekness inspires my humility.*________________

Touchstone #2: *God loves me tenderly.* ________________

Touchstone #3: *God strives to recreate, redeem, and enrich me.*________________

Wednesday: The Covering and the Way Up — Jesus Day

*Christ's Robe of Right Covers My Life.*________________

*Jesus is my Friend, my Savior, and my King.*________________

Jesus loves well and shows me how. ________________

Jesus cares well and shows me how. ________________

Thursday: Untangling the Night — Freedom Day

I *escape the darkness by remaining in God's light.* ________________

Through pain and God's light my MADFATs are made right. ________________

Papa's Love PATERNs of light dissolve my night. ________________

____

Friday: IOU Love — Love Day

*God untangles my mind to understand and forgive.*______________________________

*God frees my heart to love and encourage.*______________________________

*God liberates my soul to help and heal.*______________________________

Saturday: Happy You, in God's Temple of Light — Joy and Rest Day

*God's Spirit illuminates His temple of light.*______________________________

*God urges gratitude amidst the struggles of life.*______________________________

*God revives with daily delights—water, nature, love, motion, food, worship, work, rest, and play.*____

Prayer and Learning Journal: ______________________________

You may copy our words or paraphrase each day's treat sheet into your own Spirit-led expressions. Be creative. Connect with and write to God directly. Know His love. Listen. Transcribe inspirations. Be honest. Be gritty. Cry. Laugh. Use pain and temptation to trigger God's light. Be patient. Repetition and practice are key to your unending renewal and growth.

Sunday: Planting My New MADFATs — God Loves Me Day

God's soul-enriching love and care breathe His ways into all my motives.

God's loving-kindness warms my affections for Him, myself, and others.

God's enduring faithfulness energizes my desires to know, obey, and honor Him.

God's soothing fruit of love, joy, peace, and patience seasons all my feelings.

God's life-supporting laws of love mother my improving actions.

God's tender love shepherds my thoughts with captivating wisdom.

Monday: The Good Soil Promise — Spirit Day

The Holy Spirit's soil of power, love, and self-control nourishes the roots and fruits of my soul.

Tuesday: Amazing Grace and the Touchstones — Grace Day

God's amazing grace corrects all my mistakes.

***Touchstone #1:** God's willing meekness inspires my humility.*

***Touchstone #2:** God loves me tenderly.*
***Touchstone #3:** God strives to recreate, redeem, and enrich me.*

Wednesday: The Covering and the Way Up — Jesus Day

Christ's Robe of Right Covers My Life.

Jesus is my Friend, my Savior, and my King.

Jesus loves well and shows me how.
Jesus cares well and shows me how.

Thursday: Untangling the Night — Freedom Day

***I** escape the darkness by remaining in God's light.*

Through pain and God's light my MADFATs are made right.

Papa's Love PATERNs of light dissolve my night.

Eden Treats for the week of: ____________

"Rejoice in the Lord always; again I will say, Rejoice." Philippians 4:4 ESV

Friday: IOU Love — Love Day

God untangles my mind to understand and forgive.

God frees my heart to love and encourage.

God liberates my soul to help and heal.

Saturday: Happy You, in God's Temple of Light — Joy and Rest Day

God's Spirit illuminates His temple of light.

God urges gratitude amidst the struggles of life.

God revives with daily delights—water, nature, love, motion, food, worship, work, rest, and play.

Prayer and Learning Journal:

You may copy our words or paraphrase each day's treat sheet into your own Spirit-led expressions. Be creative. Connect with and write to God directly. Know His love. Listen. Transcribe inspirations. Be honest. Be gritty. Cry. Laugh. Use pain and temptation to trigger God's light. Be patient. Repetition and practice are key to your unending renewal and growth.

Sunday: Planting My New MADFATs — God Loves Me Day

*God's soul-enriching love and care breathe His ways into all my motives.*____________________

*God's loving-kindness warms my affections for Him, myself, and others.*____________________

*God's enduring faithfulness energizes my desires to know, obey, and honor Him.*____________________

*God's soothing fruit of love, joy, peace, and patience seasons all my feelings.*____________________

*God's life-supporting laws of love mother my improving actions.*____________________

God's tender love shepherds my thoughts with captivating wisdom. ____________________

Monday: The Good Soil Promise — Spirit Day

*The Holy Spirit's soil of power, love, and self-control nourishes the roots and fruits of my soul.*______

Tuesday: Amazing Grace and the Touchstones — Grace Day

God's amazing grace corrects all my mistakes. ____________________

Touchstone #1: *God's willing meekness inspires my humility.*____________________

Touchstone #2: *God loves me tenderly.* ____________________

Touchstone #3: *God strives to recreate, redeem, and enrich me.*____________________

Wednesday: The Covering and the Way Up — Jesus Day

*Christ's Robe of Right Covers My Life.*____________________

*Jesus is my Friend, my Savior, and my King.*____________________

Jesus loves well and shows me how. ____________________

Jesus cares well and shows me how. ____________________

Thursday: Untangling the Night — Freedom Day

I *escape the darkness by remaining in God's light.* ____________________

Through pain and God's light my MADFATs are made right. ____________________

Papa's Love PATERNs of light dissolve my night. ____________________

Friday: IOU Love — Love Day

God untangles my mind to understand and forgive.

God frees my heart to love and encourage.

God liberates my soul to help and heal.

Saturday: Happy You, in God's Temple of Light — Joy and Rest Day

God's Spirit illuminates His temple of light.

God urges gratitude amidst the struggles of life.

God revives with daily delights—water, nature, love, motion, food, worship, work, rest, and play.

Prayer and Learning Journal:

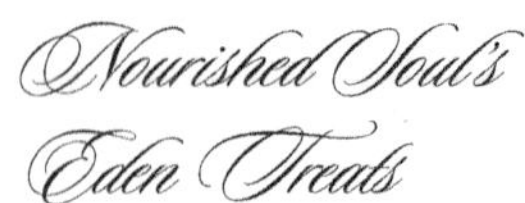

You may copy our words or paraphrase each day's treat sheet into your own Spirit-led expressions. Be creative. Connect with and write to God directly. Know His love. Listen. Transcribe inspirations. Be honest. Be gritty. Cry. Laugh. Use pain and temptation to trigger God's light. Be patient. Repetition and practice are key to your unending renewal and growth.

Sunday: Planting My New MADFATs — God Loves Me Day

God's soul-enriching love and care breathe His ways into all my motives.

God's loving-kindness warms my affections for Him, myself, and others.

God's enduring faithfulness energizes my desires to know, obey, and honor Him.

God's soothing fruit of love, joy, peace, and patience seasons all my feelings.

God's life-supporting laws of love mother my improving actions.

God's tender love shepherds my thoughts with captivating wisdom.

Monday: The Good Soil Promise — Spirit Day

The Holy Spirit's soil of power, love, and self-control nourishes the roots and fruits of my soul.

Tuesday: Amazing Grace and the Touchstones — Grace Day

God's amazing grace corrects all my mistakes.

Touchstone #1: *God's willing meekness inspires my humility.*

Touchstone #2: *God loves me tenderly.*

Touchstone #3: *God strives to recreate, redeem, and enrich me.*

Wednesday: The Covering and the Way Up — Jesus Day

Christ's Robe of Right Covers My Life.

Jesus is my Friend, my Savior, and my King.

Jesus loves well and shows me how.

Jesus cares well and shows me how.

Thursday: Untangling the Night — Freedom Day

I *escape the darkness by remaining in God's light.*

Through pain and God's light my MADFATs are made right.

Papa's Love PATERNs of light dissolve my night.

____

Friday: IOU Love — Love Day

God untangles my mind to understand and forgive.

God frees my heart to love and encourage.

God liberates my soul to help and heal.

Saturday: Happy You, in God's Temple of Light — Joy and Rest Day

God's Spirit illuminates His temple of light.

God urges gratitude amidst the struggles of life.

God revives with daily delights—water, nature, love, motion, food, worship, work, rest, and play.

Prayer and Learning Journal:

You may copy our words or paraphrase each day's treat sheet into your own Spirit-led expressions. Be creative. Connect with and write to God directly. Know His love. Listen. Transcribe inspirations. Be honest. Be gritty. Cry. Laugh. Use pain and temptation to trigger God's light. Be patient. Repetition and practice are key to your unending renewal and growth.

Sunday: Planting My New MADFATs — God Loves Me Day

God's soul-enriching love and care breathe His ways into all my motives.

God's loving-kindness warms my affections for Him, myself, and others.

God's enduring faithfulness energizes my desires to know, obey, and honor Him.

God's soothing fruit of love, joy, peace, and patience seasons all my feelings.

God's life-supporting laws of love mother my improving actions.

God's tender love shepherds my thoughts with captivating wisdom.

Monday: The Good Soil Promise — Spirit Day

The Holy Spirit's soil of power, love, and self-control nourishes the roots and fruits of my soul.

Tuesday: Amazing Grace and the Touchstones — Grace Day

God's amazing grace corrects all my mistakes.

***Touchstone #1:** God's willing meekness inspires my humility.*

***Touchstone #2:** God loves me tenderly.*
***Touchstone #3:** God strives to recreate, redeem, and enrich me.*

Wednesday: The Covering and the Way Up — Jesus Day

Christ's Robe of Right Covers My Life.

Jesus is my Friend, my Savior, and my King.

Jesus loves well and shows me how.
Jesus cares well and shows me how.

Thursday: Untangling the Night — Freedom Day

***I** escape the darkness by remaining in God's light.*

Through pain and God's light my MADFATs are made right.

Papa's Love PATERNs of light dissolve my night.

Friday: IOU Love — Love Day

God untangles my mind to understand and forgive.

God frees my heart to love and encourage.

God liberates my soul to help and heal.

Saturday: Happy You, in God's Temple of Light — Joy and Rest Day

God's Spirit illuminates His temple of light.

God urges gratitude amidst the struggles of life.

God revives with daily delights—water, nature, love, motion, food, worship, work, rest, and play.

Prayer and Learning Journal:

You may copy our words or paraphrase each day's treat sheet into your own Spirit-led expressions. Be creative. Connect with and write to God directly. Know His love. Listen. Transcribe inspirations. Be honest. Be gritty. Cry. Laugh. Use pain and temptation to trigger God's light. Be patient. Repetition and practice are key to your unending renewal and growth.

Sunday: Planting My New MADFATs — God Loves Me Day

*God's soul-enriching love and care breathe His ways into all my motives.*____________________

*God's loving-kindness warms my affections for Him, myself, and others.*____________________

*God's enduring faithfulness energizes my desires to know, obey, and honor Him.*________________

*God's soothing fruit of love, joy, peace, and patience seasons all my feelings.*________________

*God's life-supporting laws of love mother my improving actions.*________________________

God's tender love shepherds my thoughts with captivating wisdom. ________________________

Monday: The Good Soil Promise — Spirit Day

*The Holy Spirit's soil of power, love, and self-control nourishes the roots and fruits of my soul.*______

Tuesday: Amazing Grace and the Touchstones — Grace Day

God's amazing grace corrects all my mistakes. __________________________________

Touchstone #1: *God's willing meekness inspires my humility.*________________________

Touchstone #2: *God loves me tenderly.* ____________________________________
Touchstone #3: *God strives to recreate, redeem, and enrich me.*______________________

Wednesday: The Covering and the Way Up — Jesus Day

*Christ's Robe of Right Covers My Life.*______________________________________

*Jesus is my Friend, my Savior, and my King.*__________________________________

Jesus loves well and shows me how. ______________________________________
Jesus cares well and shows me how. ______________________________________

Thursday: Untangling the Night — Freedom Day

I *escape the darkness by remaining in God's light.* ______________________________

Through pain and God's light my MADFATs are made right. __________________________

Papa's Love PATERNs of light dissolve my night. ________________________________

Friday: IOU Love — Love Day

God untangles my mind to understand and forgive.

God frees my heart to love and encourage.

God liberates my soul to help and heal.

Saturday: Happy You, in God's Temple of Light — Joy and Rest Day

God's Spirit illuminates His temple of light.

God urges gratitude amidst the struggles of life.

God revives with daily delights—water, nature, love, motion, food, worship, work, rest, and play.

Prayer and Learning Journal:

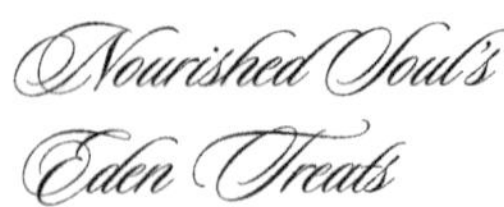

You may copy our words or paraphrase each day's treat sheet into your own Spirit-led expressions. Be creative. Connect with and write to God directly. Know His love. Listen. Transcribe inspirations. Be honest. Be gritty. Cry. Laugh. Use pain and temptation to trigger God's light. Be patient. Repetition and practice are key to your unending renewal and growth.

Sunday: Planting My New MADFATs — God Loves Me Day

God's soul-enriching love and care breathe His ways into all my motives.

God's loving-kindness warms my affections for Him, myself, and others.

God's enduring faithfulness energizes my desires to know, obey, and honor Him.

God's soothing fruit of love, joy, peace, and patience seasons all my feelings.

God's life-supporting laws of love mother my improving actions.

God's tender love shepherds my thoughts with captivating wisdom.

Monday: The Good Soil Promise — Spirit Day

The Holy Spirit's soil of power, love, and self-control nourishes the roots and fruits of my soul.

Tuesday: Amazing Grace and the Touchstones — Grace Day

God's amazing grace corrects all my mistakes.

***Touchstone #1:** God's willing meekness inspires my humility.*

***Touchstone #2:** God loves me tenderly.*
***Touchstone #3:** God strives to recreate, redeem, and enrich me.*

Wednesday: The Covering and the Way Up — Jesus Day

Christ's Robe of Right Covers My Life.

Jesus is my Friend, my Savior, and my King.

Jesus loves well and shows me how.
Jesus cares well and shows me how.

Thursday: Untangling the Night — Freedom Day

***I** escape the darkness by remaining in God's light.*

Through pain and God's light my MADFATs are made right.

Papa's Love PATERNs of light dissolve my night.

"Our mouths were filled with laughter, our tongues with songs of joy. Then it was said among the nations, 'The LORD has done great things for them.'" PSALMS 126:2 NIV

Friday: IOU Love — Love Day

God untangles my mind to understand and forgive.

God frees my heart to love and encourage.

God liberates my soul to help and heal.

Saturday: Happy You, in God's Temple of Light — Joy and Rest Day

God's Spirit illuminates His temple of light.

God urges gratitude amidst the struggles of life.

God revives with daily delights—water, nature, love, motion, food, worship, work, rest, and play.

Prayer and Learning Journal:

Mr. Paul's Testimony

I was blessed to be raised in a home with Christian parents who really loved the Lord. I remember getting up in the morning and finding my parents in the living room on their knees praying for my brother and I. Praying that God would use us and that we would become what He created us to be.

Early on, we learned to read by reading the Bible. My Dad loved the Old Testament because it had all those genealogies with Jewish names that we had to sound out by using phonetics. We learned to read in the Bible.

My mom made a real effort to have us memorize Scripture. We memorized a lot of the Word as kids growing up. I tell you, that was such a blessing to me because as I got older, I was drafted and sent to Viet Nam to fight a war my country didn't want to win. I was really blown away. I was raised in a very patriotic home, and I thought, what's up with this? This is unjust. I am packing really awesome young men in body bags onto choppers. They were dead for no reason, and I got really bitter. Instead of trying to find balance, I flipped to the other extreme because I thought, "Well, I got lied to by my country; I probably got lied to about God as well." So, I started smoking marijuana, taking LSD and other psychedelics. Through the use of those drugs, I destroyed my memory. I forgot everything I learned in school.

What was interesting, as I sought to develop philosophies to out rule God and try to see how everything made sense without Him, every time, the world would just blow up. It was so tiring to try and chase the reality of God away. I came back to Him out of sheer exhaustion. I could not escape His Word. He is so awesome. I couldn't forget Scripture! I forgot everything else, but I couldn't forget Scripture. With His Word, God brought me back to Him because; it was the answer. I couldn't argue because it is the truth.

And so, I came back to God. I began memorizing Scripture. As I memorized Scripture, God restored my memory. I got all my memory back.

My mom used to work at the USC Medical Center in the Psychiatric Ward in Los Angeles. And Psychiatrists will tell you that once you destroy brain cells, they are not renewed. But I'm telling you, God renewed my mind. His Word tells you how. The Word renews your mind. It's awesome! As I began memorizing the Word, God renewed my mind. It was such a blessing. It was so good, and I'm just so thankful.

And then, I got married, we had two children, and were living in Los Angeles. I wanted to raise food for my family because my parents raised food for us. It's such a great way to live. You walk outside when you're hungry and eat. I wanted that for my family because I felt like it was a good way to live. But in Los Angeles, by the time I got married, property was very expensive, and it was really getting unsafe to live there. I read a statistic in that one woman out of three gets raped in Los Angeles. I had a wife and two daughters, and I'm thinkin' like, uh-uh. Then in 1978, on Christmas Day, we were sitting in our house when a drunk driver came by and hit both our vehicles with no insurance. I said, "Carol, we're outta here. This is not the place to live."

What had happened before that, was raised in a family that taught me the importance of saving money. My parents told me, "Life will bring you challenges you don't expect but need to prepare for, and it's nice to have savings in place to deal with those. So, I had a thousand dollars saved in the bank, and I wanted to buy real estate. I had seen how people made big money in real estate. Real estate was a safe investment. You see, real estate is the only safe investment. It can't fail. They aren't making any more of it. Where everything else can fail, real estate is tangible. I thought, "If I could buy property in a growing area, that would be a good deal."

So, there was this pilot who would fly over Sequim from the Naval Base who wrote an article in Sunset Magazine about this blue hole. He wrote that no matter how cloudy it was in the area when I fly over Sequim, there is this blue hole from the sunny skies. This started getting people's attention, and they began moving here because of the mild climate.

A friend of mine's dad bought a home in the Sequim area and planned to retire there. He planned to go up there in February to help his dad get the house ready. I said, "I want to go with you and check the place out." In February, in Sequim, the sun is really low, the place is damp and wet. I'm there looking at all this property; it's all wet and shady, but I came to the place where we now live, and it's open. It has a beautiful mountain view where the sun sets. I think, "Someone will pay for this view." In real estate, it's all about location. Location, location, location. And this is a good location.

Interestingly, the price was $12,500; the requirements were $1,000 down and $100 per month payments. I thought, "This is perfect. I can have a savings account I'll never touch, and I can add $100 per month to it. This will work for me." I never thought I would live here. That was the last thought in my mind. That was in 1976. Then as things progressed, God said, "You know that place you've got up there in Washington. That would be a good place to live."

So, we moved up here. But I encountered a real challenge when we got this place. We drilled a well. We got down 213 feet and only got ½ a gallon per minute of water. I said, "God, how am I going to grow fruit trees without water?" He said, "Come on out to the woods with Me, and I'll show you." That day changed my life. God opened me up to His incredible power. It was August. All the trees in the woods around me were shallow-rooted but bright green. I started moving the covering on the ground, and the soil was soft and damp. I said, "God, I get it. I can put wood chips over the orchard and keep my trees alive. Thank you."

I tell people, "One of the greatest gifts God ever gave me was that lousy well because it opened me up to Him and how He operates in nature. If I had a good well, I never would have got it." I wouldn't even have a garden; I'd still be rototilling. Because I thought that's how you did it.

I can't even walk anymore, but I'm able to maintain a large garden because it's not hard. All I need is a rake, and I use my rake as a cane. I love God! He made it so easy! The things I'm seeing are His principles demonstrated in nature. It says in the Word: "It's good for a man to bear the yoke in his youth." What God is saying is if you want something of value, do the work when you are young. If you do it right up front, as you get older, it will carry you.

Do you know what's sad today? In America, the commercial farmer is spending more and more each year and getting less and less return. That's his reality. It's a pathetic reality. Imagine looking at your future, and your investment is declining. How pathetic. My reality here, in my orchard and garden, I'm doing less and less work and getting a higher and higher return. Because that's God, that's His economy. I love God! He's awesome! It's so beautiful to see all His principles demonstrated in nature when you follow His principles. It's so good. I'm so blessed.

I feel closest to the Creator when I'm in the garden, and He talks to me. God is so awesome! He's just so awesome! He spoke to me as I was digging out an old tree in my soil that was transformed from rocky, hard clay as a result of being covered for years with wood chips. He said: "As we behold the Lord, we are being changed from glory to glory." What a revelation! I said, "Wow, God! This is huge!"

So often, when I'm in the garden talking to Him, He gives me the Word. Jesus is the Word. "In the beginning was the Word." And He made everything. It's such a connection. It's all about Him. All of nature reveals the Word. God made it so easy and so available to us if we're just looking.

Today I never feel distant from God because I maintain a close connection. I talk to Him all day long. I used to think I couldn't hear God. My wife hears Him. But I never thought I could. I was frustrated because I would read the Word. I would pray. Why can't I hear Him? The Word says that "His sheep hear His voice." And, "Today, if you hear His voice." I said, "God, how come I can't hear?"

My wife got this teaching from a guy named Mark Virkler. He shared about how you hear the voice of God. It was so cool because he shared what I felt. He said: "I read the Word. I pray, but I don't hear the voice of God." And all of a sudden, the Holy Spirit opened up to him how he could hear the voice of God. And this one statement changed my life. He said, "God's voice comes as a spontaneous thought."

All of a sudden, the door was opened! It's not a still, small voice! It's a thought! Suddenly I started connecting! And what I'm finding about God's voice is; how I know it's Him—He will always confirm it. If God is speaking, He is faithful to confirm it. And when you get confirmation—you know you heard.

The Scripture states that "He who is faithful with a little will be faithful with much." With God, the more I pay attention to what I hear and acknowledge it—the more it comes. Now I hear on a regular basis all day long. It's just so fun! Because He is present. I love that Scripture, "Today, if you hear His voice, harden not your hearts." Today is a very present tense. How we harden our hearts—we have unbelief, we have doubts, we have preconceived ideas, and we are not paying attention. And it's pathetic because God has such great ideas.

Do you know what's interesting about God? It's how honorable He is. He never overrides our free will agency. If you look in the Word, it says, "Draw near to God, and He will draw near to you." And "Work out your salvation, for God works in you." What I'm seeing is; God made the first move by sending His Son. So the ball is in our court. And He waits on us to ask. He never intrudes. Man, that's huge. That is huge.

People say, "Well, I don't know God." I say, "Did you ever ask?" They say, "No." I say, "That's the problem. He's not going to barge in. He's waiting on you." What I find is that when you ask, He enjoys it. He gets excited and says, "Can I show you this?" Like, He goes on! You can tell He really enjoys that you asked!

* The one thing I'm most grateful for is the knowledge that God's voice comes as a spontaneous thought. That opened that door for me to hear God. That changed everything in my life. My wife just busts up laughing when I'm on the phone talking to people, teaching them how to hear God. She laughs and says, "You always said that you could never hear, and now you're teaching people how to."

It's so amazing to be talking with someone on the phone when the Holy Spirit inspires them with a spontaneous thought, and they come to understand how God communicates. It's so real! It's so tangible! It happens all the time! But we're not geared in. We're not paying attention.

* Another key person who has blessed my faith journey is an awesome pastor who lived in Joyce and would drive to Port Ludlow every week, which is like a two-hour drive. He lived to be 92 years old. He had ten children. On his 90th birthday, he had a gathering of 120 of his offspring—all believers. That man believed the Word. He would claim the promise, "All your children shall be taught by the LORD, and great shall be the peace of your children." And he would not move from that promise.

That man was such an inspiration to me. He was a believer in the Presbyterian church and smoked cigarettes. God told him, "I don't want you smoking cigarettes. It's not good for you." He replied, "I can't give it up, God." God said, "I'll tell you how to give it up. You know how you carry those cigarettes in your pocket? Replace them with a small New Testament, and anytime you want to smoke, you go for my Word instead." That man memorized so much Scripture getting over that habit. Cause it was hard. It took him a long time. It was awesome. God used that experience to totally ground him in the Word.

He was a truck driver, and shortly after that, he went to a house to make a delivery, and a woman came to the door. She looked almost dead. She had major cancer. She said, "I want to go to Seattle one more time before I die." He said, "In the name of Jesus, you be healed right now." And she was totally healed. He brought her and her husband into his house and disciple them. Here's what is amazing; the couple adopted children because she had a hysterectomy. But while they were in his house, she got pregnant. God totally restored everything that was taken out.

This guy lived in that kind of reality all the time. It was just phenomenal how he walked in the Spirit, heard the voice of God, and just moved. He was out walking on the highway one day. He wasn't hitchhiking or anything. He says, "I'm hungry." All of a sudden, someone throws a loaf of bread out their car window right in front of him. He's in his house one day eating beets. He has ten children and no money. They're sitting at the table, and his wife says, "God, you said to pray for our daily bread. Can we have some bread?" All of a sudden, there was a knock on the door. The neighbor up the street was there and said, "I was awakened at three o'clock this morning and told that you guys needed bread. So she baked a bunch of bread and gave it to them. It was amazing!

Hearing that type of testimony on a weekly basis increased my faith. You see, faith comes by hearing, and constantly hearing that testimony was so awesome. So good. I was really blessed by Arthur Cory.

It all goes back to hearing God. That is significant. Being able to hear the voice of God has changed my life. God's voice comes as a spontaneous thought. He says, "Today, if you hear." It's such a call. It's so important to hear. And I never thought I could. I remember feeling like, "What's wrong with me? What am I doing wrong? I'm trying to hear. I'm reading the Word; I'm praying. I'm seeking God." I just couldn't hear. It was such a frustration for me. But when that broke, that changed everything. Nothing has been more amazing in my life.

* I keep growing. That's what it's all about. We're to grow up into the full stature of Jesus Christ. That's the design. I want to keep growing and keep seeking God. I believe in growing. My relationship with God is good. Every morning it's, "Good morning, God. What are you up to today, and how can I be a part of it?" If I had to describe my relationship with God in one word, that word would be—precious. God is precious. He's so precious. He's precious!

* What I see about God is that His principles are universal. They are in everything. If you look at nature, every single organism has a protective covering; we have skin, birds have feathers, fish have scales, animals have fur, and the soil is a living organism. Nowhere in nature where man has not been is the soil uncovered. It's huge. Covering is such a principle of God. His blood covers us. It's so significant how clear He is. He's so clear. He's so real. You gotta be brain-dead or blind not to see it.

God is good. That's all I can say. He's just good. He's all good. I love Him. He's the best.

Index

Symbols

A

B

C

D

E

F

G

H

I

J

K

L

M

N

O

P

R

S

T

U

W

Y

Resources—Access books on our website's resources page at ExploringGodsLove.com

A. Jennings, Timothy R. M.D. The God-Shaped Brain, InterVarsity Press 2013.

B. Leaf Caroline M.D. Switch On Your Brain: The Key to Peak Happiness, Thinking, and Health, Baker Books September 1, 2013

E. Swaminathan, Nikhil. Scientific American, Why Does the Brain Need So Much Power? April 29, 2008, http://www.scientificamerican.com/article.cfm?id=why-does-the-brain-need-stimulus

F. Bartz, Paul A. We Are Fearfully and Wonderfully Made! Christian Assemblies International, http://www.cai.org/bible-studies/we-are-fearfully-and-wonderfully-made

G. Wikipedia, Brain, 18 March 2012, http://en.wikipedia.org/wiki/Brain

H. The Kavli Foundation. Frontiers in Neuroscience, June 2007, http://www.kavlifoundation.org/frontiers-neuroscience

I. Jennings, Timothy R. Does Conversion Heal the Brain?, September, 3 2010, http://www.comeandreason.com/index.php?option=com_content&view=article&id=309:addictions-does-conversion-heal-the-brain&catid=52:tims-blog-archive&Itemid=70

J.Universe Review. Nerves and Nervous System, http://universe-review.ca/R10-16-ANS.htm

K. Hawthorne, Jennifer Read. Change Your Thoughts, Change Your World, 2009, http://www.jenniferhawthorne.com/articles/change_your_thoughts.html

L.Wehrwein, Peter. Harvard Health Letter: Astounding Increase In Antidepressant Use By Americans, October 20 2011, http://www.health.harvard.edu/blog/astounding-increase-in-antidepressant-use-by-americans-201110203624

M. National Institute of Mental Health, The National Institute of Mental Health Strategic Plan, 2007, http://www. nimh.nih.gov/about/strategic-planning-reports/index.shtml

N. Hansen, Dirk. Neuroaddiction: The Reward Pathway, 2010, http://dirkhanson.org/neuroaddiction.html

O. Farrenkopf, Christine. Cocaine and the Brain: The Neurobiology of Addiction, 1/4/2008, http://serendip.brynmawr.edu/exchange/node/1704

P. Nestler, Eric J. and Malenka, Robert C. Scientific American, The Addicted Brain, March .. 2004, http://wireheading.com/article/addiction.html

Q. NeuroRehabilitation & Neuropsychological Services, P.C. The Brain and Its Functions, .. http://thebrainlabs.com/brain.shtml

R. Hansen, Rick. Self-Directed Neuroplasticity: A 21st-Century View of Meditation, April . . . 2011, http://www.noetic.org/noetic/issue-nine-april/self-directed-neuroplasticity/

S. Newburg, Andrew M.D. How God Changes Your Brain: Breakthrough Findings from a Leading Neuroscientist, Ballantine Books 2009

T. Wax, Dustin M. Writing and Remembering: Why We Remember What We Write, September, 2011, http://www.lifehack.org/articles/productivity/writing-and-remembering-why-we-remember-what-we-write.html Don't Be Stupid: A Guide To Learning, Studying, And Succeeding At College, Creative Commons, 2008

U. Heyle, Hans, The Stress of Life, McGraw Hill, 1984

V. Society for Neuroscience. Adult Neurogenesis, June 2007, http://www.sfn.org/index.aspx?pagename=brainbriefings_adult_neurogenesis

W. Jensen, Eric. Teaching with the Brain in Mind, Association for Supervision and Curriculum, 2nd Edition, 30 May 2005

X. Hebb, Donald O. The Organization of Behavior: A Neuropsychological Theory, Taylor and Francis e-Library, 2009 http://en.wikipedia.org/wiki/Donald_O._Hebb, March 21, 2012.

Y. Elliot, Jim, The Journals of Jim Elliot, Revell Publishing, 1978

AA. C.S. Lewis, Mere Christianity, Harper Collins Publishers, 1952

CC. Ornish, Dean. Love and Survival: 8 Pathways to Intimacy and Health (New York: HaprperCollins, 1998) pp.2,3. 23-71.

DD. Thayer, Jane PhD. In Step With Jesus - The Power of Love (General Conference of Seventh-day Adventists, 2012 p. 83

EE. Lucado, Max. Cure for the Common Life: Living in Your Sweet Spot, Thomas Nelson, 2005

FF. Thomas, Gary, Sacred Pathways: Discover Your Soul's Path to God, Zondervan, 2000

GG. Nolan, Fredrick, Rodgers, Richard and Hammerstein, Oscar, The Sound of Their Music: The Story of Rodgers & Hammerstein, Applause Theatre and Cinema Books, 2002

HH. Lewis, C.S. The Four Loves, New York, Harcourt, Brace, 1960

II. Hemingway, Ernest, A Farewell To Arms, Scribner, A Division of Simon and Schuster Inc. 1929, 1957, 2012

JJ. Nerburn, Kent, Make Me an Instrument of Your Peace, Harper San Francisco, HarperCollins, 1999

KK. Chapman, Gary D. The 5 Love Languages: The Secret to Love That Lasts, Northfield Publishing; New Edition, 1 Jan. 2010.

LL. Ross, Elisabeth Kübler, On Death and Dying: What the Dying Have to Teach Doctors, Nurses, Clergy and Their Own Families, Scribner, A Division of Simon and Schuster Inc. 1916, 1949, 1964

MM. Franklin, Benjamin, The Way to Wealth (Little Books of Wisdom), Applewood Books Inc. 1986

NN. Morris, David B. The Culture of Pain, University of California Press, 1991

OO. Furman, Joel M.D. Eat to Live, Hachette Book Group, 2003, 2011

PP. Fife, Bruce, N.D. The Detox Book, Piccadilly Books, LTD, 1997, 2001, 2011

QQ. Clayville, Linda, Certified Nutritionist, NaturesPantryNaturalFoods.com

RR. Newburg, Andrew M.D. How God Changes Your Brain: Breakthrough Findings from a Leading Neuroscientist, Ballantine Books, 2009

AAA. Emerson, Ralph Waldo, Goodreads—Quotable Quotes, http://www.goodreads.com/quotes/416934-sow-a-thought-and-you-reap-an-action-sow-an

BBB. Aristotle, Goodreads—Quotable Quotes, http://www.goodreads.com/quotes/search?utf8=%E2%9C%93&q=Aristotle%2C+We+are+what+we+repeatedly+do&commit=Search

CCC. Aristotle, Goodreads—Quotable Quotes, http://www.goodreads.com/quotes/search?utf8=%E2%9C%93&q=Aristotle%2C+anyone+can+become+angry&commit=Search

DDD. Korb, Alex PhD, The Upward Spiral ~ Using Neuroscience to Reverse the Course of Depression, One Small Step at a Time, New Harbinger Publications 2015

EEE. Duhigg, Charles, The Power of Habit ~ Why We Do What We Do In Life and In Business, Random House 2014

FFF. Jennings, Timothy, The Aging Brain: Proven Steps to Prevent Dementia and Sharpen Your Mind, Baker Books 2018

GGG. "Mortality Rates in Patients with Anorexia Nervosa and Other Eating Disorders" by Jon Arcelus, Alex J. Mitchell, Jackie Wales, and Søren Nielsen.

Recovery Journal

Ancient Wisdom and Today's Jokes for Happy, Joyous, and Free Folks

Second Edition

Journal: *A personal record of intimate communion, inquiry, and reflection.*
Journey: *A passage from one place to another.*
This book is both.
It will prove fruitful for any seeker, especially those in recovery from addiction and co-dependency.
This playful and enlightening, spiritual quest will add color to the rich horizons of your renewing mind.
You will smile and laugh.
Your meditations will enlighten the sage inside you and brighten barricaded gardens in your soul.
Your aspiring prayers will vitalize the kingdom of God that lies within.
You will affirm your intrinsic value as heaven's child.
Your wisdom, knowledge, and understanding will strengthen.
Your hope will flourish within God's promises.
You will know the Way to your divine Father's welcoming home.

Whose Are You?

Printed in Great Britain
by Amazon